THE PHILOSOPHY OF INTERNATIONAL RELATIONS

Volume 52, Sage Library of Social Research

SAGE LIBRARY OF SOCIAL RESEARCH

THE PHILOSOPHY OF INTERNATIONAL RELATIONS

A study in the history of thought

F. PARKINSON

Volume 52
SAGE LIBRARY OF
SOCIAL RESEARCH

 **SAGE PUBLICATIONS**   Beverly Hills/London

For information address:

SAGE PUBLICATIONS, INC.
275 South Beverly Drive
Beverly Hills, California 90212

SAGE PUBLICATIONS LTD
28 Banner Street
London EC1Y 8QE

Printed in the United States of America

Library of Congress Cataloging in Publication Data

Parkinson, F
    The philosophy of international relations.

    (Sage library of social research ; v. 52)
    Bibliography: p. 217
    Includes index.
    1. International relations—History. I. Title.
JX1305.P37   327'.01   77-11197
ISBN 0-8039-0689-7
ISBN 0-8039-0690-0 pbk.

FIRST PRINTING

CONTENTS

"The students of international relations are the new philosophers."

Harold D. Lasswell

INTRODUCTION

There are numerous works on the theory of international relations, the majority of them lacking in historical depth. No comprehensive text exists on the philosophy of international relations, and only fragments on the history of thought in that field.

What seems to be required is more than just a historical narrative, as it has been long felt that a philosophy of international relations must be able to tease out the changes in basic hypotheses over the ages. The present book was written to meet that demand.

Theorising on the subject of international relations with one's back turned on the past is bound to be a wasteful exercise, as history presents a treasure-house of both experience and ideas. In the field of the study of international relations, conventional diplomatic history has taken care of the former, while the latter has been neglected. Yet, ideas of the past are far from irrelevant to current or future problems of international relations. Judiciously drawn upon, they can be helpful in constructing new theories of international relations, may open minds to fresh thought, and encourage scholars to engage in bold philosophical synthesis of old and new.

To make available a wide choice of ideas on international relations presented in historical synopsis has been the prime purpose of this work. Far from being antiquarian in intent, the work is open-minded in confining itself to an impartial presentation of ideas, and open-ended in refraining from offering any conclusions, however broad. Its central purpose is to present the evidence to those in search of the truth. In that sense, this philosophy of international relations is meant to serve as a means to an end, and not as an end in itself.

The author found that, as the structure of international society emerged before the eighteenth century, it threw up intellectual concepts to be applied to the international problems of its various periods of evolution. Examples of this are the concept of natural law in classical antiquity and the concept of the balance of power during the age of Absolutism. To have left the analysis at that, however, would have conveyed the false impression that the use of those concepts was confined to the age of their inception. To avoid such an impression it was felt essential to trace their further development through the ages, and up to the present day where appropriate. In subsequent chapters this procedure could be modified, with the narrative fastening directly to concepts which had acquired a firm identity within the structure of a much differentiated international society.

This work, based on the experience of a decade of teaching at University College London, has drawn on a wide assortment of materials. The present author would be happy to see some younger scholars improve on it in future.

December 1976   *F.P.*
London

Chapter 1

NATURAL LAW AND DIVINE LAW:

PAGANS, CHRISTIANS, AND THE COSMOS

Systematic thought on the subject of international relations is of relatively recent origin, but the broader ideas in which much of it has been embedded can be traced back into classical antiquity, and in some cases even beyond, as they form part of the wider field of philosophy proper. Though some of the big themes of classical philosophy tend to run like Ariadne's thread through the maze of thought on international relations that has sprung up over the ages, they frequently get obscured in the welter of ephemeral concepts that forms from time to time.

Classical antiquity may for these reasons be regarded as a convenient starting point in an enterprise intended to illuminate evolutionary trends in thought on international relations.

Classical Greece

Political thought in classical Greece turned round the general idea of the city-state and the relations between these city-states. As to the former, Plato (427-347 B.C.) connected its welfare with education, visualising the ideal type of a philosopher-king as the fount of political wisdom. The principle of equality among the citizenry of states was taken by him to represent a guarantee of social stability.

Aristotle (385-322 B.C.), on the other hand, while sharing much of Plato's optimism regarding the positive functions of education, could not envisage complete equality as a practical possibility, and proposed instead to apply the egalitarian principle to an élite only. It would be permissible, therefore, to regard Plato as the philosophical prototype of an idealist, and Aristotle as a realist.

Interstate relations among the Greek city-states were regulated largely by treaty and custom, without the intervention of doctrine. However, the international system of Greek city-states began to decline sharply during the fourth century B.C. and eventually fell under the domination of, first, Macedon, and subsequently the expanding Roman Republic. It was only in its declining state, and very largely because of that condition, that sustained efforts were being made to lay the basis of a philosophical cosmology capable of providing explanations transcending by far the narrow confines of the city-state. The scope of these cosmologies was meant to encompass the entire political orbit in which the drama of Greek politics was being enacted.

The salient characteristic of these comprehensive philosophic constructs was that their validity was entirely independent of any principles evolved in the course of political practice. Positive law did not enter into them. On the contrary, these cosmologies were intended to take the place of positive law, however temporarily, while the latter was inoperative. The centrepiece of the philosophical cosmology generated in those circumstances proved to be Stoicism, intended as a unifying principle to restore a measure of coherence to the crumbling cosmos of the Hellenes, within which the individual could face the universe directly, without the intervention of the Greek city-states.

Deriving its inspiration from Sophocles' play *Antigone*, which had as its theme the dramatic conflict between King Creon, representing lawful custom, and Antigone, representing natural justice, Stoicism embraced Antigone's view and made it its own. Postulating a perfectly pure type of original society, Stoic theory maintained that subsequent corruption had perverted but not invalidated the two natural principles which had upheld pristine society, namely, universality and equality. Now that Greek society was collapsing, these two principles presented the only basis of an eventual renewal.

UNIVERSALITY

To the Stoics, the world was a unit, irrespective of the manifold particularisms which it displayed, and an object from which to extract a set of laws. Philosophical cosmology concerned itself with the search for the principles of world order and existence in the widest sense, and physical cosmology and astronomy were among its earliest preoccupations. Zeno of Citium (340-264 B.C.), a prominent Stoic, believed that the conditions of world harmony were discoverable by systematic enquiries into the nature of the universe. The early conceptions of Stoicism were perfected by Chrysippus (280-207 B.C.), who wrote a treatise *On Law* and was the greatest Athenian seminarist of his time. Not an a priori moralist, he stressed on the basis of empirical observation the existing distinction and tension between the concepts of world state and world law, regarding the latter as being composed of ethical and the former of technical subject matter. Without wishing to decry the functions of the former, he allowed for, and probably expected, the ultimate formation of a world consensus of ideas to provide the ethical nucleus of world law.

World law, in Chrysippus' mind, was of a strictly meta-positive kind, and as such unamenable to the accepted technical processes of legislation. If anything, world law was a function of the power of divine providence, as manifested in the unity and perfection of nature which no profane law-maker could break, try as he might. Ethics, the intellectual discipline dealing with moral obligations, was implicitly involved in Chrysippus' search for natural justice. As conceptualised by Chrysippus, world law was equated with natural justice, and it was the latter which was to provide the unifying precept of idealism throughout the ages. Its hallmark was a preoccupation with values as against empirical facts. The same cleavage between the normative and the empirical runs right through the history of thought in international relations.

EQUALITY

Leaning on Platonic thought, Chrysippus expounded the idea that all social distinctions within the universe should be reduced to a minimum. This applied to states as much as to individuals. Harmony between states was a Stoic ideal and could conceivably be attained if all states were linked together in a system of universal values based on principles of equality. In the Stoic mind, customs were varied, but the element of reason which underpinned natural justice was uniform. For every man there were therefore two kinds of norms to observe: those of his city-state, the product of man-made legislation, and those of the world city, the product of natural justice. Since justice was not a necessary ingredient of the former, the latter had to be accorded overriding authority.

Doctrines based on and theories incorporating elements of natural justice tend, as a general rule, to be used as a leaven in times when positive political order is breaking down and its legal supports are crumbling. Natural justice in the Stoic sense has therefore come to be looked upon as a reservoir of ethical precepts to be drawn on in times of decline and collapse, to aid and if necessary replace altogether sets of practical rules put together in times of ascendancy and stability. Notions of natural justice have had their greatest appeal whenever positive law has gone unduly rigid, narrowly formal, and out of touch with existing social reality. In conditions like these, there will always be a tendency to discard the empirical and to embrace the idealistic. This explains why in classical Greece the writings of Thucydides (455-400 B.C.),[1] a severely practical-minded historian, were commanding respect whilst intercity law was at its zenith, and why Stoicism began to be popular when that same system was gradually grinding to a halt after the fifth century B.C.

Roman Stoicism

While it would be true to say that Greek Stoicism tended to identify nature with justice, some of its critics—notably the Sceptics and Epicureans—identified nature with individual self-interest. Carneades, for instance, maintained that the Stoic notion of justice was little more than a rationalisation of self-interest, at best tempered by a measure of prudence. In the ensuing debate, Panaetius of Rhodes (189-109 B.C.) restated the basic tenets of Stoicism in the light of those criticisms, streamlining the doctrine in the process. By doing so, he made it palatable to Roman upper class intellectuals tutored by Greek scholars. Panaetius and the Greek historian Polybius formed part of a Roman debating club for the discussion of these questions, and it was in this manner that Stoic thought found its way from classical Greece to classical Rome, where it was to flourish.

The prime function of *jus naturale*, as the Romans came to call the system of thought devised by the Stoics, was to soften the sharp edges of their own primitive *jus civile*, the law of the city of Rome and its surroundings, as Rome went on expanding from its relatively backward mid-Italian base into a sophisticated empire of grand proportions. It was through the agency of natural law, therefore, that the harsh Roman *jus civile* was transformed into the cosmopolitan *jus gentium*—the law common to all people making up the Roman Empire. Among the Romans, Cicero (106 - 43 B.C.), in *De legibus*, gave natural law its political definition as "right reason in agreement with nature ... of universal application, unchanging and everlasting." Cicero stressed the moral element in natural law, and played down the role of force, which he regarded as incidental in the make-up of the state. To his way of thinking, justice preceded law, and justice was implicitly egalitarian. Rome was not the only state in existence, but had to live on a footing of equality with all other states, and he deplored the relentless tendency of Rome to expand in total neglect of these precepts.

Cicero probably represented the high-watermark of Roman Stoicism in its classical universal-egalitarian form, for even as he spoke, the conquering tendency in Roman foreign policy was fast getting out of control. As the Roman Empire was nearing the peak of its power and reaching the outer limits of its expansion, Stoic idealism was merged with Epicurean realism in the philosophically inclined mind of Emperor Marcus Aurelius (121 - 180

A.D.). On the one hand, his deeply felt cosmopolitanism found expression in his dictum, "My city and country as Antoninus is Rome—as a man it is the world," but on the other hand, he believed in the free will of man, regarding the individual as completely autonomous, a voluntarism basically incompatible with Stoic deference to nature. Here was the philosophical frame within which the tragic dilemma of international relations was to pose itself time and again, with the freedom of individual states pitted against the ideal of a preordained universe. The pure wine of Greek Stoicism had been adulterated in Rome by its absorption in the *jus gentium*, which in turn was to represent an expanding system of positive law at the disposal of successive Roman legislators.

Christian Stoicism

Already stirrings of a new kind of Stoicism were felt, as the Roman philosopher Seneca (4 B.C. - 65 A.D.), affected by the early Christian version of Stoicism, and showing, like them, a sense of disenchantment in the "city of man," maintained that the City of God was not of this world. In the end Christian Stoicism triumphed because it alone had something ideal to offer to the individual confronted with the apparent and ultimately real disintegration of the Latin half of the Roman Empire. Just as Stoic egalitarianism had had a considerable attraction for minorities within the Hellenic cosmos (Syrians and Phoenicians had been numerous among the early Greek Stoics), so it appealed to the persecuted Christians in the pre-Constantine Empire. But whereas the apotheosis for the Greek Stoics had resided in the original state of man, the Christian apotheosis lay in the future, and was attainable through Messianic salvation only. Meanwhile, Christian philosophy had to rest content with adopting and adapting natural law notions handed down to them by the Greek Stoics through their Roman disciples.[2]

Once Christianity had been adopted as the state religion of the Roman Empire at the end of the fourth century A.D., Stoic notions of universality, reinforced by the powerful memory of the Roman imperial structure, were to facilitate the eventual transition from *res publica romana* to *res publica christiana*. It also led to the transformation of Seneca's conception of a universal mankind held together by universally valid moral ties to the notion of an imperial theocracy imposing a universal dogma binding on rulers and their subjects alike.

However, this seemingly neat and even brilliant solution of the cosmic problem was to raise nearly as many problems as it was attempting to solve, since—except within the granite structure of the Byzantine half of the former Roman Empire, which was able to survive unchanged until 1453—the Christian theocratic commonwealth proved unable to halt the process of disintegration. Yet, there can be no doubt that the system of uniform ethical norms now residing in Christianity did help to slow the process of disintegration and to maintain a minimum measure of political coherence by keeping the two principal ideas of universality and equality alive throughout the feudal period in Western Europe. This was accomplished in the face of great adversity, especially on the interstate level, even though the operation of the feudal system—particularly in the military sphere—required the introduction of severe social inequalities on the individual level.

The powerful persistence of the idea of a centralised empire certainly inhibited for a long time—though ultimately, as will be shown, it failed—the assertion of a pluralist international system to supplant the feudal one. Feudalism may legitimately be regarded as a vast system of emergency to provide the military, economic, and social means of defence against the ceaseless onslaught of barbarian tribes throughout the period of the *Völkerwanderung* (ca. 400-900 A.D.). It demanded the full collaboration of all rulers in a colossal war effort, and it is not surprising that under the force of these circumstances the pacifism of the Stoics should have given way eventually to the notion of a militant Christianity defending the legacy inherited from the Stoic thinkers of classical Greece and Rome. It was in this fashion that, by natural selection rather than by preconceived idea, and ostensibly in headlong collision with the fundamental principle of equality, the familiar feudal pyramid of rulers came into being, in which the place of each was determined by the contribution he was able to make to the common defence in terms of military power.

St. Augustine (354 - 430 A.D.)

It was in an atmosphere of further rapid disintegration of the now Christian commonwealth in the Latin West that St. Augustine, Bishop of Hippo and Algerian by birth, took stock of the position in *De civitate Dei*, a work in which he had invested about thirteen years of his life. An admirer of the classical Roman Empire, he despaired of the possibility of its resurrection, and a scholar steeped in the current versions of Platonism, he took a tragic view of human nature, at the root of which he perceived a lust for domination over other men as an elemental driving force.

St. Augustine's views on cosmology can fairly be regarded as representing those of the Church during the early Middle Ages, and merit treatment at some length. In his scheme of thought, human relations operate on three levels: the home, the State (*civitas*) and the *orbis terrarum,* a term left unqualified by him; but since he used the term *mundus* to denote the universe, one might be permitted to infer that *orbis terrarum* was meant to refer to world society or, even more intriguingly, to interstate society. One might rightly conclude, therefore, that international relations constituted an area of great interest to him, and that one of his endeavours was to determine their nature in the light of current theology.

St. Augustine visualised a universe divided into two. Where the Stoics had drawn a conceptual line between world law and world city, he equated the former with the "City of God" (*civitas Dei*) in an attempt to rescue the principle of universality from corruption in this world by relegating it to another, ideal world of divine character. Furthermore, and of incalculable consequence in the subsequent development of thought in the sphere of international relations, he held that the ideal of international equality was no longer realisable since peace with the dreaded enemies of Christianity was inconceivable. The impressive conjunction between Christian-Stoic substance and Roman imperial form had made it easy to identify Christendom with mankind as a whole, a habit which—when the Christian empire came under direct external attack from non-Christian tribes—was to lead gradually and almost imperceptibly to the modification of the Stoic principle of absolute universal equality, as visualised by Cicero, in favour of the notion of Christian ethical exclusiveness and superiority.

Through the force of historical circumstances, and by no means from personal choice, St. Augustine found himself at the intellectual centre of this fundamental shift of attitude. Though neither the Empire in its state of depravity nor the de facto kingdoms which had arisen out of chaos, and which he considered the products of robbery on a large scale, were worth defending in his eyes, the Church certainly was. St. Augustine was therefore faced with turning Christianity from an emphatically pacific into a fighting faith. This he achieved by (a) declaring any war waged in defence of the Church as just, and (b) turning the craft of soldiery, hitherto of an outcast nature, into a respectable one. There was a third problem. To offer effective resistance, internecine warfare among nominally Christian rulers, which unfortunately could not be prevented altogether, had to be reduced to a minimum. This end St. Augustine sought to reach by listing the conditions which had to be met before a war between Christian rulers could qualify as "just": (a) it had to be authorised by a legitimate ruler; (b) it had to have a "just cause"; (c) it had to aid Christian peace and order; and (d) it was to punish evil. Wars of this nature did not necessarily have to be of a defensive kind, and could be waged on divine command (*bellum justissimum*). More constructively, St. Augustine seems to have toyed with the idea of promoting a commonwealth of independent Christian states on confederal lines, as an alternative to the revival of the Roman Empire, but despaired of realising this idea.

St. Augustine's surgery on the body of Christian theology was the answer to the state of emergency in which Christendom found itself at a time when

Alaric stood in Rome and the Vandals in North Africa. Effectively, he took the notion of natural law and gave it divine content, a condition in which natural law was to persist until the thirteenth century when, consequent on the passing of the emergency, it was gradually to resume its classical, independent role as a secular ethical standard. Meanwhile, divine law was to provide the austere defensive ideology for fighting Christendom based on the harsh ethics of the Old Testament. The incidental effect produced by St. Augustine's action was to bestow on Christianity an exclusivist mentality which was at bottom incompatible with its Stoically derived sense of international equality. This basic antithesis in general outlook on world affairs was to beset and bedevil Christianity for many centuries to come, and to cause heartache whenever the issue of relations between Christian and non-Christian rulers threatened to cause difficulties. Numerous disputes among Christian philosophers were to ensue.

The issue was not, as will be shown, as straightforward as it appeared at first sight, since it was not just a question of dividing mankind into Christians and non-Christians. In the course of many centuries, it was noticed that among non-Christian rulers there were some whose religion, while differing from Christian belief, showed some structural affinities with it, while there were others who, if they were not altogether godless, practised a kind of religion in varying degrees repugnant to the basic tenets of Christianity. In what circumstances, then, and by what mode, were Christian rulers to live either in amity or in tension—as the case might be—with those states? The elaboration of principles governing those relations was to be exceedingly difficult, since the problem itself would not go away of its own accord, and the Church proved to be perennially divided over it. So long as it was merely a question of ensuring Christian survival, no awkward controversies could arise. The problem began to be acutely troublesome once real opportunities offered themselves to carry the Christian faith beyond its existing territorial boundaries into non-Christian lands. This would necessitate a reassessment of the two time-honoured Stoic principles of universality and equality, and that in turn meant undertaking an agonising reexamination of the principles of natural law, which was in effect divine law. Once the attacking barbarian hordes from the East and North had been tamed and, having embraced the Christian faith, were settling down to a civilised existence, a redetermination of the precise functions of natural and divine law and their respective places in the general scheme of Christian theology was inevitable.

Against the historical background of ancient Greece and Rome in their decline, and during the chaos of the *Völkerwanderung*, the content of natural and divine law had been well established and undisputed. They began to assume different meanings when set against new historical conditions forming from about 800 A.D. onwards. While the principle of universality above all—now linked to the concept of centralised political administration as embodied in the Roman imperial idea—called for taking measures to ensure the universal jurisdiction of the church—now under the increasing sway of the papacy—the principle of international equality demanded the very opposite course of wide political decentralisation. The two Stoic principles, so admirably matched to supplement and reinforce each other in the past, suddenly seemed in downright collision with each other, with universality claiming the application of divine law, and international equality that of natural law. Natural law, as originally conceived by the Stoics within the homogeneous cultural background of the Hellenic macrocosm, was of limited application in the multicultural orbit in which international problems arose from the ninth century onwards, but so was divine law. It was this antithesis that was to present new problems.

The Crusades

From the ninth century onwards, the papacy grew steadily more powerful. Augustinian doctrine, as well as promoting this development, may have been among the numerous factors responsible for the launching of the Crusades, a movement closely associated with the papacy. Originally no more than pilgrimages with the cross to the Holy Land, at the end of the eleventh century, the Crusades turned into allegedly defensive military campaigns against the Saracens advancing towards that area. To see them solely in this light is, however, unfruitful since the idea of a military Crusade presented the logical outgrowth of that of Christian exclusiveness, a notion originally fostered by St. Augustine. Yet, that notion was pregnant with psychological ambiguities which, from time to time, led to serious theological disputes. And while the mode in which these disputes were being conducted was subject to variation, the basic problem—what attitudes to adopt towards non-Christian rulers—remained constant. The very purpose of the Crusades, to take up arms offensively for a defensive purpose, contained a fundamental contradiction that highlighted the diverse characteristics of divine and natural law as evolved hitherto. The result—until the Reformation, the humanist movement and the great overseas discoveries intervened to bring the issue into the open—was that the attitudes adopted by Crusading Christianity towards non-Christian political groups were vacillating and confused. What is obvious when viewed with the benefit of hindsight and within a long-range perspective, is that right up to the Treaty of Westphalia of 1648, subtle changes were occurring in the measure to which Christianity had to give way to the concept of civilisation as the chief criterion of adjustment in the relations between Christian and non-Christian states.

In St. Augustine's days there was unanimity on what attitude to adopt towards the attacking barbarian tribes. They represented a menace to all the values that Christianity stood for, and had to be opposed *á outrance*. And while there can be no question that the fate and status of the Holy Land was a matter of great emotional as well as religious concern for most Christians— though the extent of this concern among the generality of Christians has been vastly exaggerated by historiography until recently[3]—it seems in retrospect at least doubtful whether from the seventh century onwards, the Arab Muslims could have been classified as barbarian by the same criteria as had some of the hordes moving in earlier from East Asia during the centuries of the *Völkerwanderung*. An element of nagging doubt must have crept into Christian minds, casting a pall of uncertainty on the legitimacy of their Crusading pretensions. Indeed, in time it must have been apparent—and with the onset of the age of overseas discoveries all doubt on that score must have been dispelled—that the picture of a compact Christianity, tightly organised within the precincts of the former Roman Empire, surrounded by a barbarian fringe at once highly disparate and scattered, was a false one. It became evident to most thinking Christians that their civilisation was but one of many, that these were at various stages of cultural evolution containing a variety of values, and that sooner or later Christianity would have to come to terms with them.

Not that the Stoic idea of universal equality had ever been entirely displaced even on the highest official levels of Christendom by the exclusivism originally fostered by St. Augustine. The amicable correspondence conducted by a number of medieval popes with certain Muslim rulers bears witness to this.[4] Yet it was undeniable that the element of exclusivism was gaining the ascendancy from the time of Emperor Charlemagne (lived 742 - 814; Emperor 800 - 814) onwards, who, ordering his army commanders to move from their Bavarian base into the area now taken up by the Republic of Austria, enjoined them ominously to "go out and conquer those heathens by fire and sword." His intention was plainly aggressive and his purpose to push the frontiers of Christendom eastwards. Carolingian ecclesiastics, leaning on Augustinian doctrine, developed the notion of the holy war, bequeathed by St. Augustine in somewhat rudimentary form, to provide the theological justification for the conquest and conversion of the infidels. Pre-Carolingian Christian thought had been ambiguous as to whether the mere absence of a proper belief constituted a justification for a holy war or whether unbelievers should be tolerated so long as their intentions towards Christians remained peaceful. Whilst, according to St. Augustine's theory, the holy war had to be sanctioned by God, such holy wars could, from Gregory VII (1073 - 1085) onwards, be expressly authorised by the papacy. Gregory VII's doctrines were instrumental in launching the Crusading movement.

Christian exclusivism, as reflected in the attitudes adopted by Catholic Christendom in its dealings with non-Christian entities, compared unfavourably with its mirror image, Islam, which on the whole showed greater tolerance. A mark of the Muslim faith was the basic distinction in its cosmology between *Dar-el-Islam,* the Muslim world, and *Dar-el-Harb,* the world outside with which the Muslims were at war. However, respect was shown for all religions of revelation, such as Judaism and Christianity, and members of those communities enjoyed full exemption from payment of the *jezya,* the poll-tax imposed on all other non-Islamic peoples. Moreover, the conceptual division of the world into *Dar-el-Islam* and *Dar-el-Harb* was matched by the all-embracing concept of *Dar-el-Amman,* the world at peace. The Muslim concept of international harmony was never as exclusive as the Christian one, and it was only in the idea of holy war (*jihad*) that there was a meeting of minds between the two sides.

One institution through which content could be given to divine law and medieval ecclesiastical discipline was canon law, a collection of church edicts binding on all subjects of the Catholic church, including rulers of states. It was within the framework of canon law that theological issues affecting the relations between Christian and non-Christian states were raised and decided. Almost from the outset, canonist scholars divided into two parties over those issues.[5] On one side were those taking a hard attitude in line with Augustinian precepts of divine law—though Professor Ullmann takes the view that only "a minority of canonists conceived of natural law as a mere species of divine law" at that time.[6] Their chief representative was Henry of Segusia, cardinal-bishop of Ostia (died 1271), known in canonist literature as Hostiensis,[7] who in his *Summa* would accord to the papacy the right of conquest of all non-Christians (he had however, primarily the Levantine Muslims in mind). Papal universalism was also upheld by Cardinal Petrus Bertrandi, another canonist, who in his authoritative work *De origine jurisdictionum* (Paris: Chaudière, 1520) represented the pope as the lawful owner of the whole world.

An absolute right of conquest of non-Christian communities was denied by Pope Innocent IV (1243 - 1254), a canonist scholar in his own right. He was chief spokesman of the moderate party on this issue, who confined that right to the reconquest of lands once under Christian rule. Already Innocent III had remarked that there was nothing obnoxious in the principle of infidel possession of countries, provided no sinful action was committed. Innocent IV denied the right to compel non-Christians to embrace the church.

Catholic doctrine was slow in evolving on the right of conquest and, closely connected with it, the right of conversion. Eventually, however, a compromise solution emerged in the dual rule that (a) no force was to be used to subjugate pagan countries, and (b) conversion was to be brought about by the missionary method only, the use of force being reserved to cases in which the right of entry was refused to Christian missionaries.[8]

Inevitably, these rules were too general to fit every particular instance, and on occasion this gave rise to doubt as to their interpretation in unforeseen circumstances. While there was no difficulty in the *reconquista* of the Iberian peninsula, the entire question was reopened in a fresh historical context when the Teutonic Knights attempted the forceful conversion of heathens in northeastern Europe at the beginning of the fifteenth century. This was the last major occasion—before the great discoveries of territories overseas made in the course of that century were to give it a new dimension—on which the problem of the relations between Christian and non-Christian states got a thorough airing. What happened was that the Church Council of Constance (1414 - 1418) received a complaint from the Order of the Teutonic Knights to the effect that Catholic Poland had entered into a military alliance with heathen Lithuania directed against it. This was promptly investigated by the council. While ready enough to concede the major point made by the knights in their submission that war against non-Christian states was legitimate in certain circumstances in accord with prevailing doctrine, Paulus Vladimiri, representing King Jagiello of Poland, took the line that alliances between Christian and non-Christian states were permissible provided entry of missionaries to the heathen country was not barred. Lithuania had put up no such barrier, and Poland was taking advantage of the opportunity by doing her utmost to convert the Lithuanians by peaceful means. Counsel for the knights, on the other hand, attempted to sustain the hard Hostensian argument according to which the right of conversion was absolute and could not be blocked by military interference on the part of a fellow-Catholic ruler.

The case was a difficult one to decide, and it is not surprising that the council, finding itself on the horns of a dilemma, failed to give a clear ruling, tending, on the whole, to sympathise with the knights, while refusing to pronounce against Poland. However, the record of the proceedings would suggest that extradoctrinal considerations—such as the fact that the knights were enjoying the diplomatic support of the Empire—were involved, inhibiting the council considerably in its quasi-judicial capacity in this matter.[9] When a century later Francis I, *Majesté Chrêtissime,* King of France, concluded an alliance directed against the Catholic Habsburg Empire with Suleyman the Magnificent, Mohammedan Sultan of the Ottoman Empire, in 1526, Papal protests were of no avail whatever. Church authority in political matters with a theologian slant was on the decline, as a new era in the history of thought on international relations was dawning.

The Conquista

The new mode of thought which began to affect the conduct of international relations during the period of the Reformation in matters related to

Christian doctrine in respect of non-Christian communities resulted from the advent of the humanist movement. Humanism, generally associated with Erasmus of Rotterdam (1466 - 1536), made its mark on canonist doctrine (witness the interminable debates which ensued after 1492 from the Spanish discovery and conquest of territories in the Western hemisphere inhabited by Indian communities). There was not a canon of medieval theology concerning the relations between Christendom and the infidel fringe which would be left untouched by the controversies stirred up by the Spanish conquest, as opinions divided once more over this basic issue of international relations.

Where the *reconquista*—completed in 1492 with the fall of Granada—had presented a straightforward case of the recovery of once Christian lands which was fully justifiable in terms of canonist doctrine, the *conquista,* commencing in the same year, appeared questionable in this regard, bringing disquiet to many a Spanish conscience. A number of prominent theologian-jurists, a special breed of scholars whose minds had been kindled by humanist currents, were agitated by what was happening in the Americas and began to ask leading questions about it. Were the Indian rulers entitled to retain their political and territorial sovereignty? And, if so, what were the grounds, if any, on which Spanish conquest, whether armed or peaceful, could be justified? Answers to these disturbing questions were persistently sought throughout the best part of the sixteenth century and beyond. Apart from the theologian-jurist scholars, most of whom resided in Spain, but some of whom were on active religious service on the scene of the drama out in the Americas, the controversy involved the *conquistadores* themselves, whose motives were mixed. Most of the latter looked upon their activities as being a composite of a traditional medieval Crusade and a modern treasure hunt, as revealed in the statement, made with disarming candour by one of their chroniclers, Bernal Díaz, that "We came here to serve God and to get rich." There was also the Spanish Crown itself, which, while adopting a waiting attitude, was willing to be convinced by the various arguments put before it.

By casting all the medieval solutions of the problem of the relations between Christian and non-Christian states back into the melting pot, the *conquista* made it possible, at least theoretically, to review and revise those solutions in the light of the advent of new historical circumstances. In essence, the choice was between two prototype solutions and their compounds. The prototypes were the classical Stoic and Aristotelian positions and their various derivatives. The former reached back into Greek antiquity and, if adopted in pure form, would have demanded a treatment of the Indian communities on a basis of complete international equality. Full respect would have had to be accorded to their political institutions, territorial sovereignty and cultural integrity, much in the manner in which Cicero would have regarded non-Roman communities as subjects of a universally binding and rationally based system of natural law removed from the grasp of Roman expansion. The Aristotelian position, in contrast, reflected a frankly aristocratic approach, implying a right of conquest of those communities on the ground of their intellectual inferiority. The Augustinian solution of isolated exclusiveness had no doubt coloured canonist views on the subject, but had been too closely geared to a specific historical situation to be of any relevance in the sixteenth century. Designed to fight off an external challenge, the basic terms of the problem were the reverse of that facing the Spaniards now.

From the Hostensian position had sprung the suggestive medieval image of a solid Christianity bordered by an infidel fringe, giving rise to an alleged papal right of appropriation and conversion of that fringe. Ostensibly a compound of the Stoic principle of universality and the Augustinian one of Christian exclusiveness, it contained at least the germ of Christian pretensions of superiority along Aristotelian aristocratic lines. Its relevance was as undeniable as its explosively controversial nature, but it proved vulnerable to objections from humanist quarters.

There was, finally, the canonist compromise of the fourteenth century, whereby the ruthless consistency of the Hostensian thesis was softened by the triple qualification that (a) no force was to be used in the subjugation of pagan communities, (b) that missionary methods only were to be employed in efforts of conversion, and (c) that force might be legitimately used only where missionary activity was resisted.

In the ensuing struggle for a solution fitting the present contingency, the Spanish theologian-jurists were in broad agreement that Papal universal authority was confined to the spiritual sphere, and that, under the terms of Alexander VI's bull *Inter caetera* of 1493, the king of Spain had the right of conversion of non-Christian peoples in certain, geographically well-defined portions of the Americas. What was far from clear was the political and legal status of the Indian communities encountered there, and it was on these points that opinions tended to polarise. At one end of the scale stood Juan Gines Sepúlveda, distinguished Aristotelian scholar whose views were popular with the *conquistadores*. He insisted that reason, according to humanist teaching the principal element in natural law, resided *in gentes humani-tiores*,[10] whom he equated with Christians. Because no truly egalitarian relationship was possible with the Indians, Christians were, by virtue of their superiority, under an obligation to move against those Indian communities to prevent a gap developing in world civilisation. Denying outright the validity of any doctrine of "just war" in this instance, he insisted on conquest—by force, if all else failed—in the name of Christian world civilisation, and demanded the institution of wardship over the Indians. At the other end of the scale was to be found Bartolomé de Las Casas, a Dominican who, unlike Sepúlveda, was out in the field with the *conquistadores* and who claimed for the Indian rights equal to those enjoyed by other subjects of Spain; though believing, with Sepúlveda, in the instruction of the Indians in civilised customs, he wanted them to be subjected to enlightened bureaucratic government directly from Madrid, and not at the mercy of the Spanish settlers in the Americas.

A position midway between these two was taken by Francisco de Vitoria (1483 - 1546), a Dominican theologian-jurist teaching at the University of Salamanca in Spain whose lectures on the subject of the relations between Spain and the Indian communities in the Americas were eventually published under the title *Relectiones de Indis noviter inventis* in 1534. Of all the Spanish theologian-jurists involved, Vitoria was probably the most legally minded, a trait which was reflected in his entire approach to the present problem. Vitoria's initial premise of the existence of a *jus inter gentes* which was applicable to all men, including non-Christian, would have constituted a revolutionary breakaway from traditional Christian conceptions of natural law, had it not been stringently circumscribed by three conditions having the effect of assimilating it in large, if not in total measure, to the traditional canonist compromise theses on this point. The three conditions were: (a) the application of *jus inter gentes* was to be general, not universal, and requiring the consent of a majority only; (b) that majority was to act as guardian in taking care of the minority; and (c) since the *jus inter gentes* postulated a nature-based world society in the field of transport and trade, the exclusion of foreigners from those activities, or a prohibition of their free entry without good reason, could be presented as acts in violation of natural law. It was apparent, therefore, that Vitoria was as anxious to find legitimate ways of peaceful conquest for the Spaniards as he was eager to protect the Indians from *conquistador* arms. Provided they behaved reasonably, and granted the Spaniards the right to trade and preach the Gospel, the Indians were entitled to retain the residue of their rights.

Beyond that Vitoria left no doubt that—though he discounted reports retailed by the *conquistadores* of cruelties committed by the Indians .as exaggerated, and would not on that account admit a right of armed conquest—he thought the Indians were incapable in the short run of exercising their faculties in a reasonable manner. Like Sepúlveda, therefore, he concluded that it would be to the advantage of the Indians to devise a system of wardship (*mandatum*) which included instruction in the Catholic religion and in general commerce, with a view to rendering them civilised within the shortest possible stretch of time. The only difference between the two men in their respective recommendations was that Sepúlveda, believing firmly that the Indians were beyond redemption, looked upon wardship as a permanent institution, whereas Vitoria, optimistic in this respect, considered *mandatum* of a strictly limited duration. Unwittingly, Vitoria had laid the basis of a theory of civilisation. "These people are not unintelligent but primitive; they seem incapable of maintaining a civilised state according to the requirement of humanity and law," he wrote.[11] In the age of budding humanism, "humanity and law," and no longer exclusive adherence to Christianity, presented the chief criteria of civilisation. His practical proposals rested on a moral compromise between the principles of Aristotelian aristocracy and sixteenth-century humanism. The crown eventually arranged a formal debate between him and Sepúlveda, which ended inconclusively. Humanism, though having made some inroads, was far from having triumphed. However, the emperor was sufficiently impressed by Vitoria to issue an order forbidding all further conquests. Moreover, the debate spilled over into the seventeenth century, in which the Crusading ideology at long last faded away.

What remained was a notion of intercultural relations which drew a sharp distinction between civilisation and savagery, and was to persist for as long as the Crusading ideology it was supplanting. Thus Hugo Grotius (1583 - 1645), Protestant humanist, lawyer and diplomat, while rejecting the Crusading ideology, remained silent on the status of the Indians in the Americas. At the same time he considered that Muslim rulers should be included within the international embrace of natural law, and that treaties with them should be binding: "The right to enter into treaties is so common to all men that it does not admit of a distinction arising from religion." He thought nonetheless that Christian states were morally bound to defend each other against infidel attack: "We ought not of our own will submit to the rule of the heathen." Baruch Spinoza, liberal-minded Jew and rationalist philosopher of the Netherlands, similarly enjoined caution in concluding treaties with non-Christian states but considered that, once signed, these treaties ought to be kept in principle.

By 1648 there was ample evidence that civilisation was rapidly supplanting Christianity as standard of moral assessment of non-Christian states. This continued to be the case long after Christianity had ceased to be a relevant factor in international relations, with a hard residue of Augustinian exclusiveness and Aristotelian superiority surviving in the attitudes of European powers towards political communities encountered in their expansion overseas. This was partly reflected in the terms contained in so-called "capitulation" treaties. The same mentality was epitomised in the treaty relationship between European colonial powers and African tribal chiefs, who were refused recognition as subjects of international law. It survived the termination of the colonial, mandate and trusteeship systems in the second half of the twentieth century to resurface in the form of growing racial prejudice against those originating in the former "uncivilised" fringe. In our own days, lurking behind an outward benevolence, it is manifested in a generally condescending attitude towards what we are now pleased to call the "underdeveloped countries" or, relegating it instinctively to the bottom of the scale, the "third world."

NOTES

1. See Thucydides (tr. R. Warner), *The Peleponnesian War*. Harmondsworth: Penguin, 1959 edition.

2. On these points, see E. Troeltsch, "Das stoisch-christliche Naturrecht und das moderne profane Naturrecht," *Historische Zeitschrift*, 106 (1911), pp. 237-267.

3. On this point, see N. Daniel, *The Arabs and Medieval Europe*. London: Longman, 1975.

4. Thus Pope Gregory VII (1073 - 1085) in a letter to King En Nasser of Mauritania stated that they owe each other love, while Popes Lucius III (1181 - 1185) and Innocent III (1198 - 1216) corresponded with Saladin about a durable peace between Christianity and the Muslim world.

5. This section is heavily indebted to the seminal work of W. Ullmann, *Medieval Papalism: Theories of the Medieval Papalists*. London: Methuen, 1949.

6. Ibid., p. 41.

7. On Hostiensis, see J.F. Schulte, *Geschichte der Quellen und Litteratur des canonischen Rechts*. Stuttgart: 1875 - 1880, Vol. 2, pp. 123-129.

8. Ullmann, op. cit., p. 131.

9. See S.F. Belch, *Paulus Vladimiri and his Doctrine Concerning International Law and Politics* (2 vols.). The Hague: Mouton, 1965.

10. On this point, see J.H. Parry, *The Age of Reconnaissance*. London: Weidenfeld and Nicolson, 1963, p. 312.

11. *De Indis noviter inventis*, Vol. 3, p. 12.

Chapter 2

RENAISSANCE AND REFORMATION:

THE RISE OF THE PRINCE

The Crusades were a catalyst in the process of mitigation of the rigours of divine law in the relations between Christian and non-Christian states. One of their main, albeit unintended effects was to open new markets for Italian commerce, for lying as they did across the thriving trade routes to the Levant, the Italian city-states benefited in two ways. In the first place, the rising volume of trade led to high yields from taxation, enabling Italian princes to use their new wealth in order to build a reliable civil service and to raise an efficient standing army commanded by the finest officers who could be hired. Secondly, it enabled them to behave more independently in relation to (a) their nominal feudal overlords, and (b) to each other. However, the rising tide of transit trade, which was such a boon for the revenue of the Italian city-states, necessitated the elaboration of detailed rules of interstate relations without which the smooth flow of international trade stood in danger of being jeopardised. This was done gradually through the agency of treaties by which a myriad of cumbersome feudal laws was swept away; by refining the techniques of diplomacy; and by taking measures to facilitate the conduct of international trade in general. The growing volume of interstate business, both commercial and diplomatic, was reflected in the creation of permanent, in place of ad hoc embassies and the device of a consular service, both institutional innovations of a remarkable kind.

Thanks largely to the spectacular growth in international trade occasioned by the Crusades and the handsome profits the Italian princes were deriving from it, the latter would eventually feel strong enough to slough off the coils of feudal souzerainty by which they had hitherto been restrained, by enforcing a de facto independence from the empire. As the routes of international trade lengthened to penetrate Switzerland and the valley of the River Rhine as far as Flanders and eventually England, the phenomenon of the *nouveaux riches* city-states made its appearance north of the Alps, where princes began to consolidate their territorial grasp and power also. What had been happening in the historical context of the Italian Renaissance was thus repeated in northwestern Europe, culminating in the attempt on the part of rulers in that area to sever relations with the papacy. The movement towards state sovereignty, which was eventually to generate a secular international society, was thus conceived in Renaissance Italy and dramatically completed in Reformation Europe north of the Alps. It reached its climax in the Treaty of Westphalia (1648), by which the emancipation of the princes was rendered absolute in respect of both empire and papacy. Thereafter, individual princes counted for more than either pope or emperor.

The emergence of a postfeudal system of international relations raised a number of crucial questions. Specifically, how were the new rulers to behave towards each other, and what sort of foreign policies should they pursue? What were the mechanics, and, for that matter, the dynamics of the new system? What, in any event, was the intrinsic nature of the new system?

There were two developments, closely intertwined, during that period which seemed inseparable at times, while at other times appearing independent of each other. One was the revival of natural law, and the other the steady growth of the notion of reason of state. The first was associated with the name of St. Thomas Aquinas, who gave it theological expression; the other, nearly three centuries later, with Niccoló Machiavelli. Both traditions are present in the humanist and posthumanist writers of the period of the Reformation—Suárez, Grotius, Hobbes, and Spinoza. In their writings they reflected the final emergence into broad daylight of the new, largely secular international society.

St. Thomas Aquinas (1225-1274)

St. Thomas Aquinas' views on international relations invite comparison with those of his great predecessor among the fathers of the church, St. Augustine, whom he largely supplanted as Thomism became the accepted Catholic theology.

Much of what St. Augustine had proposed made perfectly good sense in the conditions prevailing in the fifth century, but had to be jettisoned in the thirteenth as anachronistic. That century provided a great stage for the system builders in the sphere of cosmology. A number of factors accounted for this: the passing of the emergency which had caused St. Augustine to shape his own cosmology in the first place, and the gradual consolidation, through the return of normal or near-normal conditions, of developing state structures, which necessitated a general reassessment. An atmosphere of optimism began to replace the earlier one of near-despair, as fear gave way to hope as the dominant emotion. This in turn was reflected in the intellectual sphere by a renewed interest in newly discovered and newly translated works by Aristotle, a naturalist in the sense that his type of cosmology had been rooted in rationalism rather than Stoicism. His interests were decidedly "this worldly," in complete contrast to those of St. Augustine's "other worldly" orientation. All these developments resulted in a slow but spontaneous shift from faith to reason.

Yet, the time was far from ripe for a wholesale reception of Aristotelian thought resulting in a completely rational appreciation of problems of international relations. Christian cosmology prevailing in the first half of the thirteenth century insisted tenaciously that it was impossible not to believe in divine agency in all cosmic matters. What did happen was an attempt on the part of the "angelic doctor," as St. Thomas Aquinas was referred to among his followers, to reconcile Aristotelian philosophy with Christian faith in a grand synthesis. The doctor had first come across Aristotle's writings as a student at the University of Naples.

St. Augustine's theory of state was based on the assertion that political societies had come into being as a result of the fall of man and were meant as an artificial corrective to sin. By rejecting this theory, St. Thomas Aquinas made further developments in the sphere of international relations possible. The *civitas terrena* of the Thomist scheme was no longer, as it had been in St. Augustine's, entirely evil. It would have been difficult to continue to sustain such an assertion under the vastly improved conditions beginning to prevail in the thirteenth century. The atmosphere of total insecurity, so oppressively omnipresent in the fifth century, had vanished largely, if not altogether, by the thirteenth.

In effect, the Thomist synthesis amounted to a drastic modification of divine law as first expounded by St. Augustine. Natural law, representing human reason, was accepted as ranking second only to divine law, to which, in the Thomist scheme, it continued to be firmly linked; but, depending entirely on natural law, there appeared the Thomist rubric of the natural sciences, made possible by the present synthesis. From the thirteenth century onwards, therefore, the study of secular and scientific topics was pursued on an ever larger scale. Nature in the Thomist scheme was everything that existed, but it was also everything that ought to exist. "Is" and "ought" were fused into one under that category as natural law was assuming a dual aspect in being theological and scientific at one and the same time. There was a refreshing Ciceronian quality in the "angelic doctor's" definition of natural law as "a set of general principles issued by God for the guidance of men's reason." There was one part of natural law that prevailed—the law of science—and another part that commanded—the law of ethics.

The Renaissance

The second development resided in the steady growth of the notion of reason of state. This was expounded most cogently, though indirectly, by Machiavelli towards the end of the period of the Italian Renaissance at the close of the brilliant fifteenth century when writers and intellectuals at long last began to fathom the full extent of the transformation that had taken and was still taking place.

Niccoló Machiavelli (1469-1527) was not a typical intellectual. From a well-to-do Florentine family with excellent connections, he rose high in the Florentine civil service. Sent on a number of diplomatic missions to France, the empire and Italy, he experienced the French invasion of 1494 which brought about the defeat of the city-state of Florence. He saw the fall of the Medici dynasty there and heard the proclamation of the republic. Living through the republican period, he was witness to the puritan régime of Savonarola, and continued to serve until the Medici restoration in 1512. During the subsequent period of enforced idleness he wrote *The Discourses on Livy* and *The Prince* (1513).[1]

Essentially a political practitioner and not a scholar in the narrower and traditional sense, and disturbed by current diplomatic developments, Machiavelli addressed himself to the Italian princes in a prescriptive rather than a descriptive vein, in the age-old convention of the "prince's mirror."[2] He offered advice not so much on what foreign policies should be pursued, as on the basic attitudes to be adopted towards other princes, as a prerequisite of diplomatic success within the set of fresh circumstances that had arisen in Renaissance Italy.

Machiavelli still had an unclear notion of both the nature of the modern state and of the new interstate system. As has been pointed out recently, Machiavelli was thinking of *lo stato* in turn as the land, the people, or as something which could be acquired (which could not have been done in feudal times, when land was held in lease-hold), be maintained or taken away.[3] He was interested in the state as a self-sufficient entity in continual contact with other states, and therefore in need of power. Since the new type of prince personified the state, Machiavelli's arguments were directed to them as a political species. His was essentially a plea to the princes for a new outlook on politics in general, both at home and abroad. Disdaining to enter into the customary debate about the content and meaning of natural law, Machiavelli's concern was purely empirical. The conclusions he reached, while not constituting a theory as such, did provide a groundwork of knowledge for later theorists in the field of international relations.

The chief quality which Machiavelli prized in a prince was effectiveness. The effective prince was a virtuous prince, and *virtù*, the Italian word used by Machiavelli, was meant to denote the classical Latin sense of *virtus*, i.e., manliness and all that is excellent in the physical but more especially the moral constitution of man, bravery on the field of battle, and also, more subtly, the will to succeed, whether fulfilled or not.[4] He despised power seekers, while sanctifying the use of power in matters of state as a means towards an end. In this sense, then, Machiavelli was the pioneer of the idea of reason of state. The concept of *ragion di stato* was beginning to come into use from midsixteenth century only. A later writer, in what might be called the moderate, conservative Machiavellian tradition, a Jesuit by the name of Botero, was probably the first to be frank enough to equate the notion of *ragion di stato* with *ragion d'interesse*.[5]

To Machiavelli the past was important only if it could provide inspiration for the present. The feudal middle ages failed to fill this role, and he therefore passed them over altogether, preferring to draw his inspiration from the classical Roman Republic, as well as from certain contemporary princes whom he found impressive.[6] Himself impressed by the Roman Republic and its successes in the international arena, he was led to prescribe patterns of desirable behaviour for contemporary princes similar to those adopted by the ancients but lost during the feudal ages. He may well have considered the Renaissance a continuation of the classical period in which there was room for neither feudal rulers nor the type of Christianity dominant subsequently.[7] To him, feudal rulers in a Renaissance setting presented a blatant anachronism.

Just as the evolution of the relationship between Christian and non-Christian states had provided the backcloth to the process of transformation from natural into divine law, so the emergence of the interstate system from the womb of the feudal system was to give rise to the process of the separation of public and private morality. The latter was looked upon by Machiavelli as no longer relevant to the effective conduct of business of state. The morality of the Bible might continue to have a rightful place in the purely personal sphere of life, but it was the rigidly secular morality of the state which was to be dominant in public affairs. Within the general setting provided by the Renaissance, Christian ethics were irrelevant in public affairs.[8]

However, by pointing his finger at the growing political irrelevance of Christian thought, Machiavelli offended the theological precepts based in the feudal era but persisting in his times. To drive the lesson home, and to shock his contemporaries out of their complacency, he made generous use of a style both cynical and irreverent. Thus cleverness was to take the place of humility. The Roman rulers, he maintained, had expanded their domain as much by craft as by brute force. In a much-quoted passage in *The Prince* (1513), Machiavelli gave proof of his breezy style, which he employed as a polemical device, by citing the parable of the fox and the lion (itself taken from classical literature) to make his point: "A prudent ruler ought not to keep faith when by doing so it would be against his interest, and when the reasons which made him bind himself no longer exist. If men were all good, this precept would not be a good one; but as they are bad, and would not observe their faith with you, so you are not bound to keep faith with them."

This passage, alongside many others in *The Prince*, shocked not because it showed Machiavelli to be divorced from current morality, but, on the contrary, because the latter was too faithfully reflected for everyone's easy comfort. However, the new morality prevailing in the relations between states was rapidly becoming an accomplished fact. Despairing of attempts to reconcile traditional morality with the new political morality, Machiavelli merely made the latter ruthlessly explicit. In the feudal structure of international society, a comprehensive theocracy had ensured the virtue of its subjects. In Machiavelli's world, the concept of the virtuous prince replaced that of the virtuous people. Still lacking a vision of the new international society, but knowing that the death knell of the old had sounded, Machiavelli was looking forward to the emergence of fresh patterns, where Savonarola had tried in vain to revive the old. In doing so, the Florentine paved the way for a whole literature which treats the study of international politics as a purely technical affair.

The Renaissance had led to the appearance of a system of independent states in Italy, historical product of the severing of ties with the empire. It was also degrading the pope to the status of a prince, albeit one claiming rights of a *primus inter pares*. Thought in the sphere of international relations had tended to lag behind these developments, while Machiavelli, the most advanced thinker by far in this area, was still far from having succeeded in elaborating a comprehensive conception of the new type of international relations.

The Reformation

The humanists and posthumanists of the Reformation—the Spaniard Suárez, the Dutchmen Grotius and Spinoza, and the Englishman Hobbes—were for the most part still thinking and reasoning in terms of natural law of Thomist origin, where Machiavelli had boldly struck out in new directions. At the same time they were compelled to adapt themselves more and more to the idea of reason of state which, in the course of the late sixteenth and the seventeenth century it would have been rather difficult to overlook, since it began to form the backbone of diplomatic practice.

The Protestant revolt of the 1520s and the religious wars which followed in its wake raised the urgent problem of the status of Protestant rulers, an entirely new species in international relations. This was a cardinal question, since it would involve nothing less revolutionary than the determination of principles governing the relations among Christian princes of various persuasions where there had hitherto been unquestioned uniformity. The Treaty of Augsburg (1555) reflecting the military stalemate reached in the religious wars, issued in a compromise solution whereby Catholic and Lutheran princes alike were entitled to determine the religion of their subjects under the diplomatic formula of *cujus regio—ejus religio,* a settlement from which Calvinist princes were to be rigidly excluded until the Treaty of Westphalia (1648). Henceforth, Catholic and Lutheran, and after 1648 also Calvinist rulers, were to be equals in a system of international relations which, before the Reformation, had been wholly Catholic in character.

But while diplomatically convenient, the solution adopted at Augsburg in 1555 was intellectually unsatisfying since it had failed to clarify a number of points raised in connection with the prevailing cosmology. It gave occasion to a period of questioning which did not come to an end until the conclusion of the Treaty of Westphalia in 1648 spelt out in full the terms on which the new international diplomatic order was to be based. The interval between those two treaties of Augsburg and Westphalia (1555-1648) was to be one of the most formative periods in the history of thought in international relations.

Suárez and Grotius were the first to perceive the gradual but inexorable progress being made by the autonomous system of sovereign Christian states. Natural law suggested itself as the simple answer to the problem of the relations between Catholic and Protestant princes, but the real problem concerned the nature of natural law itself, in urgent need of reassessment now that Christendom was split. In a way the problem facing Suárez was similar to that with which St. Thomas Aquinas had to grapple in his day. Just as the "angelic doctor" had been compelled by historical developments to pragmatise natural law to a certain extent, so Suárez was forced to consider similar action, as Thomist cosmology came under severe pressure in the second half of the sixteenth century. For more than a hundred years before the Reformation there had been no futher collections of canon law, the instrument used by the papacy for maintaining ecclesiastical discipline. Sensing a growing divergence between the rival principles of Christian universality, now in steep decline, on the one hand, and secular international society, in buoyant ascendancy, on the other, Suárez felt anxious to fill the void caused by the now practically defunct institution of the canon law, itself the consequence of the weakening of natural law.

Though he could not afford to admit it, Suárez must also have grown resigned to the easily verifiable reality of fast developing princely power, both Catholic and Protestant. By allocating the sphere of interstate custom to the princes, he was hoping to retain the appropriate spiritual sphere for the authority of the papacy.

All the more reason for searching for a new bond that was to embrace divided Christendom in place of the lost uniformity. This is what Suárez and after him Grotius, the latter in a quasisecular way, tried to do.

Adjustment of thought on international relations to the new conditions created by the Reformation was slow. Vitoria, the Dominican scholar, was heavily preoccupied with the problem of relations between Catholic Spain and its newly conquered territories overseas. From his writings it would appear doubtful whether he was fully alive to changing international conditions, since he used the term *jus inter gentes* not to mark the emergence of a new political and legal relationship between states in general, but rather to place special stress on the universality of civilised values which, to him, the weak but well established Roman law term *jus gentium* could not do.

Both he and Francisco Suárez (1548 - 1617), a Spanish Jesuit teaching at the university of Coimbra in Portugal—Portugal was a part of Spain in those days—though humanists in the sixteenth-century sense, were essentially Thomists still in their basic outlook. It was Suárez, not Vitoria, who first gave terminological expression to the changing state of international relations by bestowing a dual meaning on the Roman law concept of *jus gentium*. As employed by the Romans, *jus gentium* was that law which was common to all peoples under Roman dominion. Suárez, setting out his views in the second volume of his work *Tractatus de legibus ac Deo legislatore* (1612), divided the world's laws into (a) eternal, (b) natural, and (c) *jus gentium*. The first of these could, according to him, be called "divine," in so far as it was ageless and timeless. This was clearly still the divine law of old. Natural law was distinct from eternal law in being human in quality. Made known to man through natural reason it was nonetheless rooted in the decalogue of the Mosaic tables. It was "the natural right of the intellect," "that which right reason dictates." Consisting of moral principles, it operated on the stimulus of instinct, without due reflection, and was applicable to conditions which were changeable. Man could have no part in its formation, since "in the case of every precept of natural law, God is the law-giver." Its prime social function was to meet the changing conditions on which the civilisation of the world depended. Its most important precept was good faith in the keeping of promises, such as those contained in contracts, including agreements between states.

At the bottom of Suárez' hierarchy was to be found *jus gentium*. Where eternal law was of divine and natural law of moral content, *jus gentium* was based on human custom, "founded upon the common usage of mankind." But just as in his scheme—in agreement with Thomist precepts—natural law was closely linked to eternal law, so *jus gentium*, though separate as a category, was intimately related to natural law—the three categories forming part of an interconnected whole. Of those parts, *jus gentium* was the one in which human free will could find its expression, meant as it was to provide scope for considerations of purely human experience. *Jus gentium* was to be the channel through which human history could flow and unfold. Acknowledging the separate but, to him, not isolated existence of states, Suárez recognised that there was a measure of interdependence between them which manifested itself in the existence of a "universal society."

Acting on these premises, Suárez divided *jus gentium* into two parts. The first, still bearing a close resemblance to the *jus gentium* of Roman law origin, denoting notions of equity held by all peoples under Rome, represented the civilised views of humanity as a whole. Generated through "usage and tradition," it was independent of any formal and "simultaneous compact or agreement on the part of all peoples." And although "treaties of peace and truces may be placed under the head of *jus gentium*"—provided they conformed to the strict natural law principle of *pacta sunt servanda*—it was above all that branch of *jus gentium* which dealt with relations between states as they had grown spontaneously, through interstate custom. Though Suárez was careful to maintain that the *jus gentium* was not of universal character in the absolute meaning of that term, it was nonetheless difficult to change it in practice, product as it was of hardened, general consensus. As understood by Suárez, therefore, international law was grounded in custom, which, through its upward connections with natural, and ultimately eternal law, formed part of the entire structure of world law. It had, viewed in this perspective, no independent status.

Treaties made up a strictly subordinate part of *jus gentium*. It was precisely in this manner that Suárez was hoping to preserve the kind of moral and spiritual unity among states that had been guarded over by the Catholic church and theocratic empire in the past and had found its formal expression in the feudal system. He disliked the idea that states should become legislators in place of *Deus legislator*, and his elaborate cosmology of law was expressly designed to prevent such an eventuality.

Hugo de Groot (Grotius) (1583 - 1645), a Dutch Protestant scholar of quasi-Calvinist convictions interested in the reunion of the Christian church, largely accepted Suárez's cosmology, but tried to improve upon it, both substantially and technically. Though still inclined to stress the preeminence of natural law, as redefined by Suárez, Grotius was evidently impressed by the power and effectiveness of current state practice, as witnessed during the Thirty Years War (1618 - 1648). He was consequently more willing than Suárez to accept the principle of state sovereignty within the framework of *jus gentium* and to allot to the states a permanent place under the rubric of *jus gentium voluntarium inter civitates*. It is noteworthy that this type of *jus gentium* differed completely from Vitoria's *jus inter gentes* employed in the previous century, Vitoria's purpose being merely, as has been noted, to make a special point of the all-embracing global, and not just Christian character of his version of *jus gentium*. Grotius' term *civitas*, on the other hand, was meant to refer without reservations to the independent, sovereign state. His *jus gentium voluntarium inter civitates* issued from interstate consensus in respect of subject matter relating to specific sets of circumstances of time and place. It was to be capable of modifying rules of natural law up to a point.

This at once raised the issue of the interconnection between *jus gentium* and natural law, a point stressed by Suárez and, of course, St. Thomas Aquinas before him. The function of natural law in Grotius' scheme of positive international law, as one now can begin to call it, was to keep independent action on the part of sovereign rulers strictly within permissible moral bounds. Unlike Suárez, Grotius saw God as the creator of the world only, but not also as its ruler. The Dutchman was therefore willing to place much greater stress than Suárez on the Aristotelian sense of the sociability of mankind.

Taking existing interstate practice as his starting point, Grotius suggested in his work *Tractatus de jure belli ac pacis libri tres,* first published in 1625 in the midst of the turmoil of the Thirty Years War, that the status of war and peace, as well as of neutrality, be defined with as much stringency as possible, so as to ascertain with precision the exact circumstances in which sovereign states were entitled to be belligerents and neutrals respectively. This, in addition to natural law, was his means of keeping otherwise unrestrained sovereignty in check.

In previous notions of natural law, justice had been the yardstick for determining when a war could be waged legitimately. But recognising realistically that now the decision in this sphere had to be left to the sovereign states themselves rather than to the representatives of emperor and papacy, as in the past, Grotius had to acknowledge, not without some reluctance, the possibility of state neutrality. This he did discreetly by devoting Ch. XVII of his work to a discussion "On those who are on neither side in war" (the Latin for "neither" is *neuter*).

The remarkable feature in Grotius, and one which was his way of satisfying Suárez's desire of maintaining the fabric of the civilised universe, was Grotius' insistence that, to be lawful, wars would have to be waged to ensure the continued cohesion of international society as a whole, instead of for the promotion of sectional interests only. This amounted to a reaffirmation, couched in secular-legal terminology, of traditional Christian "just war" doctrine as originally expounded by St. Augustine and adopted virtually unchanged by St. Thomas Aquinas.[9]

What Grotius had done was to separate the legal element from Suárez's still mainly theological cosmos, thereby making possible the emergence of a system of purely secular, positive international law dependent for its development almost entirely on the agency of sovereign states.

Where Suárez had been reluctant and Grotius self-conscious in acknowledging current trends towards the plain sovereignty of states in relation to
empire and papacy as well as in respect of each other, Thomas Hobbes (1588 -
1679) and Baruch Spinoza (1632 - 1677) gave unreserved acknowledgement
to the existence of a society of sovereign states and turned their attention to
the intrinsic relationship between those states. While not entirely able to shed
a preoccupation with natural law altogether in the manner of Machiavelli,
Hobbes and Spinoza paid far more attention to its Epicurean aspects than
either Suárez or Grotius would have dared, thus highlighting the element of
reason of state to some extent. This they accomplished by drawing attention
to some of the distinctly political implications of the new type of relations
between states, where Suárez and Grotius would have remained the prisoners
of theology and law respectively.

The differences in approach between Hobbes and Spinoza—who were
contemporaries, though Spinoza wrote later than Hobbes—were slight, stem-
ming from their individual backgrounds rather than their differing religious
origins. Thus, excommunicated by the orthodox Jewish community in the
Netherlands for his liberalism and rationalism, Spinoza set out to provide a
coherent account of the universe and man's place within it; whereas Hobbes,
vicar's son from Westport, Gloucestershire, in England, alarmed by the havoc
and upheaval wrought by the English civil war, and therefore fearful of the
prospects of anarchy, dwelt on the importance of security to be obtained
from constitutional order.

Both men were impressed by the "general inclination of all mankind," as
Hobbes put it, towards "a perpetuall and restless desire of Power after power,
that ceaseth only in death." From this Spinoza inferred the strong sentiment
of self-preservation as the universal urge of all men. International relations,
according to him, were conducted in an environment in which the rights of
individual states reached only as far as their power.

Hobbes' distinction between (a) the state of nature and (b) the law of
nature was fundamental, that between the law of nature and the law of
nations (international law) insignificant. According to his well-known major
premise, often misunderstood because taken literally instead of metaphoric-
ally, the state of raw nature in which men found themselves "before they
entr'd Society" was "meer War, and that not simply, but a War of all men,
against all men; for what is war, but that same time in which the will of
contesting by force, is fully declar'd either by Words or Deeds. The time
remaining termed Peace."[10] The state was consequently looked upon by him
as an instrument of order needing immense strengthening if it was to contain
the beast in man. Proceeding from the liberal theoretical assumption that
sovereignty resides in the people, he developed a contract model whereby a
voluntary transfer of power was envisaged from people to sovereign by way

of a "covenant" among the people, thus ensuring political order through the mediation of the "Leviathan," the strong constitutional state.

On the international plane, however, Hobbes noted, states continued to live in the state of nature in conditions of unfettered freedom, "for the state of Commonwealths considered in themselves, is natural, that is to say, hostile; neither if they cease from fighting, is it therefore to be called Peace, but rather a breathing time, in which one enemy observing the motion and countenance of the other, values his security not according to the Pacts, but the forces and counsels of his adversary."[11] Whereas in the state of nature, men lived in untrammelled liberty, the law of nature served to instil a sense of self-enlightened reason in mitigation of the harshness of the state of nature. Not being "an Agreement of men, but the dictate of reason,"[12] the law of nature was deemed "the summe of Morall Philosophy."

Spinoza, deeply affected by the sense of material progress pervading his native Netherlands, considered the absolute authority of the sovereign to be derived from his constant devotion to the common welfare of his subjects. Both he and Hobbes were agreed that, in Spinoza's words, the sovereign "may live entirely as he pleases and is not bound to obey the will of another, or to recognise any mortal as his judge."[13] Treaties of peace or alliance could in those circumstances remain in force only as long as the motives for concluding them—listed by Spinoza as fear of loss or hope of gain—continued to hold good. Here Spinoza was touching on a sensitive point in the new system of international relations, as he detected a basic incompatibility between the principle of popular accountability at home and that of the responsibility of rulers towards other rulers. He maintained that the moment the conditions listed by him ceased to apply, the contractual bonds were dissolved and each of the parties to them had "the right to break the treaty whenever he wished." To be on the safe side, and, one suspects, to sweeten the bitter pill, Spinoza tried to strengthen this assertion by a reference to the Scriptures which allegedly taught good faith only as a general rule. It followed that "contracts for the future" were valid only so long as the cause which had produced them, the test of this being the extent to which it served the interests of the ruler's subjects. Hobbes similarly insisted that in the state of nature contractual agreements, like treaties, depended on the judgement of the parties and on their good faith.[14]

Though considering that "it were a great error to call the Law of Nature unwritten law," Hobbes nonetheless thought that "the Law of Nature and the Law of Nature is the same thing. And every sovereign hath the same Right, in procuring the safety of his people, that any particular man can have, in procurring the safety of his body."[15]

This, though Hobbes would not perhaps have admitted as much, was a possible definition of reason of state. But such was the hold of natural law on men's minds that Spinoza saw it as incumbent on himself to justify his startling thesis in respect of good faith in terms of natural law also by way of special pleading. Conceding in accordance with Christian tradition that natural law was rooted in the divine, he construed it to mean that sovereign rulers were in duty bound to promote the welfare of their subjects in the widest sense. The sovereign's duties towards his subjects, by implication both absolute and direct, were at all times to prevail over his duties towards other sovereigns, these being by implication less compelling. Sovereignty basically belonged to the whole people, and no sovereign could "keep promises to the detriment of his state without committing a sin." Thus, if he saw any promise he had made to be operating to the disadvantage of his state, he could only keep it by breaking his pledge to his subjects, for the latter was a pledge which bound him most strictly, and one moreover which men generally promise most solemnly to keep. It followed that when faced with the choice of breaking the trust placed in him by his subjects or that by his fellow-sovereigns, a popular ruler was bound to give unquestioned preference to the interests of the former.

By justifying reason of state in terms of natural law—even where the latter had to be strained by Spinoza to contain his line of argument—Hobbes and Spinoza managed to do justice to both the historical realities of the moment and Christian tradition at one and the same time.

Prescriptions

Both men seem to have been curiously unconcerned about the effects of war. It ought to be realised, therefore, that in their day war, in spite of its horrors, was considered less a threat to the fabric of society in general than internal conflict. Thus, in Hobbes—as he explained in *The Leviathan*—the disorders of the English Civil War had induced the belief that, because of their high level of organisation, states were at least potentially capable of taking care of the security of most of their subjects; there would not necessarily follow from the involvement in international war that misery which resulted from the licence of particular men possible in domestic society. Moreover, he was certain that in international conflict "a certain mean was wont to be observed,"[16] a view which, under the shadow of the French Revolution over a century later, was voiced also by Edmund Burke, according to whom international wars were less to be feared than civil wars, since the latter were more destructive.[17]

It must have been for reasons like these that it never occurred to Hobbes to suggest the need of an international covenant setting up a super-Leviathan on a universal scale on the analogy of the Leviathan proposed in his contract model. Instead, Hobbes sought refuge under the umbrella of traditional natural law as the ethical basis of relations between sovereign states. According to him, then, peace could not be achieved unless the law of nature was generally observed between states. Reason, he argued, was the principal element in the law of nature and implied a striving towards some sort of international order. It followed that "the same law, that dictateth to men that have no civil government, what they ought to do, and what to avoid in regard to one another, dictateth the same to commonwealths, that is, to the consciences of sovereign princes and sovereign assemblies; there being no court of natural justice, but in conscience only."[18]

The furthest that Hobbes would go in this direction was to recommend that, where peace seemed unattainable, alliances should be formed.[19] While Spinoza and Hobbes were at one in treating any war waged by sovereign rulers as legitimate, the eclectically minded Hobbes saw reason of state as inherent in natural law and regarded the latter as operating towards the imposition of restraints, a view reflected in his conception of the functions of war. According to him that war was rational—as distinct from legitimate—that was waged for real ends. War for the sake of glory, as in Athens and Carthage, was condemned, while wars of plunder were similarly dismissed as unreasonable.

These could hardly be called radical proposals, and Spinoza, for one, was not to be bothered with the invocation of natural law when it came to making prescriptions regarding the future of international society. Having cast considerable doubt on the value of good faith in international agreements, he felt he had to suggest a practical way out of the dilemma. If rulers could not be expected to keep good faith in all circumstances, then the remedy lay in making it difficult for them to evade their international obligations by engaging them multilaterally in collective treaties, instead of allowing them to contract bilaterally, as in the past. But in making these proposals, Spinoza enjoyed the advantage of writing some while after the conclusion of the Peace Treaty of Westphalia (1648), which, though consisting formally of a series of bilateral commitments, amounted in its aggregate to a multilateral network of legal obligations, the effectiveness of which in that instance could easily be verified whilst Spinoza was composing his *Tractati.*

In so far as they thought in terms of an absolute but constitutional state, Hobbes and Spinoza were in advance of their time; but their thought on international relations in general was germane to a period which was marked by the advent of an absolutist international society in which reason of state was the first command. After them, natural law lost all traces of its former connection with divine law.

NOTES

1. Professor M. Lerner, in a foreword to one of the latest English translation of *The Prince,* informs us that it was originally part of *The Discourses on Livy;* but that, because

of the urgency of the international situation in Italy, and especially that of Florence, *The Prince* was published separately.

2. These consisted of advice offered to a ruler on a variety of subjects of a technical kind, such as etiquette, but not excluding political matter altogether.

3. See J.H. Hexter, *The Vision of Politics on the Eve of the Reformation.* London: Allen Lane, 1973.

4. Machiavelli's virtuous prince was not by any means invariably successful. Witness his positive references to Leonidas, who was killed while fearlessly, but in vain, defending the pass of Thermopylae against overwhelming odds. Had he been alive in the early 1960s, Machiavelli would have regarded Che Guevara in the same light.

5. G. Botero, *Della ragione di stato* (1589).

6. In that category were to be found Ferdinand of Castile and the Emperor Maximilian of Habsburg.

7. The *Discourses on Livy* deal with Rome's glory in international affairs, while *The Prince* is concerned with forms of government to make such glory possible.

8. In this respect Machiavelli might be classed as the heir of developments initiated by St. Thomas Aquinas and further developed by Ptolemy of Lucca, one of the latter's disciples, who completed *De regimine principum* (1277 - 1279), a work begun by the "angelic doctor." It is significant that these developments should have been fostered by Italians.

9. On the legal history of the concept of "just war," see F.H. Russell, *The Just War in the Middle Ages.* Cambridge: Cambridge University Press, 1975.

10. T. Hobbes, *Philosophical Rudiments concerning Government and Society.* London: Royston, 1651, Ch. 1, Art. XII, p. 13.

11. Hobbes, ibid., Ch. 13, Art. VII, p. 195.

12. Ibid., Ch. 2, Art. I, p. 16.

13. B. Spinoza, *Tractatus Theologico-Politicus* (1670), Ch. 16.

14. Hobbes, op. cit., Ch. 2, Art. XI, p. 26.

15. *Leviathan,* Ch. 3.

16. Hobbes, op. cit., Ch. 5, Art. 2.

17. E. Burke, *Works,* Vol. 4, p. 81.

18. *Leviathan,* Ch. 31.

19. Hobbes, op. cit., Ch. 14.

Chapter 3

THE AGE OF ABSOLUTISM:

THE BALANCE OF POWER

While a system of independent states was gradually arising during the Renaissance and Reformation, the princes at the helm of these states were too preoccupied with the task of decision-making in a new and unfamiliar context of foreign policy to think of devising mechanisms to govern the relations among them. In making their day-to-day decisions, they relied on their tactical instincts, rather than on any broad conception of the nature of international society.

Nonetheless, the concept of the "balance of power" was to develop gradually as the structure of a society of states made its appearance, surfacing first in the context of schemes for the consolidation of that society, and later as part of investigations concerning the nature of the "balance" in which the minds of the investigators were still clouded by the political prejudices and diplomatic interests of the moment. Truly scholarly pursuit of the concept had to wait until the two World Wars of the twentieth century had made such work a matter of urgent universal concern.

Thus, Machiavelli showed little awareness of the concept as it related to Italy or other areas, although in his days a "balance of power" undoubtedly existed within the peninsula. The dominating notion in the sphere of international relations during the sixteenth century was still that of reason of state. In his monumental work of *Storia d'Italia* (first edition probably about

1537), Francesco Guicciardini (1483 - 1540), Machiavelli's contemporary, came closer to an appreciation of the "balance" when he used the term "counterpoise" to indicate the need for international balancing.[1] Gradually, as the outlines of the new, pluralist international system presented themselves in sharper relief, the mode of its operation became the subject of intense debate. During the seventeenth and eighteenth centuries, the difficult concept of the "balance of power"—for so long implicit in the foreign policies of states—was finally made explicit, and in a laborious process of definition raised to the level of a principle of international relations during the period of the French Revolution and the Napoleonic wars.

The Treaty of Westphalia laid the formal basis of the new international order. It provided a watershed in at least three senses. First, it terminated the wars of religion occasioned by the Reformation; second, it finally reduced pope and emperor to the status of mere princes on a footing of equality; and, third, it legitimised an international order based on the existence of independent, sovereign states.

It was by no means clear, however, on what principles the new international order would operate. Intellectual energies had been concentrated on the problem of sovereignty, and ratiocination regarding the essence of the new international system tended to lag behind state practice. What thought was given to the matter tended to concentrate on the stabilisation, rather than the operation of the new type of international relations. The most significant development by far in the field of state practice concerned the clumsy and increasingly unworkable attempts to stabilise the pluralist system by means of the dynastic principle. Since most dynasties of the period operated on the basis of primogeniture, lines of succession were left largely to genealogical chance. Aware of the uncertainty and unpredictability of that device, the rulers of the time sought to mitigate those effects by entering into prudent marriage arrangements and by making timely settlements by will, both devices which, in the measure to which they came to be seen as unwieldy, were resorted to less and less, though some instances were still recorded in the second half of the nineteenth century. To be truly effective, these arrangements would have had to be revised with fair frequency in the light of current diplomatic developments, and this they proved unable to accomplish. This must have been evident at the time, for Spinoza expressed the belief that royal marriages were apt to lead to war.[2]

The net effect of the application of the dynastic-genealogical principle to the field of international relations was disruption rather than stabilisation, in the form of a series of wars of succession, those of the Austrian, Bavarian, and Polish successions being good examples, and the Spanish the most prolonged and destructive.

It was in the course of the Spanish war and the period leading up to it that the principle of the "balance of power"—practised implicitly before—was rendered increasingly explicit in diplomacy. This war was waged expressly in the name of the "balance" on the part of the anti-French coalition which, by and large, succeeded in imposing its will in the shape of the separation of the French and Spanish crowns. The Treaty of Utrecht (1713), which ended the war, contained a clause by which the "balance of power" was elevated from a political slogan to a principle of international order. More important still, the treaty imposed an obligation on its signatories to maintain that balance. Henceforth the balance of power was to be a diplomatic goal to be positively sought after, and a prescription for statesmen to follow consciously.

Stabilising the Balance

There was no dearth of elaborate schemes during that period—some of an ingenious kind—for the stabilisation of the balance, all seemingly motivated by the noble desire to create permanent peace and order.[3] On closer inspection, however, it becomes apparent that many, if not all of these schemes contained features which detracted from their ostensible purpose. For one thing, many were inspired by statesmen and their advisers involved in current diplomatic issues, and did not result from disinterested enquiry on the part of detached thinkers. For another, though dressed up as impartial, or nearly so, they were intended to promote the diplomatic fortunes of their authors' masters or countries. Their impartiality was spurious, and their subjectivity transparent. All relied for their support on the creation of international political institutions varying in degree of constitutional sophistication, and were based on the unrealistic assumption that the rulers of Europe—not to speak of extra-European rulers—who had just won their protracted struggle for unrestricted sovereignty, would willingly surrender it to an untried international body of state representatives for the sake of the ideal of international stability.

Most of these schemes exhibited confederal features usually associated with alliances, and it was not always clear to what extent they were meant to be lasting. What is beyond doubt is that, in one way or another, they were concerned with stabilising the balance.

Until the end of the seventeenth century most of the authors of those schemes showed an underlying anxiety that an unstable balance of power might benefit the advancing Turks, and in two very early cases, those of P. Dubois' *De recuperatione terrae sanctae* (1306) and Marsilius of Padua's *Defensor Pacis* (1326) the main purpose was to revitalise the Crusades to the Holy Land.

The two schemes of George Podiebrad, King of Bohemia and Hussite dissident in religion, *De unione Christianorum contra Turcos* and *Traité des Alliances et Conféderations* (both from 1458)[4] resulted from the shock of the ultimate collapse of the Byzantine Empire in 1453 and the consequent fear of its Turkish conquerors. The purpose was to bring about an alliance having as its overt objective the struggle against the Turks, but the covert one of obtaining protection against pope and emperor, neither of whom was to be included in the proposed confederation. Addressed to the King of France, these schemes reveal the Bohemian King's ambition to establish a bipolar balance in which the King of France was ultimately to be emperor in the West, with Podiebrad figuring prominently as German emperor at Frankfurt and as eastern emperor at Constantinople.

Where Podiebrad had looked towards France as the promoter of his scheme, Tomassio Campanella, an Italian monk, regarded first Spain, and having fallen out with Spain, France as the *hegemon* capable of realising his plans; his ideas were embodied in *De monarchia Hispanica discursus* (1640), and *Discorsi ai principi d'Italia, ed altri scritti,* probably first composed in 1600, on the one hand, and *Le monarchie delle nazione* (1635) on the other. Campanella pleaded for an alliance of Catholic states to consolidate the Catholic position in Europe vis-à-vis the remaining states. There was also a utopian dimension to his general conception.[5]

Attributed to Henry IV of France (1553 - 1610), *Le Grand Dessein,* as it came to be called, for a *"république monarchie trés chretiénne"* was spelt out in the Duc de Sully's memoirs[6] after the King's death and presented a barely disguised edge against the Habsburgs. For this reason the scheme may be regarded as having eventual French hegemony in Europe as its object.

Among the politically disinterested schemes of the period is to be found the Frenchman Emeric Crucé's *Nouveau Cynée* (1623). Claiming that "the times of victory and triumph are over," Crucé—distrustful of lawyers and theologians alike—expressly addressed himself to "monarchs and sovereign princes of this time." It was meant to be an all-embracing, global appeal, the most unusual aspect of which was to desire to integrate, rather than to fight the Turks.

Both William Penn's *Essays towards the Present and Future Peace of Europe* (1693) and John Bellers' *Some Reason for an European State* (1710) show that, as Quakers, the foremost motive of these two was the pursuit of peace.

As to the structural features of those schemes, all contained provisions for an assembly of state representatives, with Crucé's according it universal suffrage—expressly mentioning Tartary and China as potential members— while Penn (who welcomed membership of Turks and Muscovites) and the remainder wanted it confined to Europe. Only Campanella insisted on a franchise restricted to Catholic rulers in a Senate in Rome, taking its decisions by majority vote, with the pope presiding. Podiebrad's wish was to exclude papacy and empire.

Podiebrad also envisaged the creation of a court of justice (*parlamentum seu consistorium*), while Crucé's assembly of ambassadors, conveniently sited in Venice, would have been equipped with arbitral authority, as would Penn's. As to executive powers, Podiebrad, Campanella and Penn thought in terms of a combined army as a last resort to enforce decisions of the assembly, while Cruce merely implied as much. The Bohemian King would also have imposed a financial levy in support of such a force and suggested the setting up of a special fund to finance the fight against the Turks.

Crucé still thought it proper to establish a system of precedence among existing rulers, with the pope at the top, followed by the sultan of Turkey, the emperor, the king of France and other kings after him, whereas no such provisions figured in the later schemes of Penn and Bellers, who took international equality for granted.

Among the schemes cited, those of Sully, Penn, and Bellers are the ones focussing directly on the principle of the balance of power. Thus, Sully tried to achieve a balance by dividing Europe into fifteen states of roughly equal strength, and was prepared to see a redrawing of frontiers, at the expense of the empire and Spain mainly, in pursuit of that objective. Equally anxious to stabilise the balance of power, Bellers intended to divide Europe into one hundred equal "cantons and provinces" for the purpose of achieving a balanced system of representation without tampering with the territorial integrity of the European states, so that, as Hinsley rightly comments, "the disparity in the power of States would be offset by the division into cantons."[7] Each canton or province was to contribute 1,000 soldiers to a common force, so as to extend the principle of balance into the military sphere.

The most intriguing novelty, however, was suggested by Penn, whose "Parliament or House of States of Europe" would be composed of state representatives whose number was related directly to their country's wealth. Penn estimated that, in accord with this criterion, the Empire might be represented by thirteen, Spain and France by ten representatives each, and so forth, establishing in this way a balance of economic power.

In some ways, C.I. Castel de Saint-Pierre's *Projet pour rendre la paix perpétuelle en Europe,* published during the final phase of the tortuous negotiations that preceded the Treaty of Utrecht of 1713, which terminated the War of the Spanish Succession,[8] marked the climax of past attempts to stabilise the balance, incorporating and refining as it did many of the concepts elaborated by previous writers. It seems fit, therefore, to give a separate outline of the salient features of his scheme here.

Under the provisions of Saint-Pierre's scheme, sovereign rulers were obliged to renounce recourse to war, and to seek the mediation of their confederates in the event of a dispute arising. If mediation failed, these rulers were bound to accept a decision by an international senate reached by qualified majority vote. In the event of that decision being ignored, the senate would be empowered to use force to impose the decision, using an international force drawn from contingents furnished by the confederates, and commanded by a generalissimo.

As additional safeguard against imbalances that might develop, Saint-Pierre envisaged that "in return for joining the Union, each prince will be assisted against rebels by the forces of his confederates. So that by this means . . . [rebels] will always be reduced to obedience." The last provision may justly be regarded as the *ultima ratio* of stabilising an existing balance.

Operating the Balance

A true theory of the balance of power had to advance from the sphere of imagery to that of model-building. Scientific concepts of balance taken from the mechanical sciences proved helpful in this respect. The revolution of the natural sciences in the seventeenth century thus came to the aid of those enquiring into the nature of the balance of power, for it enabled them to proceed by analogy, a facility denied to Thucydides, who, writing during the fifth century B.C., had been confined to the historical imagination. Theoretical models in the social sciences springing from the scientific as distinct from the historical imagination often, but not invariably, reflect the state of current technology.[9] It could not have been altogether a historical coincidence that speculation concerning the nature of the balance was taking place pari passu with the progress of the scientific revolution of the seventeenth century, which had begun with Kepler's publication of the laws of planetary motion in 1619 and was virtually complete with Newton's discovery of the laws of gravitation in 1687.[10] In the realms of astronomy and mechanics alike, the central principle was precisely one of balance, providing ample inspiration for the construction of fruitful analogies. On a down-to-earth level, there was also the great fascination exerted by the fine balance of the clock which was perfectly accessible for inspection in every seventeenth century middle-class home. Though Cromwell made use of the mechanical analogy in the middle of that century by referring to the principle of balance underlying all constitutional theory, the heyday of the concept was to be the following century, in which Frederick the Great of Prussia expressly compared the system of international relations to that of a clock, in which Edmund Burke called the balance of power the common law of Europe, and in which Prince Kaunitz, the modern-minded Habsburg minister, boasted of the 'arithmetical methods' employed in his diplomacy.

And yet, theorising made painfully slow progress in spite, and possibly because of the great popularity of the concept. State practice kept abreast of theorising, making it difficult at times to distinguish theory from ideology. The gap between the two was being closed by degrees in the course of the eighteenth century, during which the conceptualisation of the balance of power made some progress.

The Continental Tradition

The hub of the continental approach towards the problem of the balance rested in Germany, an area prone to manipulation by the powers since the Treaty of Westphalia and, because it was in the centre of Europe, psychologically sensitive to the dimension of territorial contiguity. The continental tradition of looking at the balance developed within the context of a growing complexity of that equilibrium, especially because in the course of the eighteenth century, both Prussia and Russia had to be considered integral parts of it. The debate on the nature of the balance reflected these conditions on the continent. More sophistication was added, though the element of diplomatic partiality was rarely altogether absent. Evidence of this is to be found in the significant tracts produced in the eighteenth century by L.M. Kahle[11] and H.G. von Justi,[12] and in the response they aroused.[13]

Kahle, who was Professor of Philosophy at the University of Göttingen, sought to provide a diagnosis of international society in the mideighteenth century by holding that "each nation in its natural state must be considered as the enemy of all others; or disposed to be such." J.P.F. Ancillon,[14] writing in response to Napoleon's policies over half a century later, added that the balance of power was an essential condition of international order. But, as in the earlier literature on the subject, the question of the management of the balance posed itself. Rigid international institutions were not a practical proposition, and so new modes of adjustment had to be considered which could ensure flexibility.

TERRITORIAL COMPENSATION

The principle of compensation was conceded by Kahle, who remarked that "the most legitimate rulers must sometimes renounce their rights in order to maintain the balance." Ancillon argued similarly, claiming that a state might justifiably be compelled by other states to sacrifice for the common good territory to which it held good legal title, just as by way of a domestic analogy a ruler could compel his subjects to give up part of their wealth for the benefit of the community.

State practice relied largely on the expedient of "territorial compensation" to render the principle of the balance flexible. Thus, territorial compensation was implicit in the Treaty of Utrecht, where territories were generously divided among Habsburgs and Bourbons, the two antagonists of the War of the Spanish Succession. Montesquieu was among the first to draw attention to newly discovered territories overseas as potentially more or less automatic equalisers among states.[15] During the second half of the eighteenth century there occurred the cynical partitions of Poland. Towards the end of the next century, these were followed by the division of China into spheres of influence affording equal access to the trade of a handful of great powers under the device of the "open door." The Ottoman Empire was finally carved up after a century of partition schemes at the close of the First World War in the twentieth century. At the end of the Second World War territorial rearrangements were affected at the expense not only of Germany, Japan, and Italy, the defeated powers, but also of Poland, Czechoslovakia and China, allied states unable to resist the major allied powers' determination to compensate each other in this manner in order to preserve the world balance.

STOCHASTIC COMPENSATION

The second means of adjustment, stochastic compensation,[16] arose out of the practical difficulty of quantifying the concept of power itself, an awkward aspect of the principle of the balance since it involved considerations of domestic developments of states. For a long time it had been tacitly assumed in the continental conception of the balance of power that it was possible to make reasonably precise comparisons of the real strength of various states. However, von Justi gave warning in the eighteenth century that power was a concept difficult to define, and a debate ensued as to the exact nature of the ingredients of which state power was composed. Von Justi was able to show that the dramatic weakening of Spain exposed the element of territorial extent as illusory; that in spite of their large populations, Persia, classical Rome and China had all fallen victim to foreign powers at one time or another; and that Louis XIV of France had ruined himself because of the heavy burdens which the great size of his armies had imposed on him. Von Justi was finally driven to the conclusion—which happened to suit him politically, as he was a supporter of the system of enlightened despotism instituted by Frederick the Great in Prussia—that the true strength of a state resided in the overall efficiency (*Vollkommenheit*) of its government. From there he went on to offer the radical but perfectly consistent proposition that if the balance of power were to be maintained effectively, this must needs lead to the international prohibition of substantial changes in the overall efficiency of important states. In such an event, von Justi pointed out with disquieting logic, a right or intervention would have to be created on the part of the remaining powers to keep the growing overall efficiency of the affected state within acceptable bounds. Thus, the inherent logic of the principle of the balance of power, as then interpreted, carried the paradoxical implication of provoking foreign intervention against well-governed states. It was, however, impossible to establish reliable criteria by which the growing power of such a state could be considered "too big." Thus, von Justi thought he had proven the absurdity of the principle of the balance which, he implied strongly, was but a rationalisation of the perceived interests of the powers.

If his hidden political purpose had been to destroy any pretext on behalf of certain European states for acting against Prussia, such reasoning could easily serve to render plausible the very opposite diplomatic intention. Thus, a quasi-state paper published in Austria in 1761—the Habsburg state was permanently aligned against Prussia during the eighteenth century—maintained that Prussia's ostensible power was enhanced through her ruler's "zeal and talent to wage war, himself taking the field and acting as supreme warlord."[17]

The Maritime Tradition

Where continentals, and especially Germans, would argue endlessly about the intrinsic properties of the balance, the British—main exponents of the maritime tradition—were above all else concerned about its management. Implicit in that notion was the idea of deliberate and calculated manipulation, the British approach towards the balance having been marked from the beginning by a sense of voluntarism which was in stark contrast to the objectivism of the continental approach.

The maritime dimension of the eighteenth century imported the increasingly prominent commercial element. Kahle, a pro-British writer, approvingly regarded British trade as forming part of the general balance of power,[18] and Daniel Defoe observed in *A Plan of the English Commerce* (1737), albeit with some exaggeration, that "to be master of the marine power is to be master of all the power and all the commerce in Europe." British policy acted on those assumptions.[19]

The new factor of commerce in the balance is attested by French pamphlet literature in which a possible restoration of a world monarchy was foreseen through the application of overwhelming naval strength, a state of affairs which could be prevented only by attending to the maintenance of the balance at sea, as well as on land. To these observations the Duc de Choiseul added the nicely antithetical comment that "the English, while pretending to protect the balance on land which no one threatens, are entirely destroying the balance at sea which no one defends." Maubert de Gouvest, in his pamphlet *Politique Danois* published in Copenhagen in 1759, passionately tried to draw attention to the need for an equal sharing of the balance at sea.[20]

Closely connected with the element of growing British seapower was the concept of the "balancer." As early as the sixteenth century, Cardinal Wolsey laid down the maxim *"cui adhaereo praeest,"* but it was in the course of the intense Franco-Spanish rivalry of the second half of the seventeenth century that the British role as balancer capable of tipping the European balance of power came into its own. Its diplomatic advantages to Britain were stressed by Lord Halifax, the political philosopher, in the *Character of a Trimmer* (1688), who was echoed by the writer and political essayist Jonathan Swift (1667 - 1745), who enlarged the meaning of the term by emphasising the special advantages accruing to the balancer. Swift added for good measure that it was not necessary "that power should be equally divided" between the two principals and the balancer, "for the balance may be held by the weakest, who by his address and conduct—removing from either scale, and adding to his own—may keep the scales duly poised."[21] To further the principle of maintaining a balance, the true function of the balancer would have been precisely to "keep the scales duly poised," as suggested by Swift. While recognising the validity of the principle of the balance explicitly from the late seventeenth century onwards, Britain claimed the right to be the balancer of the system by virtue of her imposing command of the seas. However, during the nineteenth century, Richard Cobden was to claim in his pamphlet *Russia* (1836) that Britain was playing that role "not with the blindness of the goddess of justice herself, or with a view to the equilibrium of opposite interests, but with a Cyclopean eye to her own aggrandisement."

Under the powerful impact of Napoleon's attempted overthrow of the entire system of the balance, the British pragmatic approach towards that phenomenon tended to fuse with the objective continental one. As a result, the characteristically mechanical conception of the continental type gradually ceded to the voluntarist conception of the balance favoured by Britain. In the course of this transformation, the much more sophisticated notion of a free-wheeling balance employing a multiple balancer emerged, which, it was hoped, would provide ample scope for diplomatic flexibility and manoeuvre. The process was initiated in 1803 by Lord Brougham, who in an essay notable for its detachment indicated the prime importance of the concept of balance thus: "The grand and distinguishing feature of the balancing theory is the systematic form to which it reduces those plain and obvious principles of national conduct; the perpetual attention to foreign affairs which it inculcates; the constant watchfulness which it prescribes over every moment in all parts of the system; the subjection to which it tends to place all national passions and antipathies to the views of remote expedience."

Three years later, in 1806, Friedrich Gentz, a Prussian civil servant probably "in the pay of the British cabinet to produce writings of this type"[22] and destined to be secretary to the Congress of Vienna in 1815, made a substantial contribution to the subject, by (a) elaborating the concept of the free-wheeling balance and its adjunct, the multiple balancer, and (b) casting fresh light on the interregional nature of the newly developing historical balance. Gentz's central thesis was that diversity of power, not equality, was an essential condition for its balance. Big and small powers alike had to be involved in maintaining the balance, and symmetry in this respect was positively undesirable. In presenting this thesis, Gentz was, of course, attempting to gear a particular conception of the balance of power to the diplomatic interests of Britain, Prussia, and Austria.[23] Beyond this he was hoping that by creating the new notion of free-wheeling equilibrium, he might give the mechanical continental theories of the balance prevailing during the eighteenth century the dynamic quality they so manifestly lacked. The ideal balancers in his scheme were small states in a position to shift their weight from one side to the other, in accordance with an earlier idea vented by Swift, so as to redress any imbalances that might occur.

Gentz's conception had the great advantage of leaving the definition of what constituted the ingredients of power to the discretion of the states concerned, and would not exclude action on the part of the balancers in the event of accretions of internal strength by any state, a contingency made acutely topical by Napoleon's proven ability to mobilise the material resources of France. Disliking the continental device of territorial compensation, Gentz placed heavy emphasis on the mechanism of shifting alliances. His expectations of a free-wheeling equilibrium were, however, foiled by the advent of the industrial revolution, which he never lived to witness, and which was to show that only major industrial powers would in future be capable of functioning as effective balancers. Cobden, apostle of absolute nonintervention, criticised the idea of the balancer *inter alia* on the ground that it was a recipe for involving Britain in foreign intervention. It was historical irony, therefore, that, after the creation of the German Reich in 1871, H. von Treitschke should have thought of the new and 'sated' Germany as the ideal manager of the continental balance of power, thereby saving Britain the trouble of continental entanglements and leaving her free to look after her maritime interests.[24]

Gentz also drew attention to the growing regional complexity of the balance of power in Europe. In the last year of his life (1797), Edmund Burke had divided the balance into "the great middle balance" composed of Britain, France, and Spain; "the balance of the North; the balance, external and internal of Germany; and the balance of Italy;" and he added that "in all those systems of balance, England was the power to whose custody it was thought it might be most safely committed."[25] All the more essential, therefore, that there should be small powers to grease the interacting wheels of such a complex balance, according to Gentz.

Gradually other discoveries were made about the balance; notably that, however operated, it merely preserved the independence of states. It would not guarantee peace, a shortcoming noted by Burke as early as 1760, before the partitions of Poland. The notion began to gain ground that to be lasting, the balance had to be buttressed by a political system composed of all European states. A.H.L. Heeren, a historian at the University of Göttingen, was to make a proposal of this kind in a manual on the history of the states system.[26] Lord Brougham similarly advocated the establishment of a "general union . . . of all the European powers in one connecting system—obeying certain laws and actuated by a common principle." The idea of the balance of power thus logically led to the notion of a political Concert of Europe, not unlike the one suggested during the seventeenth century in numerous writings but within a different set of historical expectations. To be effective as well as, manageable, the balance had to be subjected to central political control. The two basic notions of stabilisation and management had to march hand in hand.

Ideology

There were other complications. The French Revolution had injected the new element of ideology into the general body of politics, alerting, and in some cases alarming Europe's statesmen. Thus, Metternich, who professed an eighteenth-century belief in the existence of general laws governing the relations between states, was thoroughly alarmed at the prospect of liberal and national advance. Wishing to charge the Congress system inaugurated at Vienna in 1815 with the function of ideological surveillance, he antagonised Britain, which eventually became wedded to the principle of nonintervention. However, while Metternich's fears regarding the incompatibility of liberalism with the basic principle of the balance of power—so carefully applied in the Vienna settlement—were unjustified, he was on firmer ground in being suspicious of the forces of nationalism in this respect.

In their unadulterated form, the principles of nationalism and of the balance of power were indeed wholly incompatible. The first to note the real impact of the former on the latter was Leopold von Ranke, German historian and political scientist, who viewed the balance as a system in which movement and change were the normal conditions, and which was capable of adjusting itself accordingly. Ranke consequently made allowances for the national factor in adjustments in the system of balance in a way to which Palmerston, who pursued a conscious policy of reconciling the two principles, could hardly have objected.[27] Gentz would have had none of this as he had completely ruled out adjustments in the balance on ideological grounds.[28] The operation of the balance in the modified way suggested by Ranke was possible only so long as national forces were willing to keep their claims within moderate bounds. This was no longer the case between 1914 and 1945, and so that system broke down. It would, however, be a mistake to write it off at this point, since the post-1945 system of the United Nations was in essence an attempt to revive the Concert of Europe, guardian of the balance, on a world scale. Again it was shown that this would not work unless ideological considerations could be prevented from affecting the principle of the balance. It was only with the advent of Dr. Henry Kissinger as effective director of United States foreign policy and the simultaneous rise of a set of decision-makers in the Soviet Union willing in the final analysis to subordinate their ideological ambitions to their desire for security, that something like a multipolar Concert of Northern Hemisphere Powers—a *pentagonate*, in effect, as in 1815—could come into existence in the mid-1970s capable of operating the balance of power on a world scale.[29]

Recent Theorising on the Balance of Power

Relatively little attention was paid to the principle of the balance after 1918, mainly because it had been thought to be effectively shackled by the new political institutions of the League of Nations and the United Nations. The matter became acute once more after 1947, with the outbreak of the Cold War and the ensuing disenchantment with international political institutions. In 1948, H.J. Morgenthau, while reaffirming the traditional function of the balance as a regulator of international relations in lieu of international law, and while himself remaining sceptical as to its ultimate value to international society, held that states were in practice striving not just to maintain the balance, but because of the difficulty of assessing the quantitative element of power, to achieve a "margin of safety" over and above that of other states.[30] Morgenthau cited the eighteenth-century writer Lord Bolingbroke according to whom "it is sufficient that the deviation [i.e., the "margin"] be not too great. Some there will always be."[31]

A systematic reassessment of the nature of the concept undertaken by E.B. Haas in 1953 was still essentially within the accustomed stream of thinking on the subject.[32] From then onwards thought on the balance reflected the rapidly spreading alarm about, first, the escalation in the strength of nuclear devices and their delivery systems, and, second, the increasing potentialities of violence on the substate level. The central questions now being asked were: Was stability of the balance, whether politically desirable or not, feasible any longer? Conversely, was the very existence of these new and terrifying weapons, untried and uncontrollable as they seemed, a guarantee for stability, irrespective of whether, in theory, they upset what was now the "balance of world power"?

A spate of literature began to appear, subsumed under the generic term "strategic studies," concerned, as in prenuclear centuries, with theorising on the nature of the new balance. Now that war conducted by nuclear devices seemed inherently irrational, the first concern of theorists had to be the avoidance of war. The basis of these endeavours was the scientific treatise produced by J. von Neumann and O. Morgenstern on *The Theory of Games and Economic Behavior* in 1944.[33] The way in which psychological considerations were now beginning to overshadow the customary logistical ones was reflected in the change of emphasis from balance of power to "balance of terror" from 1957 onwards.[34] These years also saw the appearance of what were to be two classic works dealing with the strategy of conflict and— carrying on where von Neumann and Morgenstern had left off in 1944—on fights, games, and debates.[35]

As new aspects to the daunting balance of terror began to present themselves, further fields of enquiry were opened in an effort to achieve fresh theoretical refinements. Such was the case with bargaining theory, which reflected the urgent need to avoid nuclear conflict at almost any cost.[36] This in turn gave rise to thinking on the subject of crisis management.[37] Closely connected with this was the emerging literature on modes of decision-making inaugurated by R.C. Snyder, H.W. Bruck, and B. Sapin in 1962,[38] the implicit objective here being "safe" decision-making. Nor was there any shortage of ultrarealistic assessments of nuclear strategy and war, as presented in one particular imaginative but spine-chilling attempt.[39]

Within the mainstream of traditional thought on the balance, attempts—this time completely disinterested politically—were beginning to be made to elaborate typologies of balances with a view to ascertaining their relative stabilities. Drawing on biological science for inspiration and moving into the field of systems theory, M.A. Kaplan in 1957 employed the comparative method of analysis to great effect in shedding light on problems of system maintenance.[40] The central point of the exercise was to determine which type of polarity of world power could ensure maximum stability, and in this respect Kaplan's findings pointed to a multipolar system, a conclusion shared by K.W. Deutsch and J.D. Singer.[41] The latter was subsequently able to expand his findings on the basis of work done in his project "Correlates of War" to the effect that "during the nineteenth century, peace was achieved and maintained essentially through a condition of parity in the system, while preponderance of the leading actor or coalition usually constituted the condition of peace in the twentieth century." K.W. Waltz, on the other hand, preferred the bipolar system of balance as being the more stable.[42] Since, however, overall stability resting on the great powers, in whatever polar constellation, was no guarantee that world equilibrium would not be upset by the action of small or middle powers, the role of these states in the balance—reminiscent of Gentz's ideas on the subject—drew the attention of scholars also.[43]

History was to invalidate some of the basic assumptions still taken for granted by theorists of the balance as late as the mid-1960s. Two developments were responsible for this. First, the rapid development of nuclear and allied technologies made it virtually certain that the day was not too distant when nuclear weapons could be turned out with relative ease, with a minimum of technical apparatus, and, above all, in clandestine conditions. Second, it was becoming more and more apparent that the knowledge of nuclear production could not be concealed indefinitely either from states hitherto ignorant in this respect or—a more sinister prospect still—from nonstate actors, and that there was an increasing likelihood that the monopoly of force which sovereign states had enjoyed for half a millennium might be lost.

This rendered much of the work still exclusively focussed on the investigation of the world balance of *state* power somewhat irrelevant. Even the emotional element reflected in the division of scholars into optimists and pessimists regarding their expectation of the survival of particular balances of state power seemed bereft of any substance.[44] In 1957 J.H. Herz was still able to argue on the historical analogy of the evolution of military technology from the late medieval fortresses, which helped to consolidate the territorial state, to the advent of nuclear weapons that the most important change during that period was the dimension of territorial scale. In the nuclear age, according to him, the state was no longer safe in this respect, and only vast structures covering far-flung geopolitical spaces were territorially impermeable.[45] Roberta Wohlstetter tried to show the obverse, namely that the state was in danger not so much from the suprastate dimension as, on the contrary, from infrastate developments, springing from the new power of terrorist groups.[46]

States, it seemed, were becoming vulnerable in both dimensions and, far from presenting the main threat to the world balance, were themselves presenting the object of attack. If this line of reasoning were taken to its ultimate conclusion, then the centuries of state-centred balances were drawing to a close, as the horizontal, interstate dimension was being gradually superseded by a highly perplexing, vertical one.

The real prospects of a disintegration of the world interstate system and the ensuing chaos have prompted a swing back to studies of world order, as evidenced in the establishment of the Institute for World Order in New York.[47] In overt or in covert form, the problem of the balance of power—historical product of the Age of Absolutism—though having undergone many a metamorphosis, is still very much with us as regards its substance, and continuing to exercise the intellects of some of the leading scholars in the field.

NOTES

1. This term was also preferred by F. Gentz early in the nineteenth century.

2. See B. Spinoza, *Tractatus Politicus* (1677), Ch. 7, p. 355.

3. For a full discussion, see F.H. Hinsley, *Power and the Pursuit of Peace*. Cambridge: Cambridge University Press. 1963, Chs. 1 and 2. See also H. Morley, *Ideal Commonwealths*. London: Routledge, 1885; S.J. Hemleben, *Plans for World Peace through Six Centuries*. Chicago: University of Chicago Press, 1943; and K. von Raumer, *Ewiger Friede: Friedensrufe und Friedenspläne seit der Renaissance*. Freiburg and Munich: Oldenbourg, 1953.

4. See Y. Zourek, "Le Projet du Roi Tcheque Georges de Podiebrad," 10 *Annuaire français de droit international* (1964), pp. 14-37.

5. See *Città del Sole*. Modena: 1904.

The edition of his *Discorsi* published by Stevens in London in 1654 carries the following lengthy but intriguing subtitle: "A Discourse touching the Spanish Monarch: wherein we have a political glasse, representing each particular country, province, kingdome, and empire of the world, with wayes of government by which they may be kept in obedience; as also, the causes of the rise and fall of each kingdome and empire."

6. Maximilien de Béthune, Duc de Sully, *Mémoires des sages et royales oeconomies d'estat, domestiques, politiques et militaires de Henry le Grand* (1638).

7. Hinsley, op. cit., p. 35.

8. C.I. Castel de Saint-Pierre, *Projet pour rendre la paix perpétuelle en Europe.* Utrecht: 1712.

9. On the sociological aspects of the scientific revolution of the seventeenth century, see a fascinating paper read by Soviet physicist Boris Hessen at the 1931 Conference on the History of the Philosophy of Science, in which he discussed the relationship between Newtonian physics and the needs of budding seventeenth-century capitalism.

David Hume, in an essay on the "balance of power" in classical antiquity published in 1754, claimed that the balance had existed in practice, but that the concept was then unknown. See A. Lijpart (ed.), *World Politics.* Boston: Allyn and Bacon, 1966, pp. 228-234.

10. See H. Butterfield, *The Origins of Modern Science, 1300 - 1800.* London: Bell, 1950.

11. Kahle wrote a Ph.D. thesis at the University of Göttingen, entitled *Commentatio juris publici de trutina Europae, quae vulgo appellatur 'Die Ballance von Europa'* (1744); published in the same year in French, *La Balance de l'Europe considerée comme la règle de la paix et la guerre* (Berlin and Göttingen).

12. H.G. von Justi, *Die Chimäre des Gleichgewichts von Europa.* Altona: 1758.

13. See E. Kaeber, *Die Idee des europäischen Gleichgewichts in der publizistischen Literatur vom 16. bis zur Mitte des 18. Jahrhunderts.* Berlin: Duncker, 1907.

14. J.P.C. Ancillon, *Tableau des révolutions de système politique.* Berlin: 1803 - 1805.

15. Montesquieu, *Rélections sur la monarchie universelle en Europe* (1734), as published in *Deux opuscules de Montesquieu.* Bordeaux: Societé des bibliophiles de Guyenne, 1891.

16. The term "stochastic," taken from cybernetics, was first used in this connection by M.A. Kaplan in 1957.

17. See Kaeber, op. cit., pp. 108-110.

18. See Kaeber, op. cit., p. 86.

19. Thus, Britain tried to persuade the Dutch in the early 1720s to oppose the plans for the creation of an Ostend Company in Austrian Belgium. See M. Huisman, *La Belgique commerciale sous l'Empereur Charles VI. La Compagnie d'Ostende.* Brussels: 1902.

20. The same theme is contained in M. de Goubest, *La Voix d'un citoyen d'Amsterdam.* Amsterdam: 1758, for the benefit of the Dutch; and in J.N. Moreau, *Mémoires pour servir a l'histoire de notre temps, par rapport a la guerre Anglo-Gallicane. Par l'Observateur Hollandais.* Frankfurt and Leipzig: 1757 - 1758.

21. The idea of the "balancer" was implicit in an anti-French tract by Lord Somers, *Anguis in herba: on the fatal consequences of a Treaty with France,* composed in 1701, in which Britain was supposed to balance between Habsburg and Bourbon. See also H. Meinberg, *Das Gleichgewichtssystem Wilhelm III und die englische Handelspolitik.* Berlin: Duncker, 1869; and J. Viner, "English theories of foreign trade before Adam Smith," 38 *Journal of Political Economy* (1930), pp. 249-301 and 404-457.

The reference to Jonathan Swift was taken from *A Discourse of the Contests and Dissentions in Athens and Rome* (1701), Ch. 1. Oxford: Blackwell, 1957, p. 197, as quoted by M. Wight, "The balance of power" in H. Butterfield and M. Wight (eds.), *Diplomatic Investigations.* London: Allen and Unwin, 1966, pp. 149-175.

22. See A. Lijphart (ed.), *World Politics*. Boston: Allyn and Bacon, 1966, p. 245.

23. The Treaty of Chaumont of 1814 among the Allies was to state unequivocally that their policy had "for its object the maintenance of the balance of Europe." (Art. 16.)

24. See M. Cermicelius, editor of Treitschke's *Politik*. Leipzig: Hirzel, 1897 - 1898, Vol. 2, p. 527.

25. E. Burke, *Works*. London: Rivington, 1801, Vol. 3, *Third Letter on a Regicide Peace*, pp. 441-442.

26. A.H.L. Heeren, *Handbuch der Geschichte des eurōpaischen Staatensystems*, being Vols. 8 and 9 of *Historische Werke*. Gottingen: Rower, 1821 - 1826.

27. See L. von Ranke, *Sämmtliche Werke*. Leipzig: Duncker, 1867 - 1890, Vol. 24, *Die grossen Mächte*, pp. 37-38; and Vol. 49, *Zur Geschichte Deutschlands und Frankreichs im 19. Jahrundert*, p. 75

28. Lord Brougham, writing in his *General Principles of Foreign Policy* in 1843, however, was prepared to countenance intervention on ideological grounds in cases in which the "balance" was truly threatened.

29. See H.A. Kissinger, *A World Restored: Metternich, Castlereagh and the Problem of Peace, 1812 - 1822*. London: Weidenfeld and Nicolson, 1957, for data on the historical parallel.

It was A.H.L. Heeren who towards the close of the eighteenth century suggested that a system of states incorporating the existing "balance of power" should be extended from Europe to cover the entire physical globe. See *Historische Werke*. Göttingen: Röwer, 1821 - 1826.

30. H.J. Morgenthau, *Politics among Nations*. New York: Alfred A. Knopf, 1948. The passage referred to occurs in the 1948 edition but is to be found on p. 208 of the 1973 edition.

31. Henry St. John, Lord Viscount Bolingbroke, *Works*. London: 1754, Vol. 2, p. 439.

32. E.B. Haas, "The balance of power: prescription, concept or propaganda?" 5 *World Politics* (July 1953), pp. 442-477.

33. J. von Neumann and O. Morgenstern, *The Theory of Games and Economic Behaviour*. Princeton, N.J.: Princeton University Press, 1944.

34. A.L. Burns, "From balance to deterrence: a theoretical analysis," 9 *World Politics* (1957), pp. 505-529; and A. Wohstetter, "The Delicate Balance of Terror," 37 *Foreign Affairs* (1959), pp. 211-234.

35. T.C. Schelling, *The Strategy of Conflict*. Cambridge, Mass.: Harvard University Press, 1960; and A. Rapoport, *Fights, Games and Debates*. Ann Arbor: University of Michigan, 1960.

36. O.R. Young, *The Politics of Force: Bargaining during International Crises*. Princeton, N.J.: Princeton University Press, 1968.

37. C.F. Hermann (ed.), *International Crises: Insights from Behavioural Research*. New York: Free Press, 1972; E.B. Haas, R.L. Butterworth, and J.S. Nye, *Conflict Management by International Organizations*. Morristown, N.J.: General Learning Press, 1972; P. Williams, *Conflict, Confrontation and Diplomacy*. New York: Halsted, 1975.

38. R.H. Snyder, H.W. Bruck, and B. Sapin, *Foreign Policy Decision-Making*. New York: Free Press, 1962.

39. H. Kahn, *Thinking about the Unthinkable*. New York: Horizon, 1962.

40. M.A. Kaplan, "The balance of power, bipolarity and other models of international systems," 51 *American Political Science Review* (1957), pp. 684-695. See also his *System and Process in International Politics*. New York: John Wiley, 1957; and "Theoretical inquiry and the balance of power," 14 *Yearbook of World Affairs* (1960), pp. 19-39.

41. On this point, see J. Dedring, *Recent Advances in Peace and Conflict Research.* Beverly Hills: Sage Publications, 1976, pp. 43-49.

42. K.W. Waltz, "The Stability of the Bipolar World," 93 *Daedalus* (1964), pp. 892-907.

43. L.P. Bloomfield and A.C. Leiss, *Controlling Small Wars: A Strategy for the 1970s.* New York: Alfred A. Knopf, 1969, and M. Brecher, B. Steinberg, and J. Stein, "A framework for research on foreign policy behaviour," 13 *Journal of Conflict Resolution* (March 1969), pp. 75-101. The latter was focussed entirely on middle powers.

44. For the optimists, see F.H. Hinsley, *Power and the Pursuit of Peace.* Cambridge: Cambridge University Press, 1963.

Optimism regarding the world balance is not a new phenomenon. As early as 1701 Charles Davenant wrote: "As the Earth is now divided into several Kingdomes, Principalities and States, between 'em Wars will happen, but the Weaker fortifie themselves by Alliances with the stronger; so that (unless some Great Oppressor rises up to disturb the world with his Ambition) we have many more years of Peace than War." Clearly, Davenant considered the chances of the advent of such "Great Oppressor" remote. See Charles Davenant, *Essays.* London: 1701, p. 291.

As for the pessimists, see S. Hoffmann's views on roulette in the cellar with a nuclear ball in R.J. Lieber, *Theory and World Politics.* London: Allen and Unwin, 1972, p. 163.

45. J.H. Herz, "The rise and demise of the territorial state," 9 *World Politics* (1957), pp. 474-493.

46. R. Wohlstetter, "Terror on a grand scale," 18 *Survival* (May-June 1976), pp. 98-104.

47. For a general account, see J. Dedring, op. cit., pp. 54-67. As for further particulars, see A. Lepawsky, E.H. Buehrig and H.D. Lasswell (eds.), *The Search for World Order.* New York: Appleton-Century-Crofts, 1971; R.A. Falk, *This Endangered Planet: Prospects and Proposals for Human Survival.* New York: Random House, 1971; R.A. Falk and S.H. Mendlovitz (eds.), *Regional Politics and World Order.* San Francisco: W.H. Freeman, 1973; and R.A. Falk, *A Study of Future Worlds.* New York: Free Press, 1975.

Chapter 4

THE AGE OF ENLIGHTENMENT:
THE IDEA OF PROGRESS

The development of ideas on international relations during the Englightenment probably has the end of the War of the Spanish Succession (1702-1713) as its starting point. Two events, in particular, would seem to merit consideration: The Peace Treaty of Utrecht (1713) and the publication of the Abbé de Saint-Pierre's *Projet pour rendre la paix perpétuelle dans l'Europe* in 1712 in anticipation of a peace treaty. With regard to the former, it is worth noting that the Treaty of Utrecht was the first legal document to acknowledge expressly the existence of the balance of power as a regulator of international relations. The optimistic expectations regarding that principle were, however, to be disappointed as the eighteenth century turned out to be one of almost continuous, if not invariably ferocious warfare. These wars during the first half of the century could be attributed to the operation of the archaic dynastic-genealogical principle which underlay the operation of the international absolutist system since most wars were fought over problems of succession. It was only during the second half of the century that a deliberate application of the principle of the balance of power could be registered, with consequences which were not entirely happy in the event.

Of the Abbé de Saint-Pierre (1658-1743) it is interesting to note that, while manifestly failing to achieve his objective of rendering peace in Europe "perpetual" he succeeded unintentionally in laying the basis for a debate that was to go on for a century and beyond, and was to exercise the minds of some of the most brilliant thinkers of the period of the Enlightenment. And whereas the Abbé's essay had been composed in the spirit of a previous age in which mechanical solutions seemed to indicate the way to peace, subsequent thinkers—perceiving society to be moving forward in a spirit of progress—would approach the subject of eternal peace in a markedly philosophical and thoroughly methodical manner. Where the Abbé had put his faith in the goodwill of the princes, whose legitimate authority to rule he not only recognised but wished to reinforce by writing into his *Projet* a mutual guarantee of their internal tenure of power, the thinkers of the Enlightenment would, by way of contrast, challenge these bland assumptions at their very base. They attacked the idea that interdynastic solidarity was the cornerstone of world peace, thereby questioning the underlying rationality of the international absolutist system. The Abbé had been the first to establish a causal connection between the stability of internal regimes and that of the international system, and this theme was taken up eagerly during the period of the Enlightenment, but in a sense directly opposed to that of the Abbé de Saint-Pierre. The latter's innate conservatism was to prove incompatible with the spirit of the age of Enlightenment, with its accent on change.

The first to spring into action was the noted French philosopher Jean-Jacques Rousseau (1712-1778), who derived a negative inspiration from the Abbé's *Projet*, which he set out to challenge at almost every point in his *Extrait du projet de paix perpétuelle de l'abbé de Saint-Pierre* published in 1761.[2] Among his general points of criticism, two deserve to be emphasised. In the first place, the Abbé's scheme was too rigid to allow for change, and in the second place it was too rational in making insufficient allowances for those judging by the yardstick of pragmatism, in whose eyes success alone was the decisive factor. As to substance, two critical points were made by Rousseau. It was utopian to expect an unbreakable association of states, like that envisaged by the Abbé, to materialise except as a result of some major international upheaval, such as war or revolution. This could not be regarded as a constructive approach to the problem. It was, however, equally unrealistic to imagine that, on the Abbé's general assumptions, anything but such an unbreakable association could guarantee peace. A tightly organised European association of states on the Abbé's lines was in any case more to be feared than desired since, by providing guarantees for the survival of internal absolutism, the system would deliver the ruled bound hand and foot to the whims of their rulers. A peace resting on those foundations would merely enable the absolute rulers to oppress their subjects with greater ease than ever before, all restraints of behaviour dictated by external contingencies having been removed.

In making these criticisms, Rousseau was caught on the horns of a dilemma already encountered by thinkers in previous centuries. He was trying to reconcile two conflicting tendencies inherent in political life: (a) the drive towards liberty which, given free rein, would lead inexorably towards anarchy; and (b) the drive towards sociability, which, taken to its logical end, would lead to tyranny. Hobbes had chosen the contractual method to resolve the dilemma by postulating a convenant to be concluded between rulers and ruled, whereby the latter would transfer sovereignty to the ruler on a voluntary basis. Abhorring the prospect of the Leviathan which would be born out of such a covenant, Rousseau proceeded to replace the concept of the all-powerful state enjoying the exercise of full sovereignty by that of a state governed by the General Will (*volonté générale*) considered not in a narrowly explicit numerical, but in a wider, implicit material sense.

Rousseau's theory of state forms the basis of his own positive theory of international relations. Drawing an analogy between domestic and international politics, he contrasted relations between individuals *within* states with those *between* states. As he put it: "Between man and man we live in a condition of the civil State, subject to laws; between people and people we enjoy natural liberty, which renders the situation worse." Rousseau felt frustrated by this seemingly unbridgeable gap between civil society and international society. The problem was how to proceed from the natural to the civil state on the international plane. Given Rousseau's basic premises, this could have been done by allowing the General Will to dictate politics on the international as well as on the domestic level. In place of which he contented himself with offering an outspoken criticism of the working of the international absolutist system.

Rousseau's critique of the absolutist rulers was a severe one. Those rulers, according to Rousseau, had only two ambitions: to extend their rule externally and to render it more secure internally, both of which combined to make very disorderly international relations. It was absurd to expect the absolutist rulers to enter into a peaceful compact with each other. And, addressing himself directly to his long deceased predecessor, he observed: "The simplest nobleman suffering offence would disdain to take his complaint to the tribunal of the Marshal of France, and you expect a king to take his to a European Diet?"

But all was not yet lost. For the theory of international relations of the Enlightenment arose out of a combination of a heightened sense of history and a broadened philosophical scope in which movement rather than structure was being emphasised.[3] This is what set aside those willing to speculate on the nature of international relations in the age of the Enlightenment from those in the era of Absolutism. Rousseau was a case in point, for beyond the purely subjective political activities and ambitions of the abolutist rulers, which he deplored, he could discern an objective historical movement grinding on relentlessly, irrespective of the wishes and whims of these rulers. Such a concept introduced into the discussion on the nature of international relations the dimension of historical determinism, a dynamic element conspicuously lacking in any scheme that had been produced hitherto. There was something continuous, inevitable and irreversible about it, and it was not perhaps as unrelated to Calvinist doctrine as Rousseau pretended. Though potentially harsh and often cruel in the way it worked, this international historical force could have its effects mitigated by the application of natural law in the form of applied reason.

The crucial question was where—once its existence had been postulated— this historical force would take international society ultimately. On this vital point Rousseau preferred to remain somewhat vague though it would be permissible to assume that he understood it to make eventually for general progress in the direction of orderly and civilised international relations. This certainly is what Rousseau would have preferred to happen. He would have liked it best of all if the entire system of international relations based on absolutism were swept away and its place taken by an international system relying on the operation of the General Will within the individual states making up that new system. But these were images of the future, and meanwhile Rousseau could offer nothing concrete but a league of small states to defend itself against the arbitrary behaviour of the great powers.[4]

Though Rousseau failed to pursue his initial ideas to their logical ends, he had by his systematic critique of the *Projet* of the Abbé de Saint-Pierre laid the theoretical groundwork on which Immanuel Kant was to erect his majestic philosophical building *Zum ewigen Frieden* (Towards Eternal Peace), carrying on the eighteenth-century discussion on the search for international order in the tradition of the Abbé as revised by Rousseau.

Immanuel Kant (1724-1804)[5] was trying to do in the context of the French Revolution and its aftermath what the Abbé de Saint-Pierre had attempted in connection with the upheaval of the War of the Spanish Succession. Both were advanced thinkers of their age, the Abbé in the era of Absolutism, and Kant in the era of Enlightenment, each drawing the ultimate conclusions from contemporary systems of thought. Rousseau could be placed half-way between those two, with Kant reaping the full benefits of Rousseau's criticism of the Abbé's *Projet*.[6] What Kant had in common with the Abbé, on the other hand, was his "telos" (peace),[7] a matter in which Rousseau was a sceptic.

Unable to accept either a pure rationalism or a pure empiricism, Kant settled for a philosophy of practical reason.[8] Suspicious of empiricism, which he tended to equate with opportunism, Kant was firmly set against the idea that anything worthwhile could be learnt from experience, rather than from independent reasoning. He was nonetheless a thinker who believed in devising a priori schemes on the basis of morality, as well as on logic, provided only they made practical sense. Like Spinoza, and to some extent Rousseau, concerned with the place of morality in political philosophy, Kant was dealing with the interactions of natural law and free will in history, feeling strongly that the idea of a world history[9] containing an a priori clue was a legitimate speculation of reason.

For all his enthusiasm for the political ideals of the French Revolution and his efforts to create practical ideas in the field of international relations, Kant was not a creator of utopias.[10] His system of ideas of world order arose from a deeply rooted and well-reasoned, if controversial critique of the prevailing world order. Rather than contributing original ideas to the debate on the nature of the international absolutist system, Kant took Rousseau's criticisms as his basis, making them fully explicit and taking them to their logical conclusion. Central to his critique of the absolutist rulers was the charge—implicit in Rousseau and made explicit in Kant—of exploitation, defined as the irresponsible application of power for the purpose of material gain. War, according to Kant, was not just a high risk in the international absolutist system but an immanent part of it, rendering that system potentially self-destructive or at least self-disruptive. Thus, in an essay on the *Conjectural Origins of the Human Race*, an anthropological work published three years before the French Revolution, Kant had complained that the worst of the system lay not so much in its proneness to war but in the seemingly interminable preparations for war.

It would be a mistake, however, to think of Kant as an anarchist implacably opposed to the institution of the state per se. His critiques were confined to the absolutist state, and he freely recognised the right of self-defence and even the right to prepare for war, provided only this was done for a legitimate purpose. His theory of state amounted to a thorough elaboration of Rousseau's notion of the General Will.[11] Rousseau never lived to see the French Revolution, but the institutionalisation of the General Will, as it was to express itself through the constitutionalism of the French Revolution, would have been for him a positive step.

According to Kant, the new type of state—making its first appearance in the French Revolution—possessed genuine organic qualities on the analogy of the human being. This attribution of personality to the new state had nothing in common with the way in which lawyers attribute personality to a state by way of a legal fiction. States to Kant were living organisms in a real biological and psychological sense. However, viewing them in this manner, it seemed unnatural, even monstrous to Kant to suggest that the tissues of one state were capable of being grafted on to the body of another state in the expectation that the two might grow together eventually. If such a close association was nonetheless desirable in the interest of peace, other and indirect ways had to be found.

Rousseau had only had a rough idea about the connection between home and foreign policy. Kant, on the other hand, maintained that the precise manner in which home and foreign policy interacted provided the principal clue to the inadequacies of the international absolutist system. Firmly rejecting the principle of expediency, he would have attacked as frivolous the notion epitomised by Alexander Pope that "For forms of government let fools contest, whatev'rs best administered is best." To Kant, on the contrary, nearly everything depended on the precise form of government of a state. Making a basic distinction between absolutist monarchies and constitutional states,[12] he regarded as main criterion of constitutionalism the separation of powers between the legislative and executive branches of government. Constitutional rulers were on that basis considered incapable of initiating wars, not because their personal inclinations would not allow it, but because the constitutional structures on which their tenure depended would not sustain them. Not from any abstract idealist cause, but from enlightened self-interest, the people organised in popular assemblies—as in revolutionary France—would not foot the bills of war, as they had had to do under the irresponsible government of the absolutist rulers. However—and Kant implied that this would be through no fault on the part of the people—if these assemblies should find themselves involved in war, nonetheless, it would be because they had to give their consent only with heavy heart in an extreme emergency, and after the most serious reflection. Popular governments could hold in check internal causes of war in their own countries, but they were powerless to do the same in respect to other states. It followed, according to Kant, that just causes of war would in the case of popular governments be related always to external, never to internal factors, which, by implication, meant the elimination of the bulk of the causes of war. The only thing to be lamented by Kant was the fact that, as a rule, constitutional states were not as well prepared for war as absolute monarchies.

This was the period of the French Revolution, in which it was being widely and confidently assumed that the absolutist state was on the decline as the typical actor on the stage of international relations, and the place of which would before long be taken by an entirely new type of state, formed more or less in the image of revolutionary France; a state, moreover, in which the entire body politic, and not just the absolute ruler, was to be involved in the conduct of policy, including foreign policy. Living, as Kant did, during that period must have conveyed a certainty that the old absolutist international order was on the point of being supplanted by a new system of international relations based on states with a liberal constitution. Writing the bulk of his works on international relations under the stimulus of the French Revolution, Kant used its progress as a model by which to demonstrate the failure of the old and the success of the new system of international relations, and, by doing so, was tempted into drawing too many conclusions from the failure of the Bourbon monarchy to adapt to changing economic and social conditions. The sociological formula which Kant built into his model of transition from the old to the new contained the thesis that the strength and health of a state depended on the economic condition of general material prosperity and on the political condition of general liberty of its subjects. As Kant put it, "If the citizen is hindered in seeking his prosperity in any way suitable to himself that is consistent with the liberty of others, the activity of business is checked generally, and thereby the powers of the whole State are again weakened." Thus the absolute ruler will be compelled to grant greater freedoms, thereby hastening the general process of liberalisation. The absolute order was doomed to extinction.

Towards Eternal Peace

So far all that Kant had done was to spell out some of the basic notions on international relations recorded by Rousseau. However, by designing a comprehensive model of transition from the old order to the new, and, by implication—almost by definition—towards eternal peace, Kant was to go far beyond what the former had attempted. But then Kant had the advantage of being witness to the drama of the revolutionary wars, and in particular to the first major break in those wars, occasioned by the Peace of Basle between revolutionary France and absolutist Prussia in 1795, an event which affected Kant in the same way intellectually as the forthcoming Treaty of Utrecht of 1713 must have affected the Abbé de Saint-Pierre. The prospect of a peace treaty between representatives of both the old and the new political order fascinated Kant, and he seized the opportunity for expressing his views on international relations generally and on an enduring peace treaty in particular. These he embodied in his work *Zum ewigen Frieden.*

What Kant had in mind was a general treatise on the nature of international relations concluded by a draft for a model peace treaty, rather than a treaty in the traditional pattern between absolutist rulers, of which so many had been signed and broken in the past. As Kant put it in *Zum ewigen Frieden,* what was required now was not a conventional *foedus pacis* (a treaty of peace) but rather a *foedus pacificum* (a treaty for peace). The attainment of eternal peace was identified as the central problem of international relations. A formal compromise between warring rulers wishing for a more or less lengthy respite from fighting was not the way to achieve that end. Eternal peace had to be founded upon some positive action through a series of practical steps to be taken as part of a definite programme.

This Kant was hoping to achieve by blending a system of preferred universal values with the idea of historical progress. And whereas Rousseau had still looked upon natural law as a negative, mitigating instrument with which to blunt the sharp edge of international conflict, Kant—encouraged in this enterprise by the course taken by the French Revolution—gave natural law a positive political content, placing himself at the most advanced point of the natural law doctrine by doing so. As Kant was to put it in the final paragraph in *Zum ewigen Frieden*: "It may well be said that this treaty for universal and eternal peace constitutes not only a part, but the final objective in its entirety of law within the confines of common sense."

Neither Hobbes nor Spinoza had ever envisaged international society as being able to grow out of its state of nature altogether. Kant, who never bothered to speculate about the essence of human nature, saw the problem within a much wider social context, considering it absurd that civilised people should remain perpetually in a state of nature on the international plane. The analogy between interindividual and interstate relations, drawn by Rousseau without being pursued much further, was taken up again by Kant in the hope that the antithesis which it contained could be resolved somehow.

The simplest way of traversing the path was to recommend the adoption of the political ideals of the French Revolution, cherished by Kant, on a universal scale, thereby obviating any further complications and establishing eternal peace at one stroke, as it were. But, as has been shown, Kant's interpretation of the kind of change that had brought about the French Revolution rested on historical analysis rather than on spiritual transvaluation. Change by proselytisation was a prospect never seriously contemplated by him. In its place Kant postulated the existence of an impersonal historical tendency towards the "telos" of eternal peace, which was independent of human volition.[13] Rousseau had already shown an awareness of impersonal forces of this kind being at work, without exploring the matter any further. Kant believed that progress towards eternal peace would in the long run depend not on the applied faculty of reason, which man undoubtedly possessed, but on the cunning reason of nature forcing man to follow its dictates, whatever his passions of the moment might lead him to attempt. In this process human volition played a relatively subordinate part. Kant was attributing to nature an innate rationale towards progress which was ipso facto moral in intent, leading, as it would eventually, to the creation of a state of eternal peace. Men, and in particular practitioners in the art of politics and diplomacy, were blind to their real interests, and to them morality was only a theory. Their striving was directed towards the achievement of man's apparent interest, while nature was working towards the attainment of his real interest. It was nature that in this sense embodied the categorical moral imperative.[14] The contradiction between nature and civilisation—an intractable problem still in Hobbes, Spinoza, and Rousseau—resolved itself in Kant's scheme by nature acting through history, which, in its teleology, revealed nature and civilisation not to be opposites, but one and the same. Hobbes had equated civilisation with organisation on the assumption that it was only when people were organised that they could also be civilised while Rousseau had looked upon the civilising process as the product of a harsh historical progression mitigated only by man's voluntary use of natural law. In Kant's sweeping synthesis there is room for organisation, civilisation and progress, the three essential ingredients of eternal peace.

The Functions of War and Law

Kant adopted a critical attitude towards the prevailing system of international law whose moral basis he questioned, as it would lend itself to being used in justification of acts of state of dubious morality by citing authorities like Grotius, Vattel, and others. No government, he noted shrewdly, had ever been persuaded to desist from an act on account of the existence of a rule of international law that would prohibit it. Kant was particularly hard on those who considered that treaties of peace of the conventional kind and the doctrine of "just war" had any bearing on the maintenance of peace or on the improvement of international relations generally.

What, then, did Kant wish to put in the place of the balance of power and international law, the two institutional pillars of the international absolutist system? The theoretical ideal, a world state, was dismissed by him on practical grounds as comprising too large an area to cope effectively. This, one feels strongly, was a pretext rather than the real basis for his objection, which was moral and consisted in a denial of a right of states to demand union with other states on the analogy of individuals expecting other individuals to join them in a state for the common benefit of all. It was a point which Rousseau had made before Kant, but which somehow lacked logical force. Was it that Kant, who represented the values of the rising middle classes, shrank, like Rousseau before him, instinctively before the prospect of a universal Leviathan? The presumption is a strong one, but evidence in Kant's writings is scanty.

Ultimately, Kant took over ideas of international schemes already in existence which relied on the loose, confederal pattern, but by giving them fresh philosophical content and fitting them into his long-term historical perspective, found a place for them within his wider, comprehensive scheme. As regards its philosophical content, Kant was set on constitutionalism in the manner of the French Revolution. At this point Kant drew together the two essential elements of his formula in his final synthesis. A state, unitary or composite, may not find it feasible to govern too large an area, but the political principles which aim at a wider combination "and which enjoin the promotion of such union among States as may ensure a continuous approximation to Eternal Peace are not impracticable." International union had to be preceded by affinity of political principle, but the formative process making this possible might last a long time—possibly a couple of centuries.[15]

What did Kant propose should be done meanwhile? Neither a confederation based on voluntary agreement nor a universally acceptable political philosophy seemed a practical proposition in the short run. Kant, intent on being practical, proposed a compromise solution by which the learning process was to be the function of the rationale of history. And although Kant held that "the problem of establishing a perfect civil constitution is subordinate to the problem of a law-governed external relationship with other States, and cannot be solved unless the latter is also solved," there was nonetheless to be detected in Kant's scheme an implied order of priority in which internal improvement preceded external reform. Given Kant's political preferences, it seems certain that the creation of a liberal-constitutional order within as many states as possible was to be the basis of all international welfare. Both internal and international society had to be civilised in this way before they could be properly organised. It was in this manner that Kant proposed to resolve the antithesis between the moral and political interests of man, represented respectively by civilisation and organisation. But even when both civilised and organised, international society would finally require a system of positive international law to protect it from backsliding. Seen from that angle, international law was a protective device, a means of reassurance against relapses into atavistic patterns of instability and disorder such as used to be endemic in the international absolutist system.

Kant died in 1804, on the threshold of Napoleon's attempt to enshrine the values of the French Revolution within a resurrected Roman empire of French nationality and hegemony. He would have found it difficult to reconcile his theory of international relations with subsequent state practice. Essentially, Kant was the last link in an intellectual chain spanning the best part of the eighteenth century, comprising the classical phase of the Enlightenment in the course of which a number of forward-looking thinkers had wrestled with the problem of international relations. Perceiving a tendency towards progress in the internal affairs of states, they tried to devise formulas whereby this progress could be realised on the international plane also.

However, in 1815, at the latest, it was clear that—for the time being at any rate—their efforts would bear few fruits. Their expectations were shown to be too optimistic, possibly because the all pervading spirit of the Enlightenment and the euphoria engendered by the French Revolution had made them impatient. Yet, there was in their theories an element of lingering scepticism strong enough to be taken up by some theorists following in their wake.

NOTES

1. In his lectures given at the Sorbonne in Paris in 1750, Turgot elaborated a theory of persisting human progress. See Turgot, *Oeuvres*. Paris: 1844, Vol. 2, pp. 578-595.

2. Rousseau's *Jugement sur la paix perpétuelle* was published posthumously.

3. Edward Gibbon (1737 - 1794), the noted English historian and philosopher—Rousseau's contemporary—and his masterpiece, *The History of the Decline and Fall of the Roman Empire* (1775 - 1776) were typical of the period in this respect. Before Gibbon's day there had been antiquarian historians, *les erudits*, and historians who went in for general ideas, *les philosophes*. Gibbon accomplished the feat of being both.

4. On this point, see J.L. Windenberger, *La Republique conféderative des petits Etats. Essai sur la politique étrangère de Rousseau*. Paris: Picard, 1900.

5. See M.G. Forsyth, H.M.A. Keens-Soper, and P. Savigear (eds.), *The Theory of International Relations: Selected Texts*. London: Allen and Unwin, 1970, p. 192 et seq.

6. *Extrait du projet de paix perpétuelle de l'abbé de Saint-Pierre*. Paris: Pigalle, 1761.

7. On that point, see P. Hassner, "Les concepts de guerre et de paix chez Kant," 11 *Revue française de science politique* (1961), pp. 642-670.

8. See Kant, *Kritik der reinen Vernunft*. Riga: Hartknoch, 1781.

9. Kant, *Idea of a Universal History of a Cosmological Plan*. Hanover, N.H.: The Sociological Press, 1927. (Originally called *Idee zu einer allgemeinen Geschichte in weltbürgerlicher Absicht.*)

10. G.E. Lessing (1729 - 1781), poet of the German Enlightenment, with whom Kant had a great deal in common, did not believe in utopias either. See his treatment of the philosophy of history in *Die Erziehung des Menschengeschlechts*. Berlin: Voss, 1780.

11. Edmund Burke, in the course of his attacks on the French Revolution, expounded his theory of the people as an artificial, corporate idea, meaningless apart from the leaders and discipline which are essential to the agreement in which it originates. He limited the class he called "the people" for any political purposes to educated adults of "tolerable leisure," of about 400,000 in England and Scotland. This group to him was the natural representative of all the rest.

12. Constitutional monarchies would qualify under that label. Kant was not opposed to monarchy per se.

13. Kant, op. cit.

14. Hassner, op. cit., spells out the ethical problem encountered by Kant in greater detail.

15. Kant was writing this in 1784.

Chapter 5

THE DIALECTIC:

IDEALISM AND MATERIALISM

The Age of Enlightenment was passing, and with it the search for explanation analogous to that in the natural sciences, where mankind was showing a growing ability to harness physical forces for its purposes. The optimism of the Enlightenment, according to which education and science together could achieve the perfectability of individual and social development, had been given a further stimulus by the French Revolution. However, as Mirabeau gave way to the Girondins, and they to the Jacobins, Robespierre, and ultimately Bonaparte, this faith in perfectability was severely shaken.

Moreover, since the middle of the eighteenth century, there has been a shift away from the personal to the impersonal element in the philosophy of history, and it was no accident that from about 1750 onwards, historians began to show an interest in economic and social, as well as purely political factors. Absolutism had involved the formal control of all political, economic, and social forces; but gradually the view gained ground that in some areas of human activity change was inevitable, whatever man might do to hold it up, and that there were invisible forces at work shaping the destinies of men. At one stage during the eighteenth century, speculation regarding the nature of these forces was accepted as a proper intellectual pursuit, and this opened the way to theory-making on the subject.

The abandonment of controls meant the introduction of the competitive element, as the idea of a fully regulated society was discarded in favour of that of a fully competitive one. New generations of economists—Adam Smith in Britain and François Quesnay in France, for instance—would claim that the free play of economic forces was good for the general welfare. Soon the idea of the competitive spirit was widely accepted as being empirically as well as normatively sound, and the deduction was made that a general willingness to engage in competitive pursuits would lead to a true "harmony of interests."

Both Rousseau and Kant were great believers not only in freedom but also in the impersonal forces which, if not exactly acting as history's motor, were propelling mankind along some preordained trail of progress. However, neither man attempted to produce a comprehensive theory along those lines. That attempt was made by Georg Friedrich Wilhelm Hegel (1770 - 1831).[1] Furthermore, where Rousseau and Kant had tried to construct a system of universal values and link it to a theory of historical progress, Hegel boldly reversed the order, by moving the latter concept to the very centre of his system of enquiry. As a result of this, Hegel's theory of international relations was the first of its kind to be conceived wholly in terms of social dynamics.

A German philosopher who, as a student at the university of Tübingen, had become an ardent supporter of the French Revolution, Hegel was to be disillusioned fairly early with regard to the potency of ideology in politics, but remained an unwavering supporter of revolutionary France on nonideological grounds. Concentrating his intellectual powers in the field of the spiritual, in which he saw the essential basis of the social fabric, he regarded philosophy as the key to all historical explanation.[2] He consequently attempted the enormous task of providing a comprehensive philosophical explanation of world history, in which the universe was visualised as a systemic whole with subordinate parts.[3] Believing, as Kant before him, in the organic unity of political life, Hegel regarded the isolated individual as an abstraction, only historical totality assuming concrete form in his mind. However, the real subject matter of history lay in universal reason, defined by him as "divine, absolute reason" as manifested in history,[4] which could be comprehended by establishing a correlation between human spirit and human consciousness. The appropriate technique to achieve this consisted in identifying philosophical reflection with the development of real consciousness towards self-knowledge, *Selbstbewusstsein*. Only in his full state of *Selbstbewusstsein* could man be truly free. Viewed in this manner, history ceased to be meaningless, as it represented "progress in the consciousness of freedom" and contained a purpose: the gradual realisation of human freedom. The spirit thus reveals consciousness no longer as isolated, critical and antagonistic, but as fully liberated.

Setting himself firmly against a priori rationalism in the Kantian manner, but proving himself equally hostile to British empiricism, Hegel proposed that "what is must be rational," which suggested that there is a rational explanation for everything. There are no accidents. Everything is the embodiment of reason. Reality is contained in the sum total of all phenomena and assumes the shape of an organic whole composed of innumerable parts which are all related to each other. To develop his personal capacities to the full, man has to understand this world environment, the full comprehension of which alone enables him to overcome his sense of alienation.

The Dialectic: Hegel

Seeing world reality as a reflection of eternal and unchanging ideas, Hegel sought to determine the process by which these ideas are realised in the actual world, and found it to be broadly analogous to that of intellectual debate but fundamentally different from the kind of logic hitherto accepted as valid. Whereas in the system of formal logic there was a strict sequence of cause and effect, or at least some correlation between the two, the dialectical method of thinking implied a movement of reasoning propelled by the contradiction of opposites. To Hegel there were three stages in that process by which reason moved through history: thesis, antithesis, and synthesis. Thus, any assertion one can make is never wholly true, and because of this, it immediately seems to involve its opposite. Out of these two assertions—thesis and antithesis—there arises the synthesis. This synthesis, which is still not wholly true, becomes a new thesis, and thus the process is repeated until all contradictions are resolved. To Hegel, it was contrary to the nature of reason to accept a contradiction as final, since to admit this would be to admit that the universe is not thoroughly logical.[5] The only way to progress to truth was by grasping and overcoming contradictions. And though Kant and Fichte had both previously taken up the idea of the dialectic, it was Hegel who developed it fully to relate it directly to the historical process.

HEGEL'S CONCEPTION OF THE STATE

Before an intelligible account can be rendered of Hegel's theory of international relations, it is essential to go into his theory of the state. Here we see Hegel further developing Kant's ideas, but giving them a definite, postrevolutionary complexion. For Hegel, as for Kant, freedom of the individual was of prime importance. But whereas classical liberalism was to varying degrees suspicious of the state and sought to limit its power, Hegel asserted that true freedom could only be attained through the state itself. In the state man may fully raise his outward self to the level of thought of the inward self. Thus,

Hegel attributes a moral purpose to the state, expecting states to live up to that task. A state must help the individual to achieve *Selbstbewusstsein* and is therefore seen as potentialiy a force for good in human life.[6] Rousseau furnished the state with a "General Will" in politics; Hegel with a conscious and thinking essence, referred to as spirit (*Geist*).

Moreover, the state was the highest ascertainable form of political existence. There was nothing above the state but an infinite void. To some extent this view of the state was the product of Hegel's theory of anthropological progression, according to which mankind had traversed three stages of institutional development, from (a) the *family,* in which the rational element was still hidden behind sentiment; to (b) *civil society,* which was using the rational principle in order to achieve ends of pure self-interest; to (c) the *state,* the only institution based on full *Selbstbewusstsein* on the basis of mutual gain and serving unselfish interests.

Viewed in anthropological perspective, this was a plausible theory. It could not be maintained once the level of analysis shifted to that of international relations. The state, for Hegel, was the framework in which human purpose had to be achieved, but set within an international framework, it had to be regarded no longer merely as a means towards an end, but as an end in itself. As Hegel put it: "The State is not there for the benefit of its subjects; one might say it represents the purpose of world history and man is only its instrument."

Hegel's constant emphasis on the superior rationality as well as on the concrete reality of the whole as contrasted with that of the parts makes him single out the *Weltgeist* as the central concept in his theory of international relations. The *Weltgeist* is the spiritual mainspring of world history. It is an abstraction, although on the highest social and political level of world society, but it remains, nonetheless, an abstraction. While the *Weltgeist* is the embodiment of the whole, the *Volksgeist* is its subordinate, representing merely the historical spirit of certain peoples. The essential difference between *Weltgeist* and *Volksgeist* is that the latter is capable of finding its institutional expression in the form of the state, whereas the former is not. Hegel never defines the term *Volk* (people), and one ought to be on one's guard against confusing *Volk* with nation. However, Hegel notes, in perfect logic, that a *Volk* lacking the institutional framework of the state is "unhistorical" in the sense that it is incapable of acting on the stage of political world history. The *Weltgeist,* however, is world history and therefore requires no institutional framework. The *Volksgeist* is supraindividual reason finding its incarnation in the institutions of *Volk*-society.[7] The *Weltgeist*, on the other hand, cannot incarnate supra-*Völker* reason by way of analogy because there is no world state within which to accomplish that task.

At this point Hegel is faced with a contradiction, which is also the basic problem of international relations: that between state and world order, between interstate society and world society. He tries to resolve this dilemma by applying the notion of the dialectic. In this he succeeds only partially, seeming at all times unable to make up his mind about the level of priorities between on the one hand, *Volksgeister,* represented by their states, and on the other, the *Weltgeist.* Faced with the classical "chicken or egg" problem, he hesitates somewhat, now according priority to the one, now to the other, without rising beyond establishing a simple correlation between the two. Strongly implying that the *Volksgeist* is a link in the chain of the *Weltgeist,* he maintains that though individual *Volksgeister* may perish, the *Weltgeist* is indestructible. If, on the other hand, it is the dialectic which supplies the dynamics of world history, then the *Weltgeist,* representing the sum total of the opposing wills of states, is the embodiment of the collective but undefined destiny of all states, a kind of inchoate *volonté générale internationale,* but all the same, a function of the sum total of *Volksgeister,* its very life constantly regenerated by the continuous actions of the states.

HEGEL'S THEORY OF CONFLICT AND ITS RESOLUTION

Since a simple correlation between *Weltgeist* and *Volksgeister* seemed a somewhat meagre result to achieve, Hegel went on to examine the function of the dialectic in the genesis and resolution of international conflicts. The dialectic was the spring of international relations, producing endless clashes of opposite wills of *Volksgeister* between the states making up international society. Seen from this angle, the *Weltgeist* was no more than an abstraction of the total opposing wills of states. By its very nature, however, the dialectic was not necessarily destructive, though destructiveness was undeniably one of its functions. Seen from a higher vantage point, it was a perceptive device for observing history as a continuously unfolding process admitting of no eternal truth. The dialectic was therefore at best a substitute for the traditional notion of natural law. It could not be confused, let alone identified with it. The *Weltgeist*—similarly, being devoid of all normative content—in no way resembled natural law.

While accepting the historical dialectic as an explanatory tool, Hegel rejected the traditional discipline of history in this capacity. There was not much to be learnt from a study of history. "What experience and history teach is that governments never learn anything from history or are willing to adjust their actions on the basis of insights gained from history." It was therefore useless to make prescriptions in the hope that they would be followed by governments. It was only the statesman of format (*der grosse Charakter*) who would know how to hit on the right solution and be willing to transcend the narrowness of the social framework.[8]

The role of the state vis-à-vis its *Volk* was the moral one of conciliator. Within the context of international society, however, the state had no other duty than self-preservation and maintenance. It was completely freed from the ordinary precepts of morality by which it was bound to its *Volk*. Judged by the canons of this type of international morality, the successful state was the one which emerged unscathed from the dialectical processes in which it would be inevitably involved with other states. Echoing the German Romantic poet Friedrich von Schiller, Hegel remarked that world history was in this respect the world court which would impose its verdict. If a state was thus successful, it had to be in accord with the implicit dictates of the *Weltgeist*. This seems to indicate that Hegel—unlike Kant—saw no clear way to the formation of a world state since this would be incompatible with the law of the dialectic.

Yet, Hegel was no worshipper of power. In his earlier writings especially he would not condone power per se, feeling that a state relying on the use of power would create a static society, whereas he was seeking a definition of the state which would fit into the changing context. Like Machiavelli, he considered the strongest state to be the fittest one in general terms, among which military fitness was only one element. The real basis of power was administrative efficiency, and revolutionary France, which compared so favourably with backward Germany in this respect, was taken as his model.[9]

THE FUNCTIONS OF WAR

In the final analysis, the dialectic of international relations was fully revealed in the phenomenon of war.[10] Whether one liked it or not, the function of war in man's development was undeniable, and a place had therefore to be found for it within the dialectical process. Kant had claimed that war was an essential attribute of the international absolutist system, and that it tended to disrupt international society. Hegel, on the other hand, came very close to saying war had a positive function.

War was outside the realm of ethics, and general condemnations of war and conflict were regarded by Hegel as mischievous. War transcended all material values in joining men together in the pursuit of meta-material values. Morality, to Hegel, resided in the transcendental, as in revolutionary France, and not in the narrowly conventional, as in rotten Prussia. Yet, there was no glory in war. Hitler had a romantic attachment to war. Not so Hegel, to whom war was simply a fact. It was a mistake to consider war desirable simply because it was capable of leading men to seek meta-material values.

Since there are no accidents in history, war cannot be an accident either and must be accounted for somehow. War cannot be considered a matter of right meeting wrong, but rather a clash between two subjectively perceived rights. "Each party claims to have right on its side; and both parties are right. It is just the rights themselves which have come into contradiction with one another." Where there is a dispute or a conflict, therefore, it is useless to worry about formalities, or, for that matter, even about realities. For the nature of a dispute or conflict depends not so much on real grievances as on subjective perception of an alleged threat posed, or injury received by any particular state.

In view of the above, there could not be any generally accepted way of adjudicating between warring states, and there was no point in setting up international machinery for settling international disputes and conflicts. War cannot decide, it can only regulate. Within a dialectical perspective the only value judgment is passed by world history. No believer in abstract international equality, Hegel recognised that the fitter state would emerge from a dispute in better shape.

A THEORY OF WORLD ORDER

Hegel was completely at one with Kant, however, in maintaining that, though the individual might owe a duty to the state, as embodying a community, states themselves were under no obligation in respect to one another. The state owed no duty to anyone, and it was therefore useless to moralise about the principles that should govern the relations between states. In this he was far more consistent than his two predecessors, Rousseau and Kant. It was not for him to suggest the easy way out by prescribing a system of natural law, however up-to-date in content. It was not for him to recommend schemes of federation and confederation such as suggested, however half-heartedly, by Rousseau and Kant for the sake of rounding off a coherent scheme of international relations; not for Hegel to create a set of political imperatives such as set out by Kant as the essential basis of all international order.

The essence of a state's existence, like that of an individual, was in its relationship with other states, and this relationship was regulated by the principle of negation. Legal ties among states would last only so long as states would abide by their rules. International law had a purely voluntary basis, as it lacked the coercive element which alone was capable of providing its ultimate set of sanctions. It was thus different from municipal law.[11]

Hegel was equally sceptical about formal international institutions as solvents of disputes and conflicts. Federative structures were unlikely to materialise except on a short-term basis, and then usually only for the purpose of diplomatic or military alliances. Such international institutions as did survive might, he conceded, prevent this or that war, but in order to be fully effective in the final analysis,[12] they would have to be willing to wage war.

Rather like Kant, however, Hegel believed in very long-term solutions springing from a drawn-out learning process. Kant had believed the learning process could be made explicit through the purposive application of the relevant educational techniques and be steered by the rationale of history in the direction of progress in spite of occasional appearances to the contrary, whereas Hegel considered that cumulative dialectical experiences would enable states gradually to narrow down their differences to a point at which no further international disputes of potential danger could arise. This was not so much a determinist hypothesis as a 'necessitarian' one, in which the actors on the international stage were unaware of the scenario. Nonetheless, the cunning of history, in the disguise of the dialectical process, would in the long run extract the final product of a learning process—the synthesis following in the wake of thesis and antithesis: diplomatic custom.

There is a distinct rationale to be discerned in Hegel's scheme of seemingly meaningless successions of dialectical developments, and in this (though probably not consciously), he followed Edmund Burke, who similarly regarded the bond of habitual international intercourse as a more reliable basis of world order than any number of formal engagements, such as treaties.[13] Hegel claimed that the learning process engendered by the frequent experience of conflict might lead statesmen to realise that war was ultimately disruptive, but that this was an inevitable part of dialectical reasoning. It follows that Hegel's dialectical process operates rather in the form of a spiral in an upward direction, than as a cyclical returning forever to its original position. The negative aspect of sovereignty would be overcome ultimately, as sovereignty itself was being phased out in the universal movement towards the *Weltgeist*. It is important to realise that Hegel's implicit teleology postulates not international integration but a spontaneously evolved unity of state behaviour based, not on a universal system of liberal values, such as Kant would have envisaged, but on universal diplomatic custom.

Hegel's amoral approach towards problems of international relations represents a break with the immediate past. Where those before him had long relied on the credibility of natural law, Hegel abandoned that concept altogether, putting in its place the idea of the dialectic. In this he was typical of the revolt against the formal rationalism of the Enlightenment. Individuality was everything. Natural law was nothing. The *Weltgeist* was realised through the action of the dialectic operating through the states in an eternally recurring conflict of ideas. Ultimate harmony was to be obtained through clashes of opposites. This was a novel interpretation of history, and one, moreover, that was not lost on those who followed Hegel. And among these, none was more outstanding than Marx and Engels.

The Dialectic: Marx and Engels

The Hegelian concept of the dialectic was adapted by Marx and Engels in their own scheme of thought on international relations, which was similar in some, but dissimilar in other respects to Hegel's.

The contrast with Hegel can be attributed to a difference in generations. Hegel, who died in 1831, had no inkling of the revolutionary impact of impending industrialisation, whereas Marx (1815-1883) and *a fortiori* Engels (1820-1895) were to experience its full weight. In addition to differences in generation, there were differences in temperament: Hegel was cautious in approach and, as an academic, conservative, never venturing far beyond the strictly observable, and—though willing to give free rein to his immense powers of imagination—always insisted that, at least in the short and medium term, the dialectical interplay of forces was moving history along uncharted routes.

Marx and Engels, particularly the latter, were very different from Hegel in temperament. Bold and speculative in their approach, generous in their conceptions, and sweeping in their conclusions, they were first and foremost political activists,[14] and academics only incidentally, intent as they were on using theory as a means towards an end, rather than, as did Hegel, an end in itself. They were, in this sense, theoreticians rather than theorists. Where Hegel had been extremely careful to keep academic and political pursuits apart, theory and practice were inextricably fused in Marx and Engels.

Contrast was not the only significant element between Hegel on the one hand and Marx and Engels on the other. There was also philosophical continuity, as the latter inherited from Hegel the fundamental concept of the dialectic, a teleological device to enable men to see the movement of history in perspective. Marx and Engels combined the dialectical method of thinking, elaborated by Hegel, with the philosophy of materialism, derived from the writings of Ludwig Feuerbach (1804-1872),[15] to produce the explosive mixture of "historical and dialectical materialism." Like Hegel before him, Marx dissolved thought and action into the relativism of the dialectic, but turned Hegel's idealism into materialism, so that world history was seen not to be made on the spiritual level but determined by material and, above all, economic considerations. A link existed between Hegel's idealism and Marx's materialism since the latter had made the teleological element—still cautiously implicit in Hegel—cheerfully and stridently explicit in the sphere of international relations. Where Kant had postulated universal peace as the "telos" of his scheme and Hegel intimated that refined diplomatic custom might be the ultimate answer to the problem of international conflict, the telos implicit in the scheme of Marx and Engels was to be nothing less than the creation of a world association in which, in the words of the *Communist Manifesto* of 1848, "the free development of each" was "the condition for the free development of all."

This was not perhaps very different from what Hegel would have liked also. However, where he and Kant had left the task to a set of unidentified impersonal forces acting in world history, Marx and Engels, claiming to have identified the social forces of world history, proceeded to show how they could be guided in desirable directions. Where Kant and Hegel had been cautiously determinist and predeterminist respectively—the former optimistically, the latter sceptically—Marx and Engels proved to be lusty interventionists. By constructing a transcendentalist scheme, they were hoping to effect that transformation of all values which was essential if their "telos" was to be reached. At the end of the process there was to be a breath-taking general explanation of all social and economic phenomena, including those in the sphere of international relations. To achieve this ambition, Marx adopted the Hegelian concept of the dialectic but gave it a positive direction by pairing it with the concept of the class struggle which, in response to initiatives taken which left little to historical chance, would lead to the final solution of the dialectical process.

MARXIAN INNOVATION: THE CLASS STRUGGLE

For Marx, world society was composed of layers of classes, and world history had to be seen as a progression of class struggles. To eliminate the element of conflict in world society was possible through the elimination of the class character of world society. Only the class which—in the words of the *Communist Manifesto*—had "nothing to lose but its chains" could summon sufficient energy and courage, born of desperation, to accomplish that historical task, and it was only at the lowest rungs of the class ladder, therefore, that the "progressive" forces of history were to be found. Once these basic premises had been established, all was plain logic. Whenever a lower order scored a victory over a higher order of class, that represented historical progress. Since the lowest order was that of the modern factory proletariat, the ultimate victory of that order, if it could be achieved—there was nothing automatic about it—would mark the point in history in which all contradictions would dissolve. Society would cease to be class society and, unencumbered by any dialectical contradictions, be rid of all elements of strife. Since international relations formed an integral part within the wider orbit of activity of world society, a positive outcome of the class struggle in the Marxist sense would also solve the problem of international conflict. International relations, like all other social relations, were merely a function of the class struggle. "Abolish the world class system and you will have world peace" appeared to be the implicit message of classical Marxism.

ENGELS' CONCEPTION OF THE STATE

To state the problem and its resolution in those abstract terms was one thing. To relate it to the concrete world of international relations was quite another. The most intractable obstacle to a neat and wholesale Marxist solution in the sphere of international relations was the undeniable existence of the institution of the state.[16] Marx and Engels were not so foolish as to close their eyes to the prominence of states in world society, and to relate the concept of the class struggle to the institution of the state seemed the only way of expounding a theory of international relations consistent with the basic premises of Marxism.

In accordance with classical Marxist precepts, the world economy operated as a single unit, whereas world polity did not. The development of the world's productive forces would eventually determine the shape of world politics, but meanwhile the states would continue to present an obstacle in the path of historical progress, as conceived by Marx and Engels. The precise nature of the state had therefore to be determined if any progress was to be made.

The state was, in Engels' words, "the executive committee of the ruling class," an interpretation which differed profoundly from that suggested by Hegel, for whom the state was the institution through which individual men might attain a liberating sense of *Selbstbewusstsein*. To Engels the state was the instrument through which the dominant class could maintain its hold over other classes, thereby achieving its own, wholly sectional and entirely selfish kind of *Selbstbewusstsein*. The salient point in Hegel's theory of the state had been that *Selbstbewusstsein* attained through the agency of the state was entirely unselfish and socially unifying. And where Hegel—pardonably, because writing on the eve of the industrial revolution—saw the state as the highest form of political and social institution, Marx and Engels, witnesses of the industrial revolution, discovered in the fast developing factory proletariat a force capable of bursting the confines of the class state. The child of world productive forces, the proletariat was at once a potential political force of world dimensions, and the harbinger of the classless world society of the future—its function in world history akin to that of the *Weltgeist* in Hegel's teleology. And just as in Hegel's scheme, the states were the chief actors on the international plane, so the classes performed an identical function in that of Marx and Engels.

Yet, there were some significant, if subtle divergences of view between Marx and Engels regarding the precise nature and functions of the state in international relations. To Marx—trained lawyer, competent economist and original sociologist—political institutions tended to be at a discount, whereas to Engels—interested more in political science and anthropology than in either economics or sociology—political institutions were at a premium. Engels was concerned with elaborating an explicit theory of the state which would fit into the wider Marxist scheme of thought, and which was ultimately contained in his work on *The Origin of the Family, Private Property and the State*, published in London in 1884. Intent on furnishing scientific proof of the class character of the state, Engels tried to show on the basis of contemporary anthropological theory, that the genesis of the state had coincided with the genesis of class society, and that preclass society was stateless. From having proved this, it was only one more step to argue by analogy that, since prestate society had been classless, poststate society would be classless also—*quod erat demonstrandum.*

Engels' method of investigation consisted in constructing an empirically based model of transition from primitive, semiorganised to civilised, organised society—a technique which, in a purely speculative manner, had been used in the field of political philosophy by Hobbes in the seventeenth century. Drawing his anthropological data mainly from L.H. Morgan, whose work, *Ancient Society* (in the sense of primitive society) had made a considerable impact when it was first published in 1877, Engels portrayed a classless primitive society which knew no state and existed in a condition of pristine communism. Outside the institution of the family every activity was public, and all political decisions were taken collectively by an assembly composed of the people as a whole, and not just by their representatives. Public affairs were managed informally by a public authority composed likewise not of a central agency but of the entire adult, male population, self-organised and armed. Public sanctions were applied in the first place through the coercive effects of spontaneous public opinion. Primitive society, as shown by Engels, was wholly decentralised, classless, and stateless.

The crucial moment in the development of those societies came when they began to embody the political institution of the state in their social fabric. Engels was at pains to show that this could not be done without introducing social cleavages. The sole purpose of the emerging dominant class was to use the institution of the state as an instrument of class coercion. As Engels put it forcefully: "An essential characteristic of the State is the existence of a public authority (*öffentliche Gewalt*) separate from the mass of the people." The centralisation of power in the hands of the state was the direct outcome of the genesis of class society henceforth beset by internal discord.

The important theoretical lesson to be learnt from Engels' demonstration of the genesis of the state was that the process could be reversed. Since the state was the product of class society, it could be made to disappear alongside dissolving class society. In Engels' famous phrase, the state would "wither away" (*absterben*) as a coercive instrument, retaining purely administrative functions only. "Society . . . relegates the State machine where it belongs: into the museum." It was precisely in order to effect the overthrow of world class society that Marx had devised the concept of class struggle. Applied on a world scale, the class struggle would bring about a stateless world bereft of class antagonisms.[17]

CLASS AND STATE IN INTERNATIONAL RELATIONS

Marx's conception of the state was less fully rounded than that of Engels. Having initially adopted Hegel's notion of the state, he changed his mind after service on the staff of the *Rheinische Zeitung* had revealed to him the darker sides of the state. He jettisoned the idea of the positive function of the state in exchange for that of the positive role of classes. But while Engels was far more explicit than Marx as to the nature of the state, Marx was more sensitive than Engels to the problem of the class character of states on the international plane. Marx seems to have been in great doubt as to whether peace or war was better suited to furthering the cause of the proletarian or any other, objectively progressive class. At one point he seems to have come down in favour of peace; as, in connection with the annexation of Alsace-Lorraine in 1871, he wrote: "If frontiers are to be fixed by military interests, there will be no end of claims, because every military line is necessarily faulty and may be improved by annexing some more outlying territory: they can never be fixed fairly or finally because they always must be improved by the conqueror or the conquered, and consequently carry within them the seeds of fresh wars." And he added, "History will measure its contribution not by the extent of square miles conquered from France, but by reviving in the second half of the nineteenth century the policy of conquest."[18]

This was the quintessence of petty-bourgeois radical wisdom in the field of international relations, and it should not cause surprise to learn that at one stage Marx actually recommended the application of the rules of ordinary civil law (*bürgerliches Recht*) to the conduct of interstate relations.[19] The working classes were enjoined to do their utmost to keep international peace.[20] Writing in the context of the Russo-Turkish war then in progress, Marx failed to determine whether or not a collapse of the Russian autocracy, which he was envisaging, was desirable because it might precipitate a Russian revolution.[21] This was no longer the same Marx who had lightheartedly advocated revolutionary war against Russia in 1848. It was as if Marx were implying three things: (a) that there was no necessary causal link between the class struggle and interstate relations; (b) that international relations constituted a separate system of social relations altogether and were therefore subject to a different set of rules; and (c) that, if anything, peace rather than war was the catalyst that would hasten the coming of world revolution. Conversely, and again by implication only, war might delay the revolution by its generally disruptive effects from which neither the revolutionary movement nor the autocracies could benefit.

Engels, by way of contrast, retained some of Marx's earlier *insouciance* when it came to assessing the functions of war, looking upon it in a neo-Hegelian manner as capable of achieving positive historical effects. He appears to have held on firmly to his conviction that by its actions on the international plane, the class state could not help bestowing class character on the international system. In the 1890s he seems to have sensed a revolutionary situation in the making on the international plane when, perceiving Germany as the potential victim of diplomatic encirclement, he advocated a people's war, "like 1793," in defence of the Reich. Late in his life he also felt confident enough to address the decision-makers of the international system in anticipating rhetoric as follows: "This, my lords, princes and statesmen, is where in your wisdom you have brought old Europe. And when nothing more remains to you but to open the last great war dance—that will suit us alright."

COMBINING THEORY AND PRACTICE OF INTERNATIONAL RELATIONS

How did Marx and Engels apply their theory to specific practical issues of international relations? After all, convinced of the need for combining theory with practice, with the one constantly feeding on the other, they could hardly stand aside as firmly committed politicians and practising journalists, to contemplate the course of international relations in academic isolation, as Hegel had done. The current problems of international relations would in any case force themselves constantly on their attention. To apply this theory to concrete international problems should not have presented any difficulties at all. Whether at war or at peace, the fate of governments—the "executive committees of the ruling classes"—in their relations with each other could have remained a matter of supreme indifference to them. In practice, however, Marx and Engels found it difficult to decide what attitudes to adopt in any particular international crisis. Marx's growing malaise over the problem of the levels of analysis has been noted earlier. What was even more tantalising than the levels of analysis was the problem of the levels of development.

Marxist historical materialism had always maintained that there was an evolutionary progression from primitive communism towards the feudal, bourgeois, and proletarian state, leading ultimately to the emergence of a world society both classless and stateless. Would it not therefore have made good sense in any specific international situation to back the historically "progressive" state, in the class sense, against "reactionary" ones, while staying scrupulously neutral in conflicts between states located on the same level of historical progression? Would it not have been natural, for instance, to back "bourgeois" states, historically superior to "feudal" or "semifeudal" ones by definition, against the latter type of state? Pure theory would have dictated such a decision.

In practice such a course would have appeared at once too simple and too complicated for Marx and Engels. And perhaps they were right in making the tactical interests of the working class movement—as interpreted by them—the principal yardstick of their political judgements, assessing each concrete international situation in the light of the existing balance of power between the various working class movements and states involved. That some of these judgements turned out to be far from personally disinterested was shown when, towards the end of his life, and convinced at that time that the French Socialists were not averse to entering into an alliance with Tsarist Russia in order to regain Alsace-Lorraine from Germany, Engels warned Paul Lafargue, leader of the French Socialists, not to tie himself to French revanchism on the grounds that a French victory would result in the violent destruction of the Socialist movement in Germany "whilst peace would lead us to certain victory." Writing to Engels during the Franco-Prussian war of 1870-1871, Marx similarly pointed out that the defeat of Germany, which would have strengthened Bonapartism and crippled the German working class movement for many years to come, might have been more disastrous than a German victory. By transferring the centre of gravity from Paris to Berlin, Bismarck was doing their work for them. For the German working class, being better organised and better disciplined than the French, was consequently a stronger citadel of socialism than a French one would have been.[22] On both occasions the interests of the German working class, "being better organised and better disciplined than the French," were perceived to be the overriding consideration.

As regards the relative strength of states in international society, Marx considered revolution in Germany impossible, since Russia would intervene, as she had done with telling effect in Hungary in 1849.[23] And though Russia was always seen by him as a bulwark of reaction, he never attempted to justify his opposition to her on the international plane in terms of her semifeudal internal order, as against Germany's semibourgeois one. Would Marx have lent his wholehearted support to a revolutionary government in semifeudal Russia—a possibility considered real by him in 1877[24]—in a war of intervention launched by semibourgeois Germany against it? What, in any event, were the rules laid down by classical Marxism determining the timing and siting of revolution in the context of international relations? What, moreover, was to happen if a revolutionary state were to be established in isolation—a problem that was to agitate Marxists a great deal after 1917?

Kant, Hegel, Marx, and Engels on International Relations

Marx and Engels were the last in a series of thinkers on international relations who set great store by the meaning of historical progress. But whereas Kant had sketched out a movement of history in which predetermination was implied, though only discreetly, there was nothing predeterministic about either Hegel's or Marx's scheme of international relations, despite outward appearances to the contrary, since the element of volition, still rather muted in Kant's thesis, was essential to the operation of their schemes. For, while the mainstream of international history appeared to be fixed—perhaps less according to Hegel than to Marx—crucial shifts could be brought about by human intervention in its substreams. This task was performed in Hegel's scheme by the *grosse Geister*, who alone were capable of steering the ship of state intuitively along uncharted seas in desirable directions, while in Marx's theory of international relations, the same task was performed with preconceived positivism by the organised working class movement through the device of the class struggle.[25] Viewed in this light, the concept of the class struggle in Marx was pragmatically rather than analytically useful. The analysis was contained in the teleology, not the other way round, as in Hegel.

A fixed theory of international progress was still lacking in Hegel's philosophy, though dimly indicated in Kant's. Moreover, Hegel's intrinsically idealist quality resided in the spiritual sphere where it was expressed in the concept of *Geist*. And where in Hegel's scheme of world history the *Weltgeist* always remained ethically neutral, it was in unabashedly partisan fashion equated with the international working class in Marx's scheme. Writing on the eve of the industrial revolution, Hegel was unable to attribute institutional shape to the *Weltgeist*, seeing in the state the highest institution, expressing the spirit of a *Volk*. Marx, fully caught up in the maelstrom of the industrial age, saw the organised world proletariat as the institutional incarnation of the *Weltgeist*, capable of conquering the partial autonomy of the *Volksgeist*, if unable to do away at once with the institution of the state. That task was to be accomplished eventually by shifting the emphasis in Hegel's dialectic from idealism to materialism, which would allow world productive forces to be seen as overflowing state boundaries, ushering in the victory of the world proletariat on a world scale, thereby terminating, once and for all, the dialectical contradictions of history.[26]

Judged on their own stated premises, Marx and Engels were moderately successful in establishing within an evolutionary context an explanatory theory of international relations with operational intent. It is fair to assume that, if they had not been perplexed by the twin problems of the level of analysis and development, they might have furnished successive generations of Marxists with reasonably reliable guidelines by which to find their bearings in the unpredictable currents of international politics.

NOTES

1. See B.T. Wilkins, *Hegel's Philosophy of History*. New York: Cornell University Press, 1974.

2. See J. Loewenberg (ed.), *Hegel: Selections*. Cambridge, Mass.: Cambridge University Press, 1929, p. xii.

3. G.W.F. Hegel, *Naturrecht und Staatswissenschaft im Grundrisse: Grundlinien der Philosophie des Rechts*. Stuttgart: Reclam, 1870. (Original German edition: 1821.)

4. G.W.F. Hegel, *Die Phänomenologie des Geistes*. Frankfurt: Ullstein, 1970. (Original German edition: 1807.) By substituting reason for divine providence. Hegel was enabled to produce a philosophy based on a conception of a rational historical process.

5. Hegel's contemporary, the English romantic poet, William Wordsworth (1770-1850), in *The Prelude* (written in 1804) alludes to the dialectic by speaking of

> "dark
> invisible workmanship that reconciles
> discordant elements, and makes them move
> in one society."

Charles Dickens, using the simile of the movement of the sea, spoke of "constancy in nothing but eternal strife."

6. See E. Weil, *Hegel et l'Etat.* Paris: Vrin, 1950; and F. Rosenzweig, *Hegel und der Staat,* 2 vols. Berlin: Oldenburg, 1920. Z. A. Pelczynski (ed.), *Hegel's Political Philosophy* (London: Cambridge University Press, 1971) contains two useful essays on Hegel's theory of the state. See also S. Rosen, *G.W.F. Hegel.* New Haven, Conn.: Yale University Press, 1974. Jürgen Habermas, leading contemporary philosopher of the Frankfurt School, *Theory and Practice* (London: H.E.B., 1974) contains three stimulating essays on Hegel.

7. The *Volksgeist* is seen by Hegel as the "collective will" much in the way Rousseau used the term *volonté générale.* Concretely, decisions are taken on behalf of the *Volk* by the *Geistreichen* (those possessed of the *Volkgeist*; literally, those rich in spirit). They direct the people.

8. An unemotional man where his intellect was concerned, Hegel—unlike Carlyle after him—was far from being a hero worshipper. The remark he made on this occasion was strictly in the abstract.

9. Hegel spoke with admiration of Napoleon's "Weltseele" and with satisfaction of the impending defeat of Prussia.

10. Z.A. Pelczynski (ed.), *Hegel's Political Philosophy* (London: Cambridge University Press, 1971) contains an essay by D.P. Verene on Hegel's treatment of the phenomenon of war.

11. Hegel referred to public international law as "Staatenrecht" as distinct from "Staatsrecht," which was public municipal law.

12. These barbed remarks were directed not only against Kant's *Ewigen Frieden* in the abstract, but also against the Holy Alliance, which had been formed between the Habsburg, Romanov, and Hohenzollern empires for the purpose of preserving the rigid international status quo of 1815.

13. E. Burke, *Letters on a Regicide Peace* (1796 - 1797), in *Works* (5th ed., Boston 1877), Vol. 5, p. 317.

14. Engels had been an infantryman in one of the revolutionary armies of 1848. He retained a lifelong interest in military affairs, and became for this reason known to his fellow-socialists as "the general."

15. See E. Kamenka, *The Philosophy of Ludwig Feuerbach.* London: Routledge and Kegan Paul, 1970.

16. The only present-day Marxist theorist to have focussed his investigations on the state is Clodomiro Almeyda, Chilean academic sociologist and Minister of Foreign Affairs and Defence successively in Allende's government, 1970 - 1973. He now lives in exile. See C. Almeyda, *Hacia una teoría Marxista del estado.* Santiago: Prensa Latino-americana, 1948.

17. Grudgingly but firmly, Marx and Engels accepted the need for the further existence—on a strictly temporary basis—of the state even beyond the revolution, justifying their attitude by asserting that in a classless society the state had to remain for a while to ensure the permanence of classlessness and to give the latter a basis of legitimacy. Ultimately, however, the state had to fade away.

Engels once expressed the fear that the old repressive state machine might make its reappearance even in a proletarian state, and therefore counselled that the proletariat should "safeguard itself against its own deputies and officials by declaring them all, without exception, subject to recall at any moment."

18. See Sir Isiah Berlin, *Karl Marx.* London: Oxford University Press, 1949, p. 237.

19. The irony of the matter is that in the German language the word "bürgerlich" could mean both "civil" in the strictly legal sense, and "bourgeois" in the sociological one—something that could hardly have escaped Marx's attention.

20. See G.A. Wetter and W. Leonhard, *Sowjetideologie heute*. Frankfurt: Fischer, 1962, p. 98.

21. See his famous letter to Sorge, his secretary, dated 27 September, 1877.

22. See Berlin, op. cit., pp. 236-237.

23. Ibid., pp. 158-159.

24. Letter to Sorge cited above.

25. At the International Hegel Congress held in Antwerp in 1972, Eastern Europe's "official" Marxist spokesmen accepted the idea of Hegel's élitism unhesitatingly, while maintaining that the working class in power constituted the élite today. See *Der Spiegel*, 11 September, 1972.

26. This may account for the sterility of contemporary Soviet political thought, which represents no more than an arrested system of ideas that were once in full motion. To apply Marxist criticism to the present Soviet system would be a contradiction in terms, since it would mean questioning the claims of dialectical materialism to have effected the final solution of all political contradictions. On this point, see H. Marcuse, *Soviet Marxism*. Harmondsworth: Penguin, 1971.

Chapter 6:

FUNCTIONALISM:

COMMERCIAL AND INDUSTRIAL

During the second half of the eighteenth century, the critique of the international absolutist system began to gather strength. By the time of the French Revolution, the system had become widely discredited. During that period the emphasis of informed criticism shifted more and more from purely political considerations to the economic element, and in particular to the system of mercantilism generally referred to by its critics as "the colonial system"—the economic pillar of political absolutism.

Related as it was to the perennial search for a monopoly of colonial trade, to a perpetually favourable balance of trade in general, and to the amassing of as large a stock of bullion as possible, mercantilism might indeed be regarded as an essential part of the absolutist system.

The Antimercantilist Case

The main point in the antimercantilist argument was not only that it served to prop up the international absolutist system in general but also— more potently—that mercantilism valued wealth mainly as an instrument of power, and that the economics of mercantilism tended to reinforce the bellicose tendencies in the politics of absolutism. Pointing to the predatory nature of the absolutist state and to the fatal nexus between wealth and power, these critics questioned the precise function of international trade within the wider system of international relations under absolutism. Providing ample material for their strictures, the English mercantilist economist Sir William Mildmay (1751 - 1775) wrote in 1765 that "a country cannot exist in security without power; power cannot be obtained without riches; nor the riches without trade." This was a ruthless justification for carrying on international trade for the sake not of enhancing world welfare, its only morally permissible function, but towards the aggrandisement of state power. Viewed in this perspective, wealth and state power were two sides of the same coin. As Professor Silberner, a stern twentieth-century critic of mercantilism, who provides a useful summary of antimercantilist arguments, maintained: "The object of mercantilism is not to increase wealth in order to improve the material life of the nation, but to organise production in such a manner as to ensure State predominance over other peoples."[1] The result was an unhealthy striving towards autarky akin to the permanent preparations for war of which Kant and other writers of the Enlightenment were complaining.

Professor Silberner went on to contrast the relationship that existed between international politics and international economics in the age of absolutism with that in the subsequent age of liberalism, concluding that, in the former, international economics was strictly subordinate to international politics, whereas no such dependency existed under liberalism. Abhorring state interference in the economic sphere as leading to conflict, he praised the eighteenth-century French liberal economists Quesnay and Dupont de Nemours for thinking that international organisation based on the close integration of states was unnecessary. The mercantilists, on the other hand, drew his wrath for being centralisers who believed that the economic interest of states were unalterably opposed to each other, and for encouraging the absolutist rulers to make full use of their wealth for military purposes.[2]

The two related, yet separate schools of British and French functionalism grew logically out of the criticisms levelled at mercantilism, as well as out of the writings of the Enlightenment concerning the political aspects of the international absolutist system. Taking over the intellectual baggage of these critics, the nineteenth-century functionalists on either side of the Channel concentrated on criticising the economic aspects of the international absolutist system, and in so doing, progressed from criticism to some constructive thinking about the future of international relations. The difference between the British and French schools of functionalist theory in the field of international relations was one of emphasis, rather than substance, reflecting the relative stage in economic development reached by either in the two spheres of commerce and industry, the two areas of principal economic advance during the nineteenth century. Representatives of both schools of thought believed firmly, if implicitly, in the "harmony of interests" within the state, and saw no reason why this laudable state of affairs should not profitably be extended to the international sphere, in which the institution of the state alone seemed to stand in the way of functionalism benefiting world society as a whole.

Largely an elaboration of the classical economic doctrines of liberalism as expressed through the magic formula of laisser faire at home and free trade abroad, the British functionalist conception culminated in the belief that a widely uniform system of international relations would spring from the adoption of its principles. Two kinds of expectations were fostered: (a) that, breaking down all barriers in its course, free trade would lead to the creation of a smoothly functioning world trading system; and (b) that the period of continued prosperity resulting directly from this would act as a formidable disincentive to war, issuing in an essentially pacific system of international politics.

Instead of concentrating on the mollifying properties of international trade, as the British functionalists tended to do, their French counterparts set great store in the internationally conciliatory powers of the rational management of industry by a class of technocrats operating under the guidance of an internationally assembled team of highly trained scientists, acting either independently of the states or striving to gain an intellectual ascendancy over them. The general idea common to both British and French functionalist approaches to world problems was to render the existing states innocuous through by-passing them.

The British Functionalist Approach

The classical age of British functionalist thinking began about 1840 and had its heyday in the third quarter of the nineteenth century. British functionalism, it must be pointed out, was affected by the spirit of the French Revolution and its intellectual antecedents, as well as by the newly unfolding drama of the industrial revolution, which was pioneered by Britain. Radicals imbued with a reforming zest were anxious to create close bonds between welfare and peace, and men like Cobden, Bright, the younger Mill, and Green all served as members of Parliament in order to achieve this. Bentham would have loved to do likewise, had he found a sponsor.

Derived from the remnants of the natural law school of the Enlightenment, as expressed in Britain by Adam Smith, Professor of Moral Philosophy at Edinburgh, and from early nineteenth-century utilitarianism as represented by Jeremy Bentham, the pure strain of British functionalist thinking during the nineteenth century was characterised by the strength of the amoral element in its approach to the subject of international relations, in which marked scepticism, if not outright hostility regarding the role of the state in that sphere, provided the keynote. There was basic agreement between the utilitarians and the classical liberal economists of the Manchester School on at least three points: (a) that there was a "harmony of interests" between all states; (b) that free trade was intimately connected with the achievement of peace; and (c), following from (a) and (b), that the first priority was to abolish the monopoly of trade that was part and parcel of the "colonial system."

Later in the nineteenth century two diluted strains served to adulterate the purity of the midcentury wine of British functionalism, where international relations were concerned. In the first place, J.S. Mill (1806-1873), a disciple of David Ricardo, began to adopt a positive attitude towards the role of the state, taking the view that it could be made to serve the real needs of society after all in certain ways, rather than the glory of the rulers exclusively.[3] He thereby laid the foundations for the subsequent Fabian-Liberal functional integrationist theories expounded by David Mitrany in the twentieth century. In the second place, in spite of a certain revival of Hegelian thinking, mainly at Oxford, occasioned by the advent of the new school of "social Darwinism" with its central notion of the "survival of the fittest"—a term coined by Herbert Spencer in 1852—there was to be a moralist revival, fostered by the Liberals. Their position but for that crucial difference was, at least in theory, close to that of the functionalists, where international relations were concerned.

The Classical Economists

It is commerce which is rapidly rendering war obsolete.
　　　　　　　　J.S. Mill, *Political Economy* (1848)

War is on its last legs—universal peace is as sure as the prevalence of civilization over barbarism, of liberal government over feudal forms.
　　　　　　　　Ralph Waldo Emerson, in a lecture delivered in 1838

That the interest of all businessmen dictated the establishment of an international division of labour obtainable only during universal peace was a message implicit in the writings of the classical liberal economists,[4] and more especially in the writings of their founder, Adam Smith (1723-1790), as set down in his masterpiece *The Wealth of Nations* (1776), a large part of which was taken up by an assault on the mercantilist system. Adam Smith's suspicion of the role of the state was based not so much on an abstract model of economic behaviour as on a well-justified suspicion of the monopolising aims concealed in "the clamour and sophistry of merchants and manufacturers" and on the dangerous expediency of "that insidious and crafty animal, vulgarly called a statesman or politician, whose councils are directed to the momentary fluctuations of affairs." There was a hint here of a conspiracy between state and capitalist.

Adam Smith's faith in the basic beneficence of the natural order made him think that in pursuing his own advantage, each individual was "led by an invisible hand to promote an end which was no part of his intentions."[5] Order would arise spontaneously and interference would only do harm. Left undisturbed, the natural order would bring in its train a "harmony of interests," and the best way to speed this development was to remove all obstacles to trade, both at home and abroad.

It was because of their belief that a "harmony of interests" existed that Richard Cobden (1804-1865) and John Bright (1811-1889) argued so strongly for nonintervention and free trade as essential and mutually reinforcing ingredients of a pacific system of international relations. John Bright demanded "as little intercourse as possible between governments," while Richard Cobden called for "as much connexion as possible between the nations of the world." Between them they brewed the pure wine that the commercial functionalism of nineteenth-century British origin was made of. Cobden—in this respect the most representative British functionalist of all—proclaimed panegyrically in 1846 that free trade was "the international law of the Almighty."[6]

More and more the state in its old form was perceived as a stationary and increasingly outmoded element in a rapidly changing economic and social environment, badly in need of adaptation to the newly prevailing conditions. It had either to be reformed or have its former range of functions drastically reduced. Its functions in the economic sphere had to be hived off and handed over to the business community, which was seen as being held together by a sense of self-interest. By disconnecting state and economy, the fatal link between economic wealth and military potential—which the mercantilists saw as inevitable—would be severed. As a result of the ubiquitous growth of business interests with a vested interest in maintaining peace, free trade would ensure the peaceful development of interstate relations.

War and Diplomacy

THE CAUSES OF WAR

British functionalism of the nineteenth century made a powerful and possibly lasting contribution to thought on international relations. Its common denominator was the concept of the "harmony of interests," of which Jeremy Bentham (1748-1832) was one of the earliest and most academically minded promoters. An unbeliever in the feasibility of a "world republic," yet calling himself a "citizen of the world,"[7] Bentham was basically a reformer and a talented draftsman whose doctrine of "utilitarianism" resulted from systematic reasoning. Believing in the reformability of the state rather than its by-passing, he was a forerunner of the classical, midcentury functionalists of the British school rather than an integral part of it. The link between eighteenth-century rationalism and nineteenth-century functionalism, he provided a plausible confirmation of the scientism of the Enlightenment that man would infallibly conform to the moral law of nature once its content had been rationally determined.

His thesis that the same essential community of interests prevails between states as between individuals sprang directly from his philosophy of utilitarianism, which contained a number of imperatives.[8] This accorded well with his assertion that there was no real conflict between the interests of states, and "if they appear repugnant anywhere, it is only in proportion as they are misunderstood."[9]

His rationalism was most clearly manifested in his attitude towards war, which led him to believe at the close of the Napoleonic period that no moral problem was involved in it. Though fostering no illusions as to the continued prevalence of power politics,[10] he was convinced, though subsequently plagued by doubts on this score, that among civilised states—and Britain and France at any rate were so regarded by him—the deliberate element in the initiation of war could be discarded. Such wars could therefore result from the element of accident only. However, feelings could not be commanded and persuasion and enlightenment had to be relied on as the agencies to drive the lesson home.

Not a moral pacifist like T.H. Green long after him, Bentham considered that, when attacked, a state had to defend itself as a matter of broad principle. However, in tune with his amoral approach to international relations in general, the actual decision whether or not to defend itself against an aggressor should be the subject of a simple calculation of cost. He saw no reason why a state should fight in circumstances when defence seemed more costly than submission, all the more so as the frequency of war tended to encourage a spiral of mutual suspicion. This approach had something startlingly cool and detached about it, and it reflected his general preoccupation with the factor of cost found in many of his other writings. It would not be an exaggeration to regard him as the first exponent of scientific pacifism.

Richard Cobden, cotton manufacturer and exporter, and British nineteenth-century functionalist par excellence, was echoing Bentham in thinking that, in a post-absolutist society of states, wars arose out of "accidental collisions,"[11] but to his mind "the colonial system of Europe"—meaning the monopoly of trade between metropolis and colonies—"has been the chief source of war for the last 150 years." Most wars were fought for mercantilist ends, but private vested interests were opposed to war. What was needed to protect foreign trade was not the powerful navy for which the mercantilists had been clamouring, but the cheapness of goods.

This assertion enabled him to proclaim, somewhat self-righteously, that "the more any nation trafficks abroad upon free and honest principles, the less it will be in danger of wars." Free trade would, if not exactly eliminate war altogether, at least serve to minimise its incidence.[12]

Not a systematic thinker—like Bentham—but an activist in commerce and politics, and a propagandist, Cobden had no awareness whatever that the free play of the terms of trade would be bound to favour the stronger party and lead to commercial and political distortions on a world scale. A strong believer in the internationally therapeutic function of free trade, he had no time at all for annexations of new territory, which he regarded as a source of weakness. For this reason he dismissed the principle of the "balance of power," which he thought had been conceived in terms of frontiers and armaments rather than in terms of industry and commerce.

THE JUSTICE OF WAR

The attitude towards the problem of the permissibility of war varied among the British functionalists of the nineteenth century. A stern moralist approach, hardly compatible with functionalism—which is amoral almost by definition—was adopted by T.H. Green (1836 - 1882), Professor of Moral Philosophy at Oxford, according to whom war could never be absolutely, only relatively right. Not only the need but also the impulse to war had to be abolished. War was the attribute of the imperfect state.[13]

It was, however, Cobden again who poured unremitting scorn on the frequent war scares of his time, producing pamphlet after pamphlet arguing against war.[14] John Bright, a Quaker and member of Parliament, who served in several of Gladstone's cabinets, shared Cobden's views and opposed the Crimean War. W.E. Gladstone himself (1809 - 1898) was a liberal, whose thoughts on war overlapped only partially with those of the functionalists, with whom the Liberals had a certain amount in common. A statesman and not a theorist, Gladstone was not radically opposed to war in principle. He considered the danger of aggression a real one and believed that preparations had to be made to meet it, even though on utilitarian grounds he deplored the money that had to be spent in this way.[15] Even less support for Cobden's total opposition to war on functionalist grounds was provided by Lord Palmerston (1784 - 1865). Sharing the former's enthusiasm regarding the civilising mission of commerce, Palmerston believed the decrepit Chinese and Ottoman empires could be transformed by commercial penetration, but—unlike Cobden—he would not flinch from the use of force in order to achieve this object.

An early instance of a sophisticated gradation of just causes of war was elaborated by William Godwin (1756 - 1836), near-anarchist and friend of the romantic poet Shelley, who, much impressed by the rhetoric of the French revolutionaries, considered that all wars waged for commercial gain were to be condemned outright, as was the "colonial system" of monopoly trade itself. However, a defensive war against "tyrannous aggression" was always legitimate and a war in defence of liberty always just. It would have been intriguing to know whether Godwin would have considered an aggressive war in defence of liberty equally just, as, according the logic of his basic propositions, it would have had to be. The matter becomes even more fascinating when it is considered that he regarded any war as permissible that was waged against what he called the oppressive use of power, being careful to explain that neither (a) the mere accumulation of power, nor (b) the vindication of "national honour" qualified as good causes for the opening of hostilities.[16]

J.S. Mill (1806 - 1873), a political philosopher of great note, adopted an ambivalent attitude towards the principle of nonintervention. Favouring it generally, he yet felt compelled to qualify it severely. His basic premise was that all nations have a right to self-determination, both internal and international. International political harmony existed in the sense that the basic interests of states need not conflict with the interest of all mankind. In this he was at one with Cobden.

Mill, in particular, was never willing to support a foreign policy based on totally functionalist principles, and tended to mitigate the purity of functionalism by his own kind of pragmatism. Considering the intentions of continental despotism as dubious, basically militaristic, and therefore potentially dangerous, he opposed the disarmament of Britain. He was, moreover, willing to argue that, since only armies can be aggressive, the British Royal Navy should be strengthened.[17] Nor did he share Cobden's great belief in the peaceful nature of popular opinion, expressing concern in 1871 at the bellicose attitude of many British workers demanding war with Prussia.

As regards the right of intervention abroad, Mill was of two minds. For him the rules of international law made it difficult to lend a hand to national liberation struggles abroad, and though he was certain that a right of self-government existed, he could see the dangers of unbridled application of the principle of intervention in such a case. Opposed to war for the sake of an idea, he considered intervention legitimate in the case of one country interfering with the freedom of another.

He felt it incumbent, therefore, to work out a conception of intervention of his own. Intervention to enforce nonintervention was always right, if not always prudent. Moreover, the doctrine of nonintervention, to be a legitimate principle of morality, had to be accepted by all governments—a most severe qualification. Thus, in a curious way, Mill distinguished between domestic and foreign intervention, regarding domestic oppression a matter of indifference to other states.

From midcentury onwards, it was clear that a cleavage was developing between the functionalists, with their primary concern of harmony, on the one hand, and the Liberals, with their principal interest in promoting freedom, on the other. The latter would not object to intervention on behalf of freedom. Thus, Gladstone remarked during his famous Midlothian speeches that foreign policy "should always be inspired by the love of freedom," though in his eyes that meant freedom from external restraints. He would not have foisted freedom on the Turks, but was quite prepared to assist their subject nationalities in gaining theirs. Well might A.J.P. Taylor remark, "Press Bright's policy to its conclusion, and you arrive at isolation. Press Gladstone's doctrine to its conclusion, and you have universal interference."[18] Reformist Liberalism was abandoning the basic functionalist precepts of nonintervention even while it continued to cling to that of free trade.

Fabian Functionalism

Classical functionalism stressing the role of commerce in the peaceful evolution of international relations originated in Britain, where the state was to be the watchman only. This scepticism regarding the state weakened towards the end of the nineteenth century, as early Fabians and Oxford neo-Hegelians, following Mill's lead, began to urge the assumption of larger functions of the state in the field of welfare. The better organised each state, the easier would be its relations with other states.[19]

Still within the mainstream of Victorian functionalism, but connected with the Fabian Society, David Mitrany (1888 - 1975) similarly came to realise that a number of useful functions on the part of the state could be applied to international relations. Focussing on international economic institutions, Mitrany saw these not as the beginning, but as the culmination of functionalism. International political divisions were to be overlaid with a "spreading web" of such interstate agencies, in which, and through which, the interests and life of all countries would gradually be integrated.[20]

The assumption underlying Mitrany's reasoning was that an international system of welfare resting on interstate welfare institutions would eventually be seen as manifestly beneficial, resulting in a transfer of emotional attachment on the part of individuals from their state to those international welfare institutions, through which not only prosperity but also peace could be secured.[21] This was a grandiose conception which seemed to set the crown on the achievement of nineteenth-century functionalism but springing from it, it had also modified it. E.H. Carr embraced part of Mitrany's thesis by advocating the introduction of functionalism as a means of satisfying the world's economic needs, and regionalism to take care of the world's security needs, leaving the state intact as the principal focus of political loyalty.[22]

Functional Integrationism

Already in Mitrany's writings there could be discerned a shift of emphasis from the pure model of free trade, allegedly leaving the state in possession of its "watchman" function only, to one in which the state had a significant part to play in promoting welfare, both within its own boundaries and in the international system at large. More and more it became obvious that the state was capable of assuming an impressively wide range of welfare functions and was able to cater to the well-being of its subjects with something like adequate effectiveness. This was not only admitted by Mitrany, but it invalidated to a great extent the basic assumptions of nineteenth-century functionalists in Britain and elsewhere. The result was that the functionalist approach to international relations had to be considerably modified. No longer was it a question of by-passing the state, but of integrating the welfare functions of various welfare-conscious states, on a world or at least on a regional scale. The emphasis was consequently shifted from functionalism to functional integrationism. It was to theories of functional integration that subsequent thinkers tended to turn.

A big-opportunity seemed to be in the offing with the creation of the European Economic Community on January 1, 1958. This at once attracted the attention of theorists, in particular that of E.H. Haas, who argued in favour of what he called "incrementalism," the process whereby the EEC would attract to itself more and more welfare functions, leaving the states essentially with political functions only.[23] This "incrementalist" theory continued in vogue for some time until it was realised that—mainly owing to the firm stand taken against this by General de Gaulle in France—there were definite political limits beyond which most states would refuse to go on giving up their sovereignty in the vital field of economic and social welfare.

At this point the debate shifted, as functional integrationists turned away from government towards pressure groups and the bureaucracy as the main focus of their enquiries, assuming that the latter were the principal decision-makers, instead of governments.[24] The basic objectives of traditional functionalism remain; namely to revalidate the notions on the basic "harmony of interests" of the nineteenth century held by the classical economists, but to adapt these—frequently, if necessary, in the light of fresh discoveries—to present-day conditions. Since the state of the second half of the twentieth century resembles but faintly that of the nineteenth, especially in its decision-making procedures, and since other, new actors have appeared on the international stage, traditional functionalism required remodelling to meet the challenge of the new problems. The name given to the new approach is "neo-functionalism." This name has the advantage of stressing the element of continuity with classical functionalism, but it does scant justice to the shift towards integrationism. It would therefore be preferable to speak of "functional integrationism," in order to mark the transition sufficiently.[25]

In conclusion it may be said that commercial functionalism, originally intended to by-pass the state as an obstacle towards peace and welfare, has failed to do so, not so much because its logical premises were faulty, but because the state itself has changed. Admitting this to have been the case, the neo-functionalists are trying their luck in analysing the subgovernmental processes of decision-making with a view to determine at which point in the latter it would be feasible to promote international integration.

It now remains to analyse the second principal functionalist approach towards peace and prosperity, which focusses on industrial development.

French Functionalism

If British functionalism was an attempt to by-pass the state by developing the international commercial function to such an extent as to render irrelevant the political functions of states, then French functionalism, its contemporary and counterpart—considering the task of outflanking the state to be best performed by a universal technocratic, rather than a universal commercial class—approached the subject of politics through science, without preconceptions drawn from other sources. In so doing, it showed no trace of hostility towards the ideas entertained by the British functionalists or the institution of international trade. However, in spite of large areas of overlap between the two functionalist approaches, they must be separated on academic grounds, since the French tradition of *dirigisme*, with its strong belief in the directing role of the state in the management of the economy—which might equally well be called the cybernetic tradition[26]—was basically at odds with the British tradition, with its image of a highly decentralised international structure in which the states would remain in existence in an emasculated form as the "night watchmen" of law and order, stripped of any decision-making function. Retaining its belief in the cybernetic functions of the state—based on a long line of tradition in French history—the French functionalist school wished to see the decision-making function transferred from the political institution of the state to a highly qualified but at the same time strictly apolitical technocracy fostered by the state. Intervention in public affairs must be by a body of experts with the correct scientific knowledge acting on the international level, and not by politicians of doubtful knowledge or allegiance at the level of the state. The relative backwardness of the French economy and the need to by-pass a legislature based on landed wealth explains the emphasis of the French functionalists on the role of the technocrats in promoting international harmony. The apolitical technocratic élite, operating on a scientific basis, was to be the chosen vehicle of progress.

The history of French functionalism is older than that of its British counterpart.[27] As early as 1734 Montesquieu noted that prosperity depended on trade and industry, not on conquest;[28] and long before the first outspoken British functionalist appeared on the scene, the first French Jacobin foreign minister, Doumouriez, went on record in 1792 as saying that it would be his policy to avoid entangling alliances, and as justifying this by stating that a state like revolutionary France should not be tied, as a matter of principle, to the fortune of any other state. Jacobin France, he affirmed, was to enter into commercial agreements only—clear evidence of a pronounced apolitical bias.

An aversion against politics in international affairs was only one element in French functionalism, and one, moreover, which it held in common with British functionalism. What marked out French functionalism as unique was its strong belief in the social power of science. Thus, writing his *Sketch for a Historical Picture of the Progress of the Human Mind* in 1795,[29] the Marquis de Condorcet proclaimed the "unlimited perfectability of mankind." He expressed his belief in a future without wars to be achieved by the combined application of the three elements of reason, education, and science. This was in line with the optimistic expectations in the power of progress fostered by the thinkers of the Enlightenment and eagerly taken up by the intellectual supporters of the French Revolution. The period following the French revolutionary wars, however, as well as being one of intellectual and political ferment, was a time of intellectual and political confusion.

Saint-Simon (1760 - 1826)

Both elements were to be found in the exciting but at the same time somewhat muddled ideas of Count Claude Henri de Saint-Simon (1760 - 1826), one of the originators of the French technocratic school of functionalism. In essence, his idea of progress towards a pacific international society relied on the formation of an international brains trust, freed from political interference, which should (a) determine the broad principles of scientific progress, and (b) instruct a class of elected industrialists—a term wide enough to embrace owners, managers and workers engaged in industrial production—how to go about their business in a rational manner.

In 1790—only one year after the outbreak of the French Revolution—Saint-Simon, a revolutionary with definite socialist tendencies and a thinker with a pronounced sense of power, was elected President of the Electoral Assembly. When Napoleon appeared on the scene, Saint-Simon began to sense great opportunities in the offing: "The Emperor will soon conquer the world and give it laws . . . when the war has come to an end, the sciences will be the exclusive object of his attention . . . on the basis of reasoning and observation he will find general principles which will forever serve as guides to mankind ... the Emperor is the scientific chief of mankind just as he is its political head." The prospect of creating a world state had something intoxicating about it, both emotionally and intellectually, and there seemed a real chance of putting into practice Saint-Simon's ideas on a world scale.

His ideas amounted to no less than a theory of scientific universalism (or technological universalism) betraying a belief in the almost limitless possibilities of science. Saint-Simon's key concept was competence in the sphere of technology. Just as Hegel, his contemporary, was a believer in the efficient administrative state, so Saint-Simon was a believer in the efficient technocratic state, not only on a domestic scale, but also in relation to the problem of world organisation. In 1815 Saint-Simon, who was nothing if not highly imaginative, put forward a scheme for the reorganisation of Europe, which revealed in a flash what was on his mind. He wished to see the twenty-four greatest intellectuals from among the leading countries of Europe[30] elected to a "Council of Newton," an international brains trust with a provocatively original name to mark its scientific character, under whose guidance a number of similarly elected "industrialists" would exercise temporal power. Supreme spiritual power was to remain in the hands of the "Council of Newton," which would also proclaim the doctrine of the *pensateur universel*. In this peculiar division of labour, the intellectuals would determine the principles of policy, for the industrialists to put them into practice. In this way—and on the clear understanding that the politicians would be excluded—"the curse of war will leave Europe, never to reappear." With Europe thus united, a crusade would be launched to liberate the rest of the world in order to weld it into a single unit.

Industrialism, as Saint-Simon conceived it, was a social system with an international dimension. No individual country could proceed to the establishment of the industrial system of social organisation without a movement in the same direction of all its neighbours. The world's industrialists would have a solid centre of support in Britain and France, most advanced in this respect, in their endeavours to emulate the industrialists of other countries.[31] It is almost as if Saint-Simon had raised the slogan "industrialists of the world, unite."

Saint-Simon's ideology represented an interesting combination of Napoleonic megalomania and scientific progress in many ways reminiscent of a medieval order, with a secular church containing a college of secular cardinals supported by a universalist doctrine imbued with the spirit of the Crusades. He evidently expected a magnificent response to his call from at least the scientists, whom he probably regarded as the top of the intellectual tree and who were, he thought, well placed to take action; only to be disappointed by their lukewarmness towards his grandiose scheme. With the military situation of Napoleonic France deteriorating rapidly, Saint-Simon denounced the scientists for doing nothing to stop the war and subsequently pinned his remaining hopes on the technocrats, and particularly the industrialists, whom he expected to render proper assistance in bringing about a merger of the British and French parliaments, with the parliaments of other countries following suit. Impatient as always, and increasingly élitist in outlook, he finally considered that the best chance of achieving a technocratic society in France lay in a simple decree by an autocratic Bourbon king. Having lost faith in the doctrine of *pensateur universel*, Saint-Simon reverted ultimately to Christianity, which, in a refurbished form, was seen as a suitable institutional device through which to realise his universal scheme.

It would be wrong to smile indulgently at Saint-Simon. Rushed by events and half compelled to be progagandist as well as exponent of his set of ideas, he lacked the time to inject an element of coherence into his scheme. His principal claim to fame rests on the fact that he was the first thinker struck with the idea of technological determinism based on a vision of more or less uninterrupted advance, properly managed, of technological society the world over. He believed that the progress of that society would lead to a unity of interests under which states would ultimately become anachronistic and incongruous with the forward march of history. He foresaw a world unity based on the recognition of common economic interests. Towards this end he meant to substitute men of science for the clergy, industrialists for the nobility, and hence bring about the order, stability, and efficiency conducive to universal prosperity and peace. His influence on intellectual posterity was immense. Generations of creative Marxist thinkers drew on his ideas,[32] and some of his most gifted pupils in France set out to refine and develop his thought. Chief among these was Auguste Comte.

Auguste Comte (1798 - 1857)

Comte was a follower of Saint-Simon and is generally regarded as the founder of the philosophical school of positivism. Where Saint-Simon was enveloped in the whirlwind of the French Revolution and the revolutionary and Napoleonic wars that followed—a man of action as well as a thinker—Comte was more fortunate in living in relatively settled times. A well-trained intellectual, the beneficiary of Saint-Simon's spadework and more relaxed than Saint-Simon as a consequence, he was able to take stock of what had happened in the recent past before producing his own credo in the future of international society. Like Saint-Simon before him, Comte considered that the data of history, properly interpreted, could provide the means of making predictions. Scientific thought could make a contribution towards peace by putting an end to the struggle of man against man, and by setting men free to struggle against nature.

During the eighteenth century the idea of progress had been put forward cautiously and with hesitation. In the midnineteenth century such caution was thrown to the wind, as the optimistic climate then prevailing in the course of the industrial revolution generated a profusion of determinist theories. According to Comte, Napoleon had misread the signs of his age and misinterpreted the direction of history. He had been all along in conflict with the underlying force of history. Saint-Simon already had prepared the ground for Comte's belief that it was the intellectual evolution which essentially determines the main course taken by social phenomena the world over. Relying on Condorcet,[33] he had worked out a scheme of historical evolution incorporating three stages of scientific thought composed of (a) the organic, or deductive-exploratory stage, in which a triumphant set of ideas finds its expression in a general theory; (b) the critical, or inductive-empirical stage, in which this general theory is tested by way of criticism; and finally (c) the new organic, or synthetic stage, containing the quintessence of science in all its fullness, which would, inter alia, help to produce a scientific, and by implication foolproof type of politics.[34] It was intellectual evolution which essentially determined the main course taken by social phenomena.

Comte refined Saint-Simon's scheme by maintaining that the human scientific mind (a) invents deities during its theological age; (b) abstracts by scientific analysis during the subsequent metaphysical stage; and (c) predicts by scientific synthesis during the final, positivist phase of its evolution. Synthesis, a key requirement of prediction, was to be given priority over mere analysis in the age of positivism. Contemptuous of historical accidents, such as revolution, evolution, or violence, Comte thought that society would be reorganised only through a synthesis of all existing sciences, culminating in the creation of a positive science of politics. Biology, which clearly impressed Comte, was the first product of scientific synthesis. Sociology too would have to undergo the identical process of synthetic transformation. There could be no free will, and no voluntarist element, such as politics, was to be allowed to stand in the way of scientific progress.

A society existed only to the extent that its members shared the same beliefs. It was the task of the intellectual élite first to determine and then to impose the right kind of ideas. Since a shared belief in the future based on scientific synthesis was tantamount to belief in a general theory, he could see on the distant horizon the development of a world society responding to the dictates of such a general theory, the last word in positivist perfection. Comte shared Saint-Simon's élitist notions in which a corps of intellectuals trained in scientific thought according to positivist precepts would lay down general guidelines to be carried out by "temporal" agencies. Greatly impressed by the industrial civilisation that was springing up so fast around him, Comte confidently expected the technocratic-managerial revolution to sweep the globe, since it seemed far superior to all previous forms of economic and social organisation.

In complete contrast to what contemporary British functionalists were asserting, Comte considered free enterprise not to be of the essence of the new scientific-technological society. Free enterprise was rather "a pathological element, a temporary aberration in the growth of an organisation which is to be stabilised on principles other than those of unrestricted competition."[35]

World society, according to Comte, will be the by-product of spreading industrial civilisation, but the rate of progress made by that civilisation would depend on the speed with which a general theory could be formed which alone was capable of fostering industrial civilisation in an orderly fashion. The unity of world society had to be seen first and foremost as a function of the unity of world thought. The supreme directing force from beginning to end was to be what Comte called a "homogeneous speculative class" which would eventually control all countries of the world. In the short run, however, each state in Europe would retain its own peculiar "temporal" structures.[36]

It is possible to think of Comte's theory of world society, which has certain elements in common with Kant's, as the reincarnation of the medieval unifying principle of natural law brought up to date through the incorporation of the latest scientific techniques, which leave no room for idiosyncracies of a personal kind. The primacy of politics had to give way to the primacy of science under the exclusive management of the experts.

It is still early, and Comte's vision of the genesis of a worldwide technological-managerial society may well come true in the long run. Envisaging the industrial system and its by-product, the managerial society, as a catalyst between politically opposing ideologies, Comte's message to the world was to forget about its political differences and to concentrate on the solution of technical problems so that the former, the real obstacles to world unity, might fade away.[37]

Repercussions in Britain

The French school of technocratic functionalism made an impact among British thinkers also. Herbert Spencer (1820-1903), whose *System of Synthetic Philosophy* (ten volumes) began to appear in 1860 and was completed in 1896, advocated the promotion of the industrial system, as well as of international trade, as suitable catalyst toward the formation of a pacific world society. Even more deeply affected was H.G. Wells (1886 - 1945), who—although a Fabian and therefore a believer in the concept of the socialist "permeation" of the state machinery, rather than its outright bypassage, through the creation of technocratic rival structures—was close to the mainstream of French technocratic functionalism. Fond of neatly constructed systems, Wells despised the amateurishness of the British élites, and felt an affinity to French functionalist thought reflected in his insistence that adaptation was being hopelessly outpaced by scientific discovery. His *Outline of World History* published in 1901 contained a sketch of his ideas of a future world society and an inkling of how it could be attained. He believed technological progress to be making for growing world interdependence, and that the establishment of "one world State at peace within itself" would be attained ultimately, possibly only after "centuries of misunderstanding and bloodshed." Politics had a tendency to lag behind economics and "in the economic sense, indeed, a world State already is established."

Wells' belief in technological progress led him to expect the formation of a technocratic class—broadly defined—which he likened to "an informal and open freemasonry," whose prime task it would be not to overthrow existing governments but "to supersede them by disregard." If traditional representative government stood in the way, it had to be discarded, a view which was akin to that held by Comte. World government was imperative, but the political approach towards it was obsolete and would lead to useless compromises only. Science alone—and Wells meant natural rather than social science—was capable of creating a new world.[39] Wells had shed much of the optimism which still imbued the writings of Comte. He may have thought of the Fabian Society as a body of the elect in Britain and as a model organisation on a world scale, but his general approach was apocalyptic rather than ecstatic, and he died a disappointed man.[40]

Functionalism: Present Trends

Saint-Simon and Comte thought the world was progressing from a theological-military to a scientific-technological stage. Neither laid down a specific line of thought on international relations, but their design for world society was implicit in their conclusions. French functionalism hardly developed further after Comte, while British functionalism lived on in Mill's liberalism, a certain brand of Fabianism, and, in our own days, in functionalist integrationism. Both schools accepted the concept of the "harmony of interests" as valid, springing as it did from the powerful historical trend towards industrialisation and technology, as well as towards an ever-closing network of world trade.

Suprisingly, Parsonian functionalist sociology had little to say about history. The grand theory of Parsons projected a completely integrated model of the social system which, after explaining why everything was necessarily as it was, failed to go on to say why it changed.[41] Taking his cue from sociology as developed in the United States, the West German philosopher-sociologist Jürgen Habermas put forward the similar concept of a "Kommunikationsgemeinschaft," the historical end-product of universal pressures towards specialisation and professionalisation. His late colleague of the Frankfurt School,

Max Horkheimer (1895 - 1973), in extending the quintessence of Comtian positivism into the future, even foresaw in the immanent logic of history not the land of the free, but "die verwaltete Welt" (a world of total administration). One would not perhaps be far amiss in predicting, therefore, that French, rather than British functionalist traditions will shape the future course of sociological thought on international relations.

NOTES

1. E. Silberner, *La guerre dans la pensée économique du XVIe au XVIIIe siècle.* Paris: Pedone, 1939.
2. For an attempt to place critiques of mercantilism in their true historical perspective, see J. Viner, "Power versus plenty as objectives in foreign policy in the seventeenth and eighteenth centuries," 1 *World Politics* (1948), pp. 1-29. See also D.C. Coleman (ed.), *Revisions in Mercantilism.* London: Methuen, 1969.
3. For a left-wing critique of J.S. Mill, see P. Schwartz, *The New Political Economy of J.S. Mill.* London: Weidenfeld and Nicolson, 1973.
4. For a comprehensive treatment, see D.P. O'Brien, *The Classical Economists.* Oxford: The Clarendon Press, 1975.
5. *The Wealth of Nations* (1776), Vol. 2, p. 206.
6. J. MacCunn, *Six Radical Thinkers.* London: Arnold, 1910, p. 104.
7. See *Principles of International Law,* Essay I: Objects of International Law, p. 537.
    Bentham's thought on international relations were first put to paper by him in a rather fragmented manuscript between 1786 - 1789, during the years leading to the French Revolution. This was also the period in which Kant was writing on the same topic, and this was perhaps not entirely coincidental, as Bentham was thinking in terms of a "Plan for a Universal and Perpetual Peace," a title very similar to Kant's *Zum ewigen Frieden.* His notes were eventually published in 1843 under the somewhat misleading heading, *Principles of International Law.*
8. As Sir Alfred Ayer was to comment, Bentham's central utilitarian formula, "The greatest happiness of the greatest number" of people was to be seen in its social context as a guide to action. "The principle of utility is not a true, or even false proposition; it is a recommendation." See Sir Alfred Ayer, "The principles of utility," in G.W. Keeton and G. Schwarzenberger, *Jeremy Bentham and the Law.* London: Stevens, 1948, pp. 245-259, at p. 254.
9. See *Principles of International Law,* op. cit., Essay IV: "Universal and perpetual peace," at p. 559.
10. On this point, see G. Schwarzenberger, "Bentham's contribution to international law and organisation," in Keeton and Schwarzenberger, op. cit., pp. 152-184, at pp. 173-174.
11. See R. Cobden, *Speeches.* London: Gilbert, 1849, p. 101.
12. A late and unlikely convert to the "Cobden Doctrine" was Soviet Ambassador Zamyatkin, who told the press on the third day of the summit meeting between President Nixon and Mr. Brezhnev on June 20, 1973 that there was "an indirect relationship" between trade and the SALT talks because commercial agreements generated trust, making it easier to resolve disarmament questions. See *Financial Times,* June 21, 1973.

13. The Chartist, Feargus O'Connor, jeered in his own radical *Northern Star* in 1844 at Cobden's "glib philosophy and sophistry of mountebank cosmopolites who would hang this vast world upon a free trade peg." See D. Read, *Cobden and Bright.* London: Arnold, 1967, p. 37. For T.H. Green, see his *Prolegomena to Ethics.* Oxford: Clarendon Press, 1883; and his *Lectures in the Principles of Political Obligation.* London: Longmans, 1895.

14. See, for instance, *Russia.* Manchester: Ireland, 1836; and *The Three Panics.* London: Ward, 1862.

15. See W.E. Gladstone, *On Liberalism and Peace* (pamphlet). London: 1900.

16. See W. Godwin, *Enquiry concerning Political Justice and its Influence on Morals and Happiness.* London: Robinson, 1798, 2 vols. It was first published in 1793.

17. A.T. Mahan argued in 1890 that because of the new importance of naval bases and coaling stations, they ought to be secured. Indeed, in 1889 the Naval Defence Act was passed in Britain in order to protect British commerce, leading to increased expenditures in that sphere. See A.T. Mahan, *The Influence of Sea Power upon History, 1660 - 1783.* Boston: Little, Brown, 1890.

18. A.J.P. Taylor, *The Trouble Makers: Dissent over Foreign Policy 1792 - 1939.* London: Hamish Hamilton, 1957, p. 67. John Ruskin (1819 - 1900), critic of pure functionalism and author of *The Crown of Wild Olives* (1866), thought wilful isolation to be immoral.

19. See F.D. Schneider, "Fabians and the utilitarian idea of empire," *Review of Politics,* (October 1973), pp. 501-522. T.H. Green, a strong pacifist, but at the same time a neo-Hegelian of the Oxford school, held that "will, not force is the basis of the State." See *Lectures on the Principles of Political Obligation.* London: Longmans, 1895.

20. See his work on *The Progress of International Government.* New Haven, Conn.: Yale University Press, 1934.

21. See D. Mitrany, *A Working Peace System.* London: Oxford University Press, 1946.

22. See E.H. Carr, *Nationalism and After.* London: Macmillan, 1945.

23. See E.D. Haas, *The Uniting of Europe.* London: Stevens, 1958.

24. On this point, see J.W. Burton, "Functionalism and the resolution of conflict," in A.J.R. Groom and P. Taylor (eds.), *Functionalism.* London: University of London Press, 1975, pp. 238-249.

25. For some stimulating studies in this direction, see, for instance, A. Etzioni, *Political Unification: A Comparative Study of Leaders and Forces.* New York: Holt, Rinehart and Winston, 1965; E.B. Haas, "The study of regional integration: reflections on the joy and anguish of pre-theorizing," 24 *International Organization* (1970), pp. 607-646; P.C. Schmitter, "Three neo-functional hypotheses about international integration," ibid., Vol. 23 (1969), pp. 161-166; C. Mitchell, "The role of technocrats in Latin American integration," 21 *Inter-American Economic Affairs* (1967), pp. 73-87; F. Villagran Kramer, *Integración Económica Centroamericana.* Guatemala City: Universidad de San Carlos, 1967; and J.S. Nye, *Transnational Relations and World Politics.* Cambridge, Mass.: Harvard University Press, 1972.

26. Cybernetics (Greek): meaning oarsmanship, steering, and—by way of linguistic corruption—government.

27. G.W. Leibniz (1646 - 1716), the German philosopher and forerunner of the Enlightenment, held that the creation of an academy of the learned of all lands would be a means of facilitating the search for peace.

28. Montesquieu, *Réflections sur la monarchie universelle en Europe* (1734).

29. Published in English by Weidenfeld and Nicolson in London in 1955.

30. The countries involved were Britain, France, Germany, and Italy.

31. On these points, see K. Taylor, *Saint-Simon, 1760 - 1825*. London: Croom Helm, 1975, pp. 44-45 and 154.

32. Karl Marx acknowledged his debt to Saint-Simon, and Christian Georgevich Rakovsky, noted Soviet thinker and diplomat, who was one of the first to incur the wrath of Stalinism, attempted a *Life of Saint-Simon.*

33. For a recent work on Condorcet, consult K.M. Baker, *Condorcet: From Natural Philosophy to Social Mathematics*. London: University of Chicago Press, 1975.

34. On this point, see Saint-Simon's "Mémoire sur la science de l'homme," in B.P. Enfantin and Saint-Simon, *Science de l'homme: physiologie religieuse*. Paris: Librairie Saint-Simonienne, 1858.

35. See R. Aron, *Main Currents in Sociological Thought*. London: Penguin, 1965, p. 73.

36. Comte considered the question of ownership of industries as irrelevant.

37. P.J. Proudhon, Comte's French contemporary, an anarchist, provides a stark contrast with Saint-Simon and Comte, the two worshippers of industrialisation. Proudhon saw the moving forces behind the advancing industrial system as a potent menace to peace, going so far as to warn that "we are now entering a new phase in which war . . . must disappear from the scene unless there is to be a fateful regression." He was expecting the advent of an era of wars waged for economic reasons. See Proudhon, *La Guerre et la paix*. Brussels: Lavroix, 1861.

38. H.G. Wells, *The Outline of History. Revised by R. Postgate and G.P. Wells*. London: Cassell, 1972.

39. Sir Fred Catherwood, Chairman of the British Institute of Management, has recently taken the first step in banding together the cream of the country's professional institutions in a Professional Forum (PROF for short) in an effort to remove from government what Sir Fred has called the evils of "the art of the possible" and the "art of the next best thing" in decision-making on issues which are fundamentally nonparty political. See *The Sunday Times*, January 12, 1975.

40. On H.G. Wells, see N. and J. Mackenzie, *The Time Traveller*. London: Weidenfeld and Nicolson, 1973.

41. On this point, see A.D. Smith, *The Concept of Social Change: A Critique of the Functionalist Theory of Social Change*. London: Routledge and Kegan Paul, 1974.

Chapter 7

IMPERIALISM:

THEORIES MARXIST AND POPULIST

In nineteenth-century theories of functionalism the normative element tended to predominate over the explanatory one, as writers were groping for ways and means to by-pass the state in an effort to solve the central problems of international relations. By contrast, in theories of imperialism—whether Marxist or otherwise—the explanatory element comes to the fore. Most present-day theories of imperialism are drawing sustenance from previous Marxist analyses, and it is to these that our attention must be turned.

The Classical Marxists

The period of the classical Marxist writers Karl Marx and Friedrich Engels was also the age of budding competitive capitalism (1840s - 1875 approx.) and of laisser faire notions originally elaborated by the classical political economists, such as Adam Smith (1723 - 1790) and David Ricardo (1772 - 1823). The basic assumptions of the latter were being fully shared by the classical Marxists, and it was only in their conclusions that wide differences arose.

What, then, were these basic assumptions? In the first place, it was taken for granted that industrial capitalism would expand almost indefinitely in

volume of production and international trade under the stimulus of a homogeneous world market. Secondly, since according to Marxist analysis the
government of a country was merely the executive committee of the ruling
class, it followed that the interests of that class were paramount in the
policies followed by these governments. Since it was in the interest of
business communities the world over to promote the continuous expansion of
production and trade, any formal or political barriers obstructing the worldwide expansion of capitalism would have to be eliminated. Thirdly, there was
the implication that, since commercial competition was both universal and
transnational, international frontiers were irrelevant. Industrial capitalism was
worldwide in scope, and cosmopolitan rather than international in character.
The economic indivisibility of the world, as exemplified by the existence of a
homogeneous world market, determined the universality of capitalism as a
system both in its economic and its political aspects.

So much for the assumptions. As for the conclusions, the classical Marxists
differed fundamentally from the classical political economists. While admitting the inherent tendency towards the concentration of capital, and acknowledging a trend towards a falling rate of profit, the latter regarded these
as being basically compatible with the peaceful expansion of the capitalist
system the world over. The ultimate stability of the capitalist system was
unquestioned. On the other hand, the classical Marxists saw the contradictions in the capitalist system as both innate and irremediable. Far from
leading to a healthy shake-out of inefficient producers, the tendency towards
concentration of ownership of the means of production was self-disruptive,
unless capitalism were to expand abroad to engulf the entire globe. The
ultimate consequence of this development would be a world capitalist monopoly. Moreover, while the classical Marxists were at one with the classical
political economists in desiring worldwide capitalist expansion, the former
added the ominous rider that this process would be matched by the growth of
a world proletariat and a world bourgeoisie pitted against each other politically. It was clear, therefore, that the Marxists looked upon the world not
only as a fruitful field of capitalist expansion, but also as a potential
battlefield between world bourgeoisie and world proletariat. National economic systems were perceived by classical political economists and Marxists
alike as subsystems of the world economic system, and in view of the
acknowledged cosmopolitan character of capitalism there was no sense whatever in expanding the territorial frontiers of individual economic systems.
Such actions were potentially counterproductive, as they would interfere
with the innate tendency of capitalism towards worldwide expansion. What
concerned Marxists was not whether this or that state was making territorial
gains, but which class was to obtain ultimate control of the world economic
system.

In Marxist eyes, questions of territorial expansion were irrelevant to the issue of world capitalist advance. Nor were Marxists prepared to be squeamish about the methods by which this advance was being brought about. In particular they were unwilling to shed tears about the precapitalist order destined to be swept away in the advance of the capitalist juggernaut. Where territorial acquisition was the mode by which this was to be achieved, this was accepted with a certain equanimity bordering on the cynical. This is why Marx was able to characterise the role of Britain in nineteenth-century India thus: "England has to fulfill a double mission in India: one destructive, the other regenerative—the annihilation of the old Asiatic society, and the laying of the material foundations of Western society in Asia." To have restrained British or any other imperialism in the name of morality would have meant impeding the march of material progress. As Marx was to remark in 1853: "However melancholy we may find the spectacle of the ruin and desolation of these tens of thousands of industrious, peaceful, patriarchal social groups . . . suddenly cut off from their ancient civilisation and their traditional means of existence, we must not forget that these idyllic village communities . . . always provided a firm basis for oriental despotism. . . . In causing social revolution in India, England was, it is true, guided by the lowest motives, and conducted it dully and woodenly. But that is not the point. The question is whether humanity can fulfill its purpose without a complete social revolution in Asia. If not, then England, in spite of all her crimes, was the subconscious instrument of history in bringing about this revolution."[1] Marx never seemed to be concerned with the prospect of a Roman type of world imperialism or, for that matter, with the consequences of parallel forays by rival imperialisms for world domination. The final battle, he was confident enough, would be fought in the social arena and within a transnational-functional context, and not on the interstate plane within its interterritorial dimensions. Implicit in his thinking was the conviction that purely capitalist interests would always in the last resort be able to override political state interests.

The Neo-Marxists

For Marx, the process of the circulation of capital was worldwide, with capitalism developing not in isolated communities, however large, but on a world scale. Mergers of business enterprises across the frontiers were accepted by Marxists in those circumstances as inevitable, leading logically to a world division among multinational monopolies competing for shrinking markets. There was a neat symmetry in this theory, which was to be falsified by developments in the 1870s and 1880s, when the basic patterns of capitalist expansion were shown to be thoroughly asymmetrical. Marx had predicted that capitalism would develop on a world scale, but its epicentre remained in the "Western" world. Free trade was belatedly unmasked as a British quasi-world monopoly against which, understandably enough, newly industrialising countries such as Germany, the United States, Japan, and France had to guard by surrounding their infant industries with high tariff walls. Where prevailing conditions of international trade were so unequal, there was little room for international solidarity among industrialist entrepreneurs. On the contrary, the uneven nature of world economic development tended to encourage business mergers within the territorial frontiers of the newly industrialising countries, and render mergers across the frontiers the exception rather than the rule.

The conclusions flowing from these new perceptions were compelling: it was the economic subsystems—whose boundaries coincided with the political frontiers of individual states—that were dominant over the world economic system, rather than the other way round, as had been assumed by classical Marxists and political economists alike. The world market was heterogeneous, not homogeneous; capitalism was international and not cosmopolitan. The implications were equally manifest: the expanding proclivities of capitalism would remain; but instead of being given free rein on a world scale, they would be hitched to the varying political fortunes of individual states, giving rise to sharpening international rivalries and providing an impetus to the fitter and more powerful of these states to embark on policies of territorial aggrandisement. Expanding capitalism and political imperialism were coming together in a potentially explosive mixture.

This called for a frankly political theory of imperialism to graft on to the economically deduced one that could be implied from the writings of Karl Marx. The laisser faire notions which had informed Marxist assumptions on the nature of capitalism during most of the nineteenth century now had to be abandoned in the light of the shifting structures of world capitalism. And although neo-Marxist writers would continue to employ the analytical tools of their masters, they would eventually arrive at a new set of conclusions. Ironically, it was not a Marxist—nor even anyone familiar with Marxist literature—but a British Liberal, who provided neo-Marxist theory of imperialism with its clues. J. A. Hobson (1858 - 1940) stumbled into theorising about imperialism by accident. A journalist on the staff of the Conservative *Daily Telegraph*, he had been sent to South Africa to report the Boer War. What he saw there, and what he already knew about the current carving up of China by the great powers, made him refuse to accept superficial explanations as to what had caused the Boer War. In his book, *Imperialism: A Study*, published in 1902, Hobson had tried to provide an explanation of the general phenomenon of imperialism, and had found this could be done only in conjunction with an analysis of the capitalist system as a whole. Like Marx before him, Hobson approved of the expansion of capitalism into precapitalist areas as historically progressive, but saw it as a source of dangerous international friction. The central purpose of his endeavours was to uncover the social and economic springs of imperialism, and he found these to be located at home in the shape of underconsumption, or its obverse, overproduction, the result of maldistribution of income. Because of insufficient domestic demand, capital was compelled to seek outlets abroad—by force if necessary. It was financiers, the prime custodians of capital, who would induce ministers and generals to embark on those imperial policies which could degenerate into military adventures of the kind Hobson had witnessed in South Africa.

In providing a connection between capitalism and imperialism, Hobson had achieved a breakthrough which, before long, was to be eagerly exploited by a succession of neo-Marxist writers. But, besides locating the source of the connection, Hobson also suggested a remedy. Arguing that imperialism was not a necessary feature of capitalism, he claimed that the latter was eminently reformable and potentially peaceful, provided only that sufficient purchasing power could be poured into the pockets of the working classes, and the home market expanded to absorb the available surplus capital. In such an event no capitalist need go abroad, and the only beneficiaries of imperialist expansion would be monopolists. The public tax system could be used to bring about the required degree of redistribution of income at home. This was a simple technical operation, and all it needed to set it off was a display of political willpower. The imperialist rush towards foreign markets, so marked a feature of the contemporary scene, was capable of being checked by instituting internal reforms[2] within the imperialist countries themselves.

Hobson had assigned primary importance to the role of finance capital. Rudolf Hilferding (1877 - 1940), an Austro-Marxist, in his *Finance Capital: The Latest Stage in the Development of Capitalism,* published in 1910, sought to refine Hobson's analysis by showing, on the basis of numerous data, that there had been a major transformation of magnitudes in the process of capital accumulation. Because of technical progress, the amount of capital required as initial outlay in modern large-scale industry had dramatically increased to a degree at which self-financing was no longer feasible. Credit institutions had to spring to the aid of industry by providing the enormous sums required, and to secure their investments, were compelled to participate in the running of the industrial enterprises in which they had a stake. In this manner formerly mighty captains of industry would soon be degraded to mere managers, the real control being exercised by the banks, the new accumulators of capital in the age of monopoly capitalism. Finance capital was defined by Hilferding as "capital at the disposal of the banks, but for the use of industry." According to Hilferding the advent of credit institutions as the principal source of control was supplying fresh energy to the driving tendencies of the capitalist system, providing it with a dynamic of a new and superior order.

Between them, Hobson and Hilferding had laid the foundations of a neo-Marxist theory of capitalism. What came after them was largely synthesis, as a number of neo-Marxist writer-politicians tried to bend the findings of these two men to their own polemical purposes. Within the latter category, two groups may be discerned, each eager to draw sustenance from Hobson and Hilferding. Among the reformists there was, above all, Karl Kautsky, with Joseph Schumpeter (1883 - 1950) operating on the fringes of neo-Marxism; whilst among the revolutionists were to be found Rosa Luxemburg (1871 - 1919), N. I. Bukharin (1888 - 1938), and V. I. Lenin (1870 - 1924). There was a certain amount of overlap between those two groups.

Karl Kautsky (1854 - 1938),[3] scholarly Marxist and leading theoretician of the Second International, believed in conformity with Marx and the classical school of economists in the worldwide expansion of capitalism, and, in accord with Hobson, in mere maladjustments within the capitalist system as the root cause of imperialism. While still prepared to adopt the Marxian notion of the horizontal spread of capitalism, he considered that spread potentially harmonious. A firm believer in the Marxian doctrine of the class struggle, but an ardent reformist at the same time, Kautsky still envisaged the confrontation between world bourgeoisie and world proletariat as materialising eventually on the social level across the frontiers, rather than by way of interterritorial conflict. He considered the joint exploitation of the world by an internationally united finance capital in place of the mutual rivalries of national finance capitals to be perfectly feasible. Worldwide capitalism in its ultimate, monopolistic stage would be the logical end-product of peaceful capitalist expansion. Political imperialism was seen as interfering with that process, and Kautsky therefore anticipated the achievement of rational, interimperialist accommodation, which he called "ultraimperialism," to smooth the capitalist path towards world expansion. Thus, while not disputing the existence of territorial imperialism, Kautsky emphatically denied any causal connection between it and the acknowledged expansive tendencies of capitalism as a self-contained system. Political imperialism, where it occurred, he argued, was the result of the "preferred" policy of states; the choice was voluntary and in no way dependent on the well-established, innate tendency of capitalism to expand on a world scale.

Alongside this analysis, Kautsky—who had been greatly impressed by British Fabian doctrines[4]—made the startling political observation that, far from regarding apolitical "ultraimperialism" as either dangerous or undesirable, it was capable of sharing its gains with the working classes, provided only the latter were sufficiently well-organised and vocal to raise their claims insistently. Capitalist expansion and the class struggle were both inevitable;

but since world capitalism was capable of being reformed, the class struggle could be conducted peacefully. There was nothing inevitable about either political imperialism or revolutionary socialism.

For a while the intra-Marxist debate on imperialism centred on the mode of accumulating capital. Rosa Luxemburg, a revolutionary neo-Marxist wishing to bring Marx's theory of capital accumulation up to date, was the first to take up Hobson's concept of the lack of home demand as a factor leading to the search for markets abroad to absorb surplus capital generated at home.[5] The novelty of her approach lay in her perception of capitalist penetration of a basically homogeneous world market in terms of clashing international systems. Thus, trade between French and German capitalists, though conducted across the frontiers, was classed as a transaction "internal" to the capitalist system; trade between a British capitalist and a German peasant, on the other hand (or an Egyptian peasant, for that matter) was "external," since the transaction was conducted between the capitalist and precapitalist systems: it was intersystemic in nature.[6] The systemicist approach enabled her to point to the precapitalist sectors of the world (whether situated inside predominantly capitalist areas or as precapitalist areas within their own rights) as the last remaining source of surplus capital, and to prove that, in 1913, there was still a certain margin left for capitalist survival. Imperialism was consequently to her the political expression of the accumulation of capital in its competitive struggle for what still remained of the precapitalist environment. Disagreeing fundamentally with Kautsky on the possibility of political choice, she considered interimperialist rivalries inevitable and likely to lead to war. The drama of imperialism was seen by her to be acted out on the interstate level, in diplomatic and military terms, and not on the intersystemic level in economic terms. The last point is a noteworthy one, as it was to play an important part in the controversies among theorists of underdeveloped countries half a century later.

N. I. Bukharin (1888-1938) in his work *Imperialism and the World Economy*, published in 1915 with a foreword by Lenin, agreed with Rosa Luxemburg on all but one important point. In the main systemicist in his approach, Bukharin placed much heavier emphasis than Rosa Luxemburg[7] on the interstate aspect of capitalist contradictions. Unlike Rosa Luxemburg, he saw the crucial division of the world not into capitalist and precapitalist systems, but into capitalist and precapitalist states, with the latter racing to close in on the former. And while not denying the existence of precapitalist remnants within predominantly capitalist states, he insisted that, following the rule of the falling rates of profit, the capitalist dynamic was compelling the conquest of fresh markets abroad in search of higher profits. As Bukharin pointed out, if his thesis were not valid, then capitalist states would rest content at home until such time as the precapitalist remnant was absorbed in the capitalist system, rather than take the great trouble involved in going abroad. Capitalism was denied the "precapitalist" breathing space of which Rosa Luxemburg had spoken, and its self-disruptive, imperalist phase was therefore much closer at hand than she imagined.[8] Basically, the difference between Rosa Luxemburg and Bukharin amounted to an overlapping in the levels of analysis, and it is precisely in this aspect of their differences that the importance of their respective works in the history of thought in international relations is to be found.

Lenin's tract on *Imperialism as the Highest Stage of Capitalism*,[9] published in 1916, one year after Bukharin's work on the subject—from which it must have profited greatly—has made a deep impact on posterity by virtue of its timing and, above all, of its author's enormous subsequent fame as statesman and world Communist leader. Lenin's tract, far more even than Bukharin's book, gave the impression of being a polemic rather than a disinterested academic treatise, punctuated as it was by furious attacks on Kautsky.[10] Drawing heavily on Hobson's work, and to a lesser extent on that of Hilferding, it represents on the purely academic side little more than a synthesis of the major analytical findings of these two. If there is any academic novelty, it is Lenin's heightened emphasis on the uneven development of capitalism, and his awareness of the inadequacy of some of the major assumptions made by Victorian Marxists and classical economists alike. Though never mentioning either Rosa Luxemburg or Bukharin by name, Lenin tended to side with the latter in regarding the international dimension as central to the problem of imperialism, while agreeing with the former in acknowledging that "the colonial policy of the capitalist countries has *completed* (Lenin's italics) the seizure of the unoccupied territories on our planet." However, this had been motivated in the main by the search for increasingly scarce raw materials, an assertion implying little comfort to Rosa Luxemburg's concept of precapitalist breathing space afforded to world capitalism.

As a theorist of international relations, Lenin is most relevant in drawing attention to the uneven development of capitalism, already noted by Rosa Luxemburg—the logical outcome of the relentless tendency towards the concentration of capital—with its two correlated phenomena, (a) the disproportionate growth of capital, as against consumer goods industries and exports; and (b) the emerging ranking order among the imperialist or potentially imperialist world powers. Where he is less successful is in his assessment of the growing concentration of capital and its alleged impact in sharpening interstate relations. In particular, he seemed to be having difficulty in tracing a connection between the formation of private "international monopolist capitalist association," such as the cartel between German- and United States-based monopolies in the electrical industry, which—in strict logic and in accord with orthodox Marxist doctrine, should have led to a corresponding accommodation between the imperialist powers, as indeed Kautsky was saying it might—and the trend towards interimperialist conflict, so manifest in 1915 and 1916. It never occurred to Lenin that the coming international spread of capitalist cartels could be unilateral (i.e., transnational) instead of multilateral (i.e., multinational) in kind. In the end he had to content himself with noting the parallel development between international cartel formation and interstate "struggle for colonies . . . the 'struggle for spheres of influence.' "

Though instinctively following Bukharin in placing the main weight of the emphasis on the interstate, rather than the "international monopolist capitalist" dimension, Lenin was puzzled by the problem of the levels of analysis, over which Rosa Luxemburg and Bukharin were contending. On the one hand he recognised the tendency towards world monopoly capitalism through international arrangements between private monopolies; but on the other hand his insistence that this was necessarily rendering interstate conflict inevitable is intelligible only on the assumption that, for the time being at any rate, Lenin regarded the trend towards interstate conflict as stronger than the trend towards intermonopoly capitalist accommodation. However, no rational argument was adduced by him to prove the point.

The rise of the Soviet Union on the one hand and that of international political organisations, such as the League of Nations and the United Nations, on the other, to some extent took the wind out of the sails of the neo-Marxists as regards explanatory theories of international conflict, and for a while the stage of international theory was taken by non-Marxists.

The Non-Marxists

Until and during the First World War virtually all attempts to theorise about imperialism came from Marxists of various brands. Within that spectrum, Joseph Schumpeter (1883 - 1950) must be regarded as representing the rearguard, moving away from Marxism into other streams of thought.[11] An economist by profession and a Social Democrat in his politics (he was briefly Austrian Minister of Finance in the coalition government of 1919), he wrote an important article in 1921, "Sociology of imperialism"[12] in which, while claiming the right to present alternative explanations, he expressly admitted the validity of current neo-Marxist theories of imperialism.

However, he believed with Kautsky and the classical economists in the pacific nature of capitalism in its pure and fully developed form, as it existed in Britain. Most other forms of capitalism contained what he called "atavistic"[13] survivals exercising a corrupting effect on its nature and accounting for such imperialist tendencies as were registered within capitalism. The crucial element in these atavistic survivals was seen by Schumpeter—who was manifestly under the influence of Freud's teachings regarding the functions of the subconscious mind—as the relationship through the ages between nobility and bourgeoisie, with the former retaining its dominant ethos of public service, while the latter was pursuing its frankly material self-interest. The critical moment in this relationship, according to Schumpeter, was the period of transition from the age of absolutism to that of liberalism, with their respective economic concomitants, mercantilism and capitalism. It was when free enterprise was riding high and the bourgeoisie should have been in a most self-confident mood, that the possession of a public service ethos by the nobility and its consequent predominance in the armed forces and higher echelons of the civil service put the bourgeoisie at a real disadvantage in relation to the nobility. Only in Britain had capitalism reached a stage mature enough to enable the bourgeoisie to tame the nobility, replacing it by a small standing army subservient to what were essentially bourgeois governments. What was dangerous in this relationship was the combination of the age-old conquering instinct of the nobility with the newly emerging drives of expanding capitalism, with the nobility still able to call the tune. This combination contained a potentially explosive element of imperialism.

Schumpeter blamed the bourgeoisie for allowing itself to have its true interest—the peaceful expansion of the capitalist system on a world scale—to be perverted by the nobility.[14] Social forces of a bygone age were determining the choice of policies in a manner irrelevant to the issues of the present. As Schumpeter put it forcefully: "The dead are ruling the living." The remedy lay close at hand. The true nature of capitalism was pacific and rational, not bellicose and emotional. The bourgeoisie should be made to realise where its own material interests lay and remove all atavistic remnants from its body politic. However, capitalism—according to Schumpeter—would eventually perish of its own success, giving way to some form of public control.

It is perhaps no accident that it should have been a college professor in the United States, and, perhaps even more relevant, Karl Kautsky's grandson, John H. Kautsky[15] who adopted Schumpeter's conclusions as a basis of an analysis of Fascist imperialism. According to him the interwar period of 1918 - 1939 was one in which the nobility was fighting most desperately for survival in the face of powerful monopoly capitalism on the one hand, and the growing challenge from the Left on the other hand. In a situation of this sort the Fascists succeeded in bringing together the remnants of the nobility with the representatives of the most dynamic form of capitalism—monopoly capitalism—to produce an explosive mixture of imperialism. Thus Himmler was able in 1935 to persuade the German nobility to send their sons to swell the ranks of his own élite corps, the dreaded SS. Developments in Fascist

Italy were similar. Fascist imperialism, according to J. H. Kautsky, represented the nadir of corruption of the bourgeoisie by the atavistic nobility.

Where Schumpeter tended to shift the blame for the tendency towards imperialism from the shoulders of the capitalists—where the Marxists had placed it—Hannah Arendt[16] to some extent still relied on Marxist analysis in her insistence that imperialism was due to the embarrassing presence of undisposed surplus capital in the wealthy parts of the world. Critical of Schumpeter's assessment of the capitalist system as being inherently pacific and rational, she seemed closer to his position in pointing—in terms reminiscent of Freudian psychoanalysis—to "the secret desires of the bourgeoisie for violence" without actually adopting Schumpeter's sociological categories to prove her point. Breaking away from previous patterns of theorising about the nature of imperialism by introducing frankly political, rather than economic or social motivations as root causes of the phenomenon of imperialism, she saw the essence of both capitalism and imperialism to lie in the limitless desire, not so much for capital—as the Marxists would have it—as for power. Viewed in this light imperialism was merely the political form of capitalism. As she put it: "Only the unlimited accumulation of power could bring about the unlimited accumulation of capital."

The marked change of emphasis from capital to power as the spring of capitalist expansion is also implicit in Professor John Kenneth Galbraith's work on *The New Industrial State,*[17] which accounts for the phenomenal expansion of industrial corporations noted in recent decades in terms of a permanent managerial quest for power, for the sake of limitless expansion, rather than for the traditional purpose of maximising profits in gratification of the normal desires of shareholders. H. J. Morgenthau, one of the most influential academic writers of the period after the Second World War in the sphere of international relations, asserts in the same vein that "what . . . the capitalist imperialist and the 'imperialist' capitalist want is power, not economic gain."[18] This is a far more outspoken and complete refutation of economics-oriented, Marxist explanations of imperialism than Hannah Arendt ever attempted. But it is Galbraith's theory, rather than Arendt's or Morgenthau's, that might be made to dovetail neatly with some of the most radical views expounded by writers in the underdeveloped countries regarding the role of the transnational corporations in their alleged capacity as principal force of contemporary imperialism.

Developmentalism and Dependencia

Neither the classical nor the neo-Marxist theorists on imperialism seemed to bother overmuch about the short- and long-term effects of capitalist penetration of precapitalist areas in the world. In the case of the former this may be attributable to their conviction regarding the superiority of capitalism over previous forms of economic organisation. In the case of the neo-Marxists it may have been due to a preoccupation with the close prospect of interimperialist war. This marked unconcern persisted while the bulk of the underdeveloped world was still under colonial rule. It would explain why, imperfect as Lenin's diagnosis of imperialism may have been, it was able to stand practically unchallenged until the 1960s, when the argument was at long last carried further on the theoretical plane, both by implicit and unselfconscious reinforcement and by refutation. These new developments were made possible mainly by the emergence in the early 1960s of a mass of underdeveloped countries as sovereign states, which provoked a sustained debate on their place in the international system and the nature of the relationship between developed and undeveloped countries generally. A resumption of the earlier debate on imperialism whence it had left off in 1916 was inevitable in those circumstances.

The historical difference between the two debates lay in the angle. Hitherto theorists of imperialism had viewed the world from the vantage point of the developed countries and their international problems, their chief concern being to explain what was happening, and not to draft a code of action to enable the objects of imperialism to escape their fate. In the early 1960s the perspective was turned round sharply, as writers in underdeveloped countries took a worm's eye view of the phenomenon of imperialism. Traditional theorists of imperialism had pointed to the dependence of capitalist producers on markets, investments, and raw materials in and from the dominated countries. Today's theorists fear the underdeveloped countries might be relegated permanently to the fringe, and their endeavours are therefore directed towards pointing to alternatives. They tend to see a direct connection between their countries' underdevelopment and the working of the world economic and political system. Two recurring themes mark their works. First, there has been a renewed emphasis on the systemicist approach first employed by Rosa Luxemburg in her scholarly exposition of the binary nature of the world economic system, with its two contending orders, the capitalist and precapitalist, and in her insistence on the function of the latter in prolonging the life of the former. The Luxemburg thesis must have suggested the implication, at once subtle and attractive, that the underdeveloped countries of the 1960s were forming a link in the world capitalist chain at its weakest point, making it possible for them to bring down the entire capitalist world structure by a concerted withdrawal from it. Secondly, if Lenin had insisted that Victorian capitalism was characterised by the bulking importance of consumer goods, and finance capitalism by that of capital goods, would it not be equally true to say of the age of transnational corporate capitalism that it was marked by the prominence of technology?

Much of what Hilferding had noted and Bukharin and Lenin emphasised seemed to be coming true in the 1960s in the shape of the stunning horizontal and vertical spread of transnational corporations, then nearly all based in the United States. It was to the political and social implications of these startling developments that theorists of imperialism in the underdeveloped countries were turning their attention.

Kwame Nkrumah (1909 - 1972), fittingly—as his country, Ghana, had by its own emancipation sounded the signal for a virtual stampede away from colonial rule—was the first among the new thinkers to take the field in his *Neo-Colonialism: The Last Stage of Imperialism,* published in 1965. Taking the soundness of Lenin's basic analysis for granted, Nkrumah contented himself with applying Lenin's theory to the postcolonial setting. His attempt was typical of the new writing in that he insisted, with Rosa Luxemburg, that the underdeveloped countries, even when fully independent politically, continued to be a source of capital accumulation for the imperialist states.

However, and not surprisingly, the most challenging development in this sphere came not from Africa, the least experienced underdeveloped part of the world, but from Latin America, the most sophisticated and long-established one, where Raúl Prebisch, an Argentine economist, laid the groundwork of a theory which was widely adopted within the United Nations Economic Commission for Latin America (ECLA, or CEPAL, to give it its Spanish initials), subsequently to form the basis of the radical conventional wisdom of UNCTAD.[19] An empiricist in approach, Prebisch had made a study of Anglo-Argentine trade relations[20] as conducted before 1939, from which he concluded that in international trade in general there was a "centre" composed of fully developed industrialised countries and a "periphery" of nonindustrialised countries, and that the terms of trade were permanently loaded in favour of the former. The only way of breaking out of this position of economic inferiority was for the "periphery" to develop its economies and, in particular, to industrialise. This school of thought came eventually to be known as "developmentalism" or *desarrollismo* (in Spanish) or *desenvolvimentismo* (in Portuguese).

The Prebisch model had certain elements in common with previous models developed by Rosa Luxemburg and Bukharin, especially the latter. But whereas those two neo-Marxists perceived an inherent dynamic which was ultimately self-destructive, Prebisch held that the binary nature of the international system could be overcome by a series of measures on the international plane, which he listed as: a régime of deliberate commercial preferences in favour of the periphery; the conclusion of broad commodity agreements; and the granting of aid and the encouragement of foreign investments.

Implied in Prebisch' general thesis was the idea that the nascent middle classes of the underdeveloped countries, aided by benevolent state action and encouraged by world public opinion, were perfectly capable of carrying out the task of industrialisation. His analysis, like that of the classical Marxists in the nineteenth century, had the attraction of symmetry in its structure, but suffered from having left several historical dimensions out of account, which, taken into account, might have prevented Prebisch from arriving at his relatively comforting conclusions. Of these, the most important by far, as his critics were to point out, was the massive incursion of the transnational corporations into the economies of the underdeveloped countries, the impact of which began to be felt widely in the mid-1960s. A new school of thought, strongly spiced with Luxemburgist notions, but not on that account necessarily committed to dogmatic Marxism, arose before long, highly critical of developmentalism—which might roughly be termed "populist" in view of the generally prevailing political currents of the time. Historicist in approach, systemicist in analysis, and basically sceptical in temperament, the new creed fastened on the nature of world capitalism in the age of the transnational corporations, found that the underdeveloped countries were part and parcel of that system, and concluded that to find their salvation those countries must break away from the world capitalist system.

As for Prebisch's suggested remedies, these were brushed aside as at best, palliatives. International aid and foreign investments—considered beneficial by Prebisch—were regarded as mechanisms used by the dominant world powers in the interest of an international system that was generating *dependencia* and hindering development, allowing the net capital extraction from the underdeveloped countries—first stressed by Rosa Luxemburg—to proceed apace. Most damaging of all, in the view of the new school of *dependencia* theorists, was the rapidly sharpening edge of foreign over home capital, especially in the strategically important industries of scale. This had a thwarting effect on the budding middle classes of the underdeveloped countries, which, by dint of this development, were being turned into mere clients of the transnational corporations. In this way, far from being capable of managing industrialisation, as Prebisch had maintained they were, the nascent middle classes were providing essential infrastructural support to the perpetuation of *dependencia,* representing as they did the social metabolism holding together both developed and underdeveloped countries within the grip of the world capitalist system.

Those criticisms were severe ones, found in the writing of Th. Dos Santos,[21] a Brazilian, and A. Gunder Frank[22], a sympathiser from the United States. Taking over Prebisch' vocabulary with slight modifications, the latter claimed that the *dependencia* of the "satellites" on the "metropolis" (Prebisch would have used the equivalent terms "periphery" and "centre") was a chronic condition shaping the world economy in such a way as to benefit the metropolis exclusively. Even where there was demonstrable evidence of economic growth in the underdeveloped countries, this was geared to the needs of the metropolises—a mere reflex of the expansion of the dominant economies. F. H. Cardoso,[23] another Brazilian, pointed out that, while the new forms of imperialism tended both to develop and underdevelop further the dependent countries, they created centres of development within most underdeveloped countries, leaving the rest of those countries in a premodernised state and sharpening social contradictions within them ("dependent development").

If any differences have arisen within the camp of *dependencia* theorists, it is not over details of analysis, but in the realm of prescription. When it comes to the latter, a line of division can be discerned between reformists and revolutionists reminiscent of similar lines during the earlier debate on imperialism between 1902 and 1916. Thus, Celso Furtado,[24] a Brazilian economist, is perhaps most representative of the reformers. Proceeding from the basic economic proposition that the more diversified a given basket of consumer goods, the higher the income of persons consuming these goods would have to be, he goes on to claim that only by maintaining this type of sophisticated consumer demand can foreign capital be coaxed into supplying high-level technology. The persisting maldistribution of wealth, reinforced by the presence of the transnational corporations is perpetuating *dependencia*.[25] The remedy, in Furtado's eyes, is to be found by creating, in neo-Hobsonian fashion, sufficient purchasing power at the lower end of the income scale to stimulate demand for low-grade consumer goods capable of being manufactured by national industry and medium-range technology-intensive state industry, thus ensuring a healthy national-autonomous, rather than an externally dependent hothouse-type growth.

Hélio Jaguaribe,[26] his fellow countryman—perhaps Latin America's most imaginative political scientist—tends to agree with him. At one time a hopeful advocate of broad collusion between state and national bourgeoisie within the mainstream of developmentalism, Jaguaribe now sees the intrusion of the transnational corporation as the crucial aspect of the phenomenon of contemporary imperialism. The national bourgeoisie, he would argue, defeated in its attempt to obtain the requisite technology through its own efforts, and hence compelled to rely on the transnationals for its purveyance, is degraded into a *burguesia consular*,[27] constantly at the beck and call of the transnationals as they penetrate the economies of the underdeveloped countries, carrying *dependencia* in their wake—a system dubbed sarcastically by Jaguaribe in the case of his native Brazil as "colonial fascism."

Jaguaribe recommends that the state must itself take the main role in promoting actively the autonomous economic development of the underdeveloped countries. This can best be done by widening its powers of economic control and—under proper public and constitutional safeguards—entering into carefully defined contractual ventures with private, including transnational corporations, in an effort to obtain the requisite technology without loss of sovereignty.[28] Only the properly equipped and determined state is capable of dealing with the transnationals on a footing of equality.

While both Furtado and Jaguaribe proffer reformist remedies for the cure of *dependencia*, A. Gunder Frank, in *The Development of Underdevelopment*[28] approaches the phenomenon of *dependencia* in a determinist fashion, bringing to his task an apocalyptic vision of the future of world capitalism. Bringing Rosa Luxemburg up to date, Gunder Frank maintains that the penetration of the globe by the capitalist system—merely foreshadowed by Luxemburg—is now complete outside the Socialist countries. The only escape from *dependencia* in those circumstances is a breakaway from capitalism in favour of the adoption of socialism. But although Frank's work bears potentially revolutionary implications, he will not specify the actual methods by which this is to be accomplished. On the other hand, R. Mauro Marini, a Brazilian, in *Subdesarrollo y Revolución*,[30] concentrating his attacks on the state of collapse of the national bourgeoisie and proclaiming the failure of reformism, postulates the need for uncompromising armed struggle as the sole method by which the strangling world capitalist grip can be wrested from the throats of the underdeveloped countries.

This debate has quieted down somewhat recently, but will no doubt be resumed before long, possibly in different forms and against an altered background.

NOTES

1. For the general background, see C. C. Eldridge, *England's Mission: The imperial idea in the age of Gladstone and Disraeli, 1868 - 1880.* London: Macmillan, 1973.

2. John Strachey (1900 - 1962), a latter-day Hobsonian, assumed in his post-Marxist phase, which began in 1940, that the masses in Western Europe in its postimperial phase have been raised to well above starvation level at the expense of (a) profits, and (b) the export of capital as the direct result of powerful trade union pressure. See J. Strachey, *The End of Empire.* London: Gollancz, 1959.

3. His views on the subject were forcefully presented in two articles in *Die Neue Zeit* of 1914 and 1915. They are also reflected in his commentaries on *Das Erfurter Programm.* Stuttgart: Dietz (15th ed.) 1919, pp. 234-242.

4. On the Fabian political ideal of a socialist empire, see B. Semmel *Imperialism and Social Reform.* London: Allen and Unwin, 1960.

5. Marx had dealt with this problem in Vol. 2 of *Das Kapital;* Rosa Luxemburg in *Die Akkumulation des Kapitals.* Berlin: Singer, 1913.

6. Rosa Luxemburg also considered military expenditure as a prop of the capitalist system. This is a point to which a recent neo-Marxist writer has returned: see M. Kidron, *Western Capitalism since the War.* London: Weidenfeld and Nicolson, 1968.

7. Michael Kalecki, *Essays in the Theory of Economic Fluctuations* (New York: Farrar and Rinehart, 1939), pp. 45-46, points to the numerous intellectual affinities between Rosa Luxemburg and John Maynard Keynes; while Tadeusz Kowalik, "Rosa Luxemburg's theory of accumulation and imperialism," in *Problems of Economic Dynamics and Planning: Essays in Honour of Michael Kalecki* (Oxford: Pergamon, 1966) tries to rescue her from the charge of mechanical interpretation of imperialism.

8. At the fifteenth congress of the Soviet Communist Party held in Moscow in 1926 Bukharin developed the thesis that the economic development of the underdeveloped countries must be actively promoted by the Soviet Union so as "to prevent their engulfment by capitalist imperialism." See *XV Konferentsia,* October 26-November 3, 1926. Stenographic record (Moscow, 1927). At the sixth congress of the Communist International in 1928 Bukharin, who was then its Secretary-General, maintained that capitalism was incapable of reproducing itself in its own colonies.

9. *Imperializm kak vysshaya stadiya kapitalizma* was first produced in Russia in 1917.

10. It must be remembered that in 1916 Kautsky was the leading Marxist theoretician of the world, and Lenin relatively little known. A year later the position was very different.

11. See J. H. Kautsky, "J. A. Schumpeter and Karl Kautsky: parallel theories of imperialism," 5 *Midwest Journal of Political Science* (1961), pp. 101-128.

12. This essay, as well as an updated version published in 1939, are contained in J. Schumpeter, *Imperialism and Social Classes* (Edited by H. Norden). Oxford: Blackwell 1952.

13. *Atavus:* Latin for grandfather's grandfather.

14. On these points, see T. Kemp, *Theories of Imperialism.* London: Dobson Books 1967, Ch. 6, pp. 86-105.

15. *Political Change in Underdeveloped Countries.* London: Wiley, 1962.

16. *The Origins of Totalitarianism.* New York: Harcourt Brace Jovanovich, 1951.

17. J. K. Galbraith, *The New Industrial State.* London: Hamilton, 1967.

18. See H. J. Morgenthau, *Politics among Nations.* New York: Alfred A. Knopf, 1973, p. 52.

19. Prebisch was Executive Secretary of ECLA between 1955 and 1963, and Secretary-General of UNCTAD between 1964 and 1968.

20. Lenin had specifically cited the Anglo-Argentine relationship as an example of informal imperialism.

21. Th. Dos Santos, *El nuevo carácter de la dependencia.* Santiago: Universidad de Chile, 1968.

22. A. Gunder Frank, *Capitalism and Underdevelopment in Latin America.* Harmondsworth: Penguin, 1971 ed.

23. See F. H. Cardoso and E. Faletto, *Dependencia y desarrollo en América Latina.* Mexico City: Siglo Veintiuno, 1972. See also F. H. Cardoso, "Notas sobre el estado actual de los estudios sobre dependencia," in J. Sierra (ed.), *Desarrollo latinoamericano: ensayos críticos.* Mexico City: Fondo de Cultura Económica, 1974, pp. 325-356.

24. See Celso Furtado, "The Brazilian 'model' ", 22 *Social and Economic Studies* (Jamaica), (1973), pp. 122-131.

25. A similar thesis is contained in Theodore Moran, "Foreign expansion as an 'institutional necessity' for U.S. corporate capitalism—the search for a radical 'model,' " 25 *World Politics* (1973), pp. 122-131.

Dr. Moran, a Harvard political scientist, fastened his enquiries on the product-cycle of finished exports to countries with a similar demand-structure.

26. See H. Jaguaribe, *La Dominación de América Latina*. Lima: Moncloa, 1968; and H. Jaguaribe and others, *La dependencia político-ecónomica de América Latina*. Mexico City: Siglo Veintiuno, 1972.

27. Reminiscent of Trotsky's reference to the *entrepôt* merchants of Macao who interposed themselves on behalf of foreign business interests, and were denied access to Imperial China, as the *compradore* (buyers) bourgeoisie.

28. Similar conclusions were also implicit in the thesis put forward by Oswaldo Sunkel, a Chilean economist. See his paper on "Big business and 'dependencia'—a Latin American view," 50 *Foreign Affairs* (1972), pp. 517-531. On the general point raised here, see S. J. Patel, "The technological dependence of developing countries," 12 *Journal of Modern African Studies* (1974), pp. 1-18.

29. Reprinted in R. I. Rhodes (ed.), *Imperialism and Underdevelopment: A Reader*. New York: Monthly Review Press. 1970.

For a contrary view, see H. Blakemore "Limitations of dependency: an historian's view and case study," 18 *Boletín de Estudios Latinamericanos y del Caribe* (1975), pp. 74-87.

30. R. Mauro Marini, *Subdesarollo y Revolución*. Mexico City: Siglo Veintiuno, 1969.

Chapter 8

NATIONALISM AND MULTINATIONALISM:

POLITICAL AND CULTURAL

Early nineteenth-century nationalism was at once romantic in emotional appeal, liberal in politics, and egalitarian in social outlook. It combined raionalism, inherited from the Enlightenment, with the new emotional romanticism, and although clearly limited in its territorial scope, it was nonetheless cosmopolitan in ultimate intent.

Such a paradoxical position could not be maintained indefinitely. During the second half of the nineteenth century, nationalism was rapidly being corrupted, and was finally made subservient to the goals of the neo-absolutist state, which was deriving its new strength from industrialisation. Although Hegel had intended the state to be the supreme expression of freedom, the state was using his concept of the supremacy of the state to press nationalist sentiment into its service. Instead of the nationalists capturing the state—as had been anticipated—it was ultimately the state that was able to capture and subvert the nationalist ideology. Increasingly, the latter was invoked, not to develop a world balance of national sentiment on a footing of international equality, but, on the contrary, as an instrument for the attainment of diplomatic gains. Nationalism had become a prime element of dissension, rather than harmony, in international relations.

Early Populist Theories of Nationalism

It is easy, in retrospect, to trace the stages of this process of corruption. So long as a nation was still developing, liberalism tended to march hand in hand with nationalism. It was assumed without question that popular participation in political decision-making would have beneficial effects on international relations because (a) the nation was inherently peaceful (a notion taken over from Rousseau and Kant);[1] and (b) all nations were equal.

Many of the misconceptions of early nineteenth-century thinkers on the subject of nationalism spring from too close an analogy between the behaviour of persons and nations. Thus, a nation was compared to an organism possessed of a high degree of social cohesion, whose soul was represented by its culture. The chief exponent of this line of thought was Johann Gottfried Herder (1744-1803), a contemporary of Kant.

In Herder's thought, the social organism of the nation was the product of tradition. The past was important, but more important was the continuous development from past to present, which alone could ensure gradual progress down the generations. The principle of historical continuity in the life of the nation was essential to its survival: the past was part of the present. As well as an organism, a nation required a soul. The soul was a nation's spontaneous expression of cultural personality, and this was possible only by drawing on native, not foreign sources.[2] The nation's soul had to be discovered, or, if need be, created. It was only in a liberal climate that a healthy growth of the national organism was possible.

Taking Germany as his example,[3] Herder tried to show how the adoption of Latin culture during the middle ages had harmed the sound development of the German nation. No sooner had Germany overcome that disability, and no sooner was she to begin to redevelop a native culture, than her nascent culture was destroyed in the Thirty Years War (1618 - 1848), and she became culturally dependent on France. This, Herder argued, was bad not only for Germany's soul but also for its social organism. As well as being soul-destroying, the slavish imitation of French cultural patterns by the German upper classes was socially divisive, since it tended to split the nation along class lines into a Francophil upper crust and an uncultured German mass, cutting off the latter from access to culture for centuries. The history and mythology of a nation are the property of all, however, irrespective of class. Herder wished to see the creation of a true national culture in Germany which would produce a socially unifying effect by eliminating class strife. At the end of the road he foresaw the formation of a national character *(Nationalcharakter)* at once combining and expressing the tangible characteristics of the nation's collective experience.[4]

Most important of all, however, was Herder's insistence on the principle of strict international equality. Equality and nationality were two sides of the same coin. This was an emphatic enough message, but Herder would not stop there. Alone among the theoretical exponents of nationalism even of the early liberal-romantic-egalitarian type, he berated his own countrymen for their political imperialism during the middle ages, which he considered unhealthy. He objected in particular to their ruthless subjection of the Slavs, spoke up for the native populations of Latin America, and forecast a great future for the Slavs, especially the Russians, once their national spirit was aroused. It would never have occurred to him to claim cultural or any other kind of superiority over anyone, on behalf of his fellow-Germans. Nor could he imagine that nationalism was capable of developing malevolent traits. Arguing against universalism, he believed that there should be a variety of national forms of life, and that such diversity is healthy.

Herder's theory of nationalism, at once explanatory and normative, held great appeal for the newly integrating nations of early nineteenth-century Europe, and may do so again in the case of those developing nations of the second half of the twentieth century in which conditions are roughly similar. Herder's general approach towards nationalism was comprehensive, with the linguistic element representing only one element among many. Johann Gottlieb Fichte (1762 - 1814), a disciple of both Herder and Kant, singled out language for special emphasis, and gave Herder's theory of nationalism a sharp edge by his insistence that national self-realisation was to be achieved only by political struggle. According to Fichte, God had divided humanity into language groups, a divine separation violated by the absolutist rulers, who by their transnational dynastic combinations had produced multinational empires. Whereas Herder's theory could be used to reconcile nationalism with multinationalism, Fichte's could be used to disrupt existing multinational structures.

Russia, too, produced thinkers on nationalism during the first half of the nineteenth century whose ideas resembled those of Herder. Alexander Herzen (1812 - 1870),[5] a Slavophil steeped in Herderian thought, was opposed not only to absolutist rule in Russia, but also to Russian imperialism. Among an entire generation of national revolutionaries—immortalised in some of Dostoyevsky's novels—in mid-nineteenth-century Russia, were many taking their convictions to the length of revolutionary defeatism during the Crimean War. Tolstoy in his later works made a sharp definition of the moral dilemmas posed by peace, especially by pointing out that peace might not be compatible with the maintenance of high material standards of living. Yet, nothing was to be more indicative of the eventual corruption of early nineteenth-century nationalism than the tragic change of character which Dostoyevsky himself was to undergo before long.

From Nationalism to Nation-State

The romantic nationalist thinkers of the early nineteenth century tended to focus their attention on the growth of the nation, rather than on the nation's connection with the state, though some of them must have been dimly aware of the dangers lying ahead in a closer conjunction of state and nation. Thus Friedrich von Schiller, the German romantic poet, gave warning how "the German Reich and the German nation are two different things." Herder's insistence on the compatibility of nationalism with humanist cosmopolitanism, though logically consistent and theoretically plausible in the context of conditions prevailing during the first half of the nineteenth century, failed to fit the historical facts of the second half of that century, in which it became painfully apparent that national states were capable of acting abroad, and often at home, much in the same manner as their absolutist predecessors. Instead of a neat synthesis between the Hegelian concept of the liberal state and the Herderian one of the liberal nation, there was to be an ugly hybrid between Fichtean political nationalism and the neo-absolutist state.

What had gone wrong? It would be naive to suppose that there had been wilful corruption of liberal nationalism by statesmen in power in national states. More convincingly, the competitive spirit among nation-states, engendered by the quickening pace of the industrial revolution, was the critical element compelling governments to harness the national ideology to their foreign policies in order to derive additional power within an increasingly difficult international environment. Perplexed by this unexpected development, many a liberal-minded nationalist intellectual fell victim to this subtle process of corruption. Beginning as cosmopolitan liberals, these men would end as worshippers of the new power of the state. The functionalists had fervently hoped to use the industrial system to by-pass the state, only to be compelled to witness how the state was using the industrial system to consolidate, perhaps even to perpetuate, its position at home and abroad. Instead of the emergence of an inherently peaceful system of international relations, the old system continued in a new guise to operate against a new background of growing industrial and military power.

The transition from liberal to neo-absolutist nationalism was gradual in Germany, and abrupt in Russia. Leopold von Ranke (1795 - 1886), German philosopher and historian, seemed to sanction the triumph of *raison d'état* over liberal nationhood by asking ominously, "What would have been the fate of our German States, had they not derived new life from the principle of nationality on which they were based?" He was echoed by Heinrich von Treitschke (1834 - 1896), a German political scientist, who could with some justice be regarded as the ideologist of Bismarck's moderate neo-absolutism.

The tragedy of the simultaneous transformation and corruption of early nineteenth-century nationalism—liberal, romantic, and egalitarian—was faithfully mirrored in the metamorphosis of character of Fyodor Mikhailovich Dostoyevsky (1821 - 1881).[6] The Russian populist primitivists, to whom Dostoyevsky belonged, seeing in Western culture an alien intrusion and a deadly threat to the life and soul of Russia, turned to the primitive Russian peasant as a bulwark against the lures of pervasive, Western bourgeois culture. Gradually turning away from all intellectual enquiry, in the 1870s Dostoyevsky began to regard liberalism and rationalism as mortal sins. Russia, to his way of thinking, was more than a nation and could only be understood intuitively—a line of reasoning which would have been totally unacceptable to Herder. Still showing a healthy respect for Western science and technology as a general means to be used towards a specific end, in 1877 Dostoyevsky predicted that Russia would conquer the West, take over its science and technology, but reject its bourgeois civilisation. In 1880 he went even further, and—reflecting the true extent of the corruption of nationalism by neo-absolutism—advocated Russia's turning to Asia, rejecting Europe in its entirety.

It was only in the West that an enduring synthesis between nationalism and the liberal state could be achieved—possibly at the expense of subject peoples overseas. It was consequently from the West that the bulk of criticism of nationalism was to come during the second half of the century. Thus Cobden, believer in cosmopolitan capitalism, saw nationalism as reinforcing the old absolutism, while Lord Acton (1834 - 1902), the Catholic historian, dismissed nationalism as "historically retrograde."[7] More ominous in tone was T. H. Green's warning: "As nations have come more and more to distinguish and solidify themselves, and a national consciousness has come definitely to be formed in each, the rival ambitions of nations have tended more and more first to support, then perhaps to supersede the ambitions of dynasties as to the uses of war." In 1910 H. G. Wells (1866 - 1945) became convinced that nationalism would set in motion forces which the democratic state might find difficult to control: nationalism was dangerous megalomania. In France, P.-J. Proudhon (1809 - 1865), anarchist and political scientist, claimed that though respectable in theory, the principle of nationality abounded in contradictions, because there were too many prejudices tied to it, and too many interests involved. He could detect no scientific principle to support the notion of nationality.

Populist nationalism in Europe may, in retrospect, be judged as an outgrowth of the Enlightenment and the economic and social forces that had caused that movement. Outside Western Europe only ripples of the Enlightenment were to be felt, and the type of nationalism that obtained a foothold in Western Europe never succeeded in doing the same elsewhere. There may be lessons to be learnt here by writers and politicians in underdeveloped countries in which conditions today resemble those in Western Europe during the age of the Enlightenment. But even within Western Europe the liberal variety of nationalism underwent some modifications, as the conjunction of state and nation allowed the former to retain significant areas of control, above all in fields connected with foreign policy, defence and internal security. Here too states have seen fit to restrict freedom in the name of national solidarity.

Herder's theory of nationalism, conceived in response to the Enlightenment, was the product of empirical reasoning. It laid no claim to the status of scientific truth. Not so the theories of multinationalism expounded from mid-century onwards by Marxist and neo-Marxist writers, who, proceeding from Marxist premises, claimed for their theories universal applicability.

Marxist Theories of Nationalism

Marx's dictum that "the workers have no fatherland" has been widely interpreted to mean either that they lack a homeland in the political sense or that they ought not to, or need not have one because in a basically cosmopolitan creed like Marxian socialism there is no room for such a narrow concept. However, Marx never intended his remark to be understood in either of these ways. What he meant was that the workers, alienated by the development of the factory system, had been alienated from the rest of society through the formation of a class system in which they found themselves at a permanent disadvantage. He neither denied the existence of the nation nor disapproved of it as such; his only complaint was that the working class was excluded from it.

Engels, while expecting a world culture to emerge eventually as a result of the worldwide spread of capitalism, was willing to take a practical view of the national problem. This was epitomised in his attitude towards the "unhistorical nations," a notion first used by Hegel in connection with nations lacking both state and intelligentsia, as, for instance, the Czechs since their defeat at the Battle of the White Mountain of 1620. What Hegel meant to be an academic concept was turned into a polemical instrument by Engels, who was infuriated by the inexplicable behaviour of Croats and Slovaks during the revolution of 1848-1849, in which they had supported the Habsburgs against the revolutionary nationalism of the culturally advanced Magyars; because for his part Engels envisaged the "historical" nations as carrying the torch of material progress to the "unhistorical" ones, imposing their own advanced culture on the latter in the process.[8] The victorious forward march of English and French culture in Western Europe and overseas, and German, Magyar, and Polish culture in Central and Eastern Europe, might in the eyes of Engels conceivably result in the relegation of the Basques, Bretons, Irish, and Scots—as well as a host of peoples in colonial territories—in the West, and a number of "unhistorical" nationalities in Central and Eastern Europe, to the dustbin of history.

Engels' line of reasoning smacked strongly of social Darwinism, a vulgarised form of Darwinism which, postulating the survival of the fittest, was rapidly becoming fashionable in his lifetime. It was in accord with prevailing currents of thoughts and seemed to provide the right answers on the basis of the accepted notions of laisser faire. When these assumptions came to be questioned during the last quarter of the century, the answers began to lose their cogency also. For though it was true that the materially strong nations tended to predominate in the economic sphere owing to the rapid spread of capitalism, it was equally true that the weaker ones were put on their guard because of this, throwing up tariff walls to protect their own nascent industries. This process had its counterpart within multinational empires, such as the Ottoman, Russian and Habsburg ones, in which the uneven spread of capitalism began to arouse the fears of precisely the "unhistorical" nations, rendering the problem of nationality acute and, in time, threatening the very foundations of those multinational structures. What was emerging in those conditions, however, was no longer a national but a multinational problem, calling for specifically multinational solutions.

Multinationalism

The first to see the complexity of the problem and to recognise the need for its systematic examination was Karl Kautsky (1854 - 1938), who sought to lay a suitable basis for a thorough debate by seeking a technical definition of the concept of nationality. By establishing the two criteria of (a) territory and (b) language, he was leaning on Herder and Fichte, rather than on Marx and Engels for support. However, it soon became evident that prescription as well as analysis was required, as a political debate ensued side by side with this academic investigation.

The course of the political debate was to some degree predetermined by the contrasting ethnic patterns of the Austrian half of the Habsburg empire on the one hand, and of the Romanov empire on the other. Within the former, there was first of all the patchwork quilt of nationalities in Bohemia and Moravia, where Germans, Czechs, and Jews were living cheek by jowl, in cultural and to some extent in economic separateness, yet in constant social contact with each other; and there were secondly the German-, Slovene-, and Italian-speaking parts, which formed ethnically homogeneous and therefore territorially continuous blocks. In Russia, on the other hand, the homogeneous-territorial type clearly predominated, allowing for the development of compact national units.

As a consequence of this pattern of distribution of nationalities, most Russian Marxists tended to advocate a multinational solution along lines of either a federation or outright independence, while Austro-Marxists—less resolutely opposed to the Habsburg monarchy than their Russian counterparts to that of the Romanovs—cast round for a saving formula for the imperial structure. Their complex multinational schemes aimed at the separation of political and cultural affairs in multiethnic areas in ways which would ensure the continued multinational administration in political matters on an imperial-territorial basis, while creating centres for the administration of cultural matters on a basis of individual nationality. In this synthesis of the principles of multinational territoriality and personal nationality, the Austro-Marxists saw the only hope and guarantee of the survival of the multinational empire.

Within Austrian Social Democracy two camps of theorists emerged, the territorialists and the cultural autonomists, threatening to tear each other apart within the centrally organised party.[9] Things came to a head at the Brno party congress in 1899, where the Polish section of the party, considering the relatively bright prospects of a future independent Poland, was favouring the territorial principle, while the Slovene component, which saw no such prospects, opted for the principle of cultural autonomy. The ultimate decision was founded on an uneasy compromise which highlighted the continued need of further theorising on the subject. It was in Austria, rather than in Russia, therefore, that original thought on the subject was being fostered among Marxist intellectuals. In Russia, Lenin and Stalin committed themselves to the federal-independent formula based on voluntary decision, with only Rosa Luxemburg—who was both Polish and Jewish—firmly opposed to independence, her doctoral thesis on the state of the Polish economy having convinced her that Polish industry needed the Russian market as an outlet.[10]

The two outstanding exponents of the principle of cultural autonomy, Karl Renner and Otto Bauer, were both Austrians from the ethnically diverse region of Moravia.[11] Far more than Renner, Bauer tended to view the whole question of conflict among nationalities in the light of the doctrine of the class struggle. His chief intellectual merit lay in boldly turning Engels' argument concerning the "unhistorical nations" upside down. He felt justified in doing so after drawing conclusions diametrically opposed to those of Engels regarding the cultural consequences of the spread of industrialisation. Engels, it will be recalled, who considered the cultural differential between "historical" and "unhistorical" nations unbridgeable, and welcomed the forward march of the former in the name of material progress, was willing to see the disappearance of the latter. Bauer, on the other hand, maintained that industrialisation was impossible without creating a technical infrastructure comprising a modern educational system. To stimulate the educational impulse meant stirring the national consciousness, hitherto dormant, among the newly arising working and lower middle classes of the "unhistorical" nations. According to Bauer, socialism itself, the product of industrialisation, was an important factor in awakening these "unhistorical nations." The task of international socialism, Bauer concluded, was "not to iron out national peculiarities, but to bring international unity through recognition of national diversity."[12] Bauer must hence be regarded as one of the first German-speaking Marxists to realise that the multinational Habsburg empire was doomed in the long run, not for its failure to satisfy the demands of the "historical nations" but, on the contrary, because of the awakening of the "unhistorical" ones in its midst. The impact of industrialisation within multinational structures was divisive, not integrative, and the international socialist movement could not hope to escape from the process of cultural differentiation engendered by that process.

To resolve this dilemma, Bauer saw himself compelled to fall back on Herder's organic theory, according to which nationality was the product not so much of a synthesis of territorial and linguistic considerations as of a general participation in a cultural community *(Kulturgemeinschaft)*. Applying his neo-Marxist insights to the Herderian theory, Bauer underlined the contrast between "historical" and "unhistorical" nations in this process. In the case of the former, culture under precapitalist conditions was the monopoly of the ruling class, and the net effect of industrialisation was merely the cultural integration of the masses into the nation, going some distance to correct their former state of alienation. In the case of the "unhistorical nations," however, assimilation was impossible, as the ruling classes were of a different nationality altogether. The only salvation of those national groups lay in developing a national consciousness of their own if they were to avoid being swamped by the "historical" nations in the manner envisaged by Engels. It was futile, Bauer argued, to expect a merger of national cultures to result from capitalist progress, as Engels had forecast.

Karl Renner was a full-time civil servant with a conventional legal training and a fairly moderate neo-Marxist who realised the folly of applying the territorial principle in all its rigour to the multinational problems of the Habsburg empire. He consequently proposed a solution along lines of cultural autonomy half a decade before Bauer was to produce a more elaborate version along identical lines.[13] As well as in time-span, there was a difference in purpose marking the theories of these two men. Bauer, more academic in outlook than the pragmatically minded Renner—who had been content with working out a political strategy—attempted to provide an intellectually satisfying explanation in Marxist terms.

Renner's central device for solving the multinational problems of the empire so as to preserve its territorial integrity was to replace the territorial principle of nationality by a purely personal-cultural one. Members of different nationalities, irrespective of their place of residence, would be organised under separate national councils for purposes of education and taxation, leaving unaffected all remaining governmental functions of the central power. Renner's scheme, which enjoyed Bauer's full support, had a mixed reception. It appealed to Jewish Socialists already organised in the *Bund* in Poland and Russia, where the Jewish proletariat was scattered far and wide amidst other nationalities. It also found echoes among Social Democrats in Latvia and the Caucasus. Having designed their theories to save the Habsburg empire from disintegration, Renner and Bauer clung to their theories until a point was reached during the First World War when the survival of that empire was no longer a practical possibility.

Renner and Bauer have been accused of using their scheme of cultural autonomy on a personal basis as a prop for German cultural hegemony within the Western half of the empire and within Europe itself.[14] This cannot be either proved or disproved, but their concept of cultural autonomy may have been, consciously or subconsciously, inspired by the edicts of religious toleration pronounced during the enlightened rule of Joseph II in the 1780s, when religion rather than general secular education was the central criterion of culture, and when a neat separation of politics and religion was perfectly feasible.[15]

Among the Russo-Marxists, Lenin argued fiercely against the Renner-Bauer conception of the nationality problem, basing himself firmly on Kautsky's territorialist approach and directing his main critical thrust against Bauer's Herderian conception of the nation. In 1902 a draft programme of Russian Social Democracy included a demand for the "recognition of self-determination of all nations belonging to the State," which was reinterpreted in 1913 as meaning the right to secede. Also in 1913—and probably at Lenin's behest— Stalin produced the classical tract *Marxism and the National and Colonial Question.* Proceeding from Kautsky's technical definition, which had postulated territory and language as the two central criteria of a nation, Stalin added two of his own: a common history and a common economy—both surprising omissions by Kautsky, the classical Marxist theoretician. In its final form, the Stalinist definition of nationhood was both comprehensive and neat, and liable on that account to supersede any that had gone before. Intended to outclass the Renner-Bauer theory of nationhood, the Stalinist definition anticipated objections from that quarter by making one important concession to the formers' concept of cultural autonomy: any group failing to answer the territorial criterion was qualified to be a "nationality," rather than a fully rounded "nation."

The higher purpose of the Austro-Marxist theory of multinationalism was pragmatic and conciliatory; that of the Russo-Bolsheviks was historicist and dialectic. The former regarded their theory as a contribution towards the resolution of international conflict; the latter as an instrument with which to sharpen existing conflicts in order to hasten the revolutionary process. As Stalin explained: "A nation is not merely a historical category, but a historical category which is part of a definite epoch—the epoch of rising capitalism." Unlike Bauer, who was strongly influenced by the organic concept of nationhood as elaborated by Kant and Herder, whose doctrines he had tried to marry with the social and economic thought of Karl Marx, Stalin continued to rely for a while on Engels in his anticipation of the genesis of a specifically Socialist culture and language.[16] However, during the last couple of years of his life he began to relent, and during the so-called "linguistics" debate launched in the late 1940s conceded that language was a phenomenon having a life separate from social and economic relations.[17] Stalinism too was becoming Herderian.

There was one thing that Marx, Engels, and Stalin had in common: their expectation that, as far as it was possible to see ahead, world society would be international and not cosmopolitan, calling for national solutions above all. This may be one reason why Stalinist Marxism—rather than its Trotskyist variety or, for that matter, anarchism, with their markedly cosmopolitan appeal—has persistently proved an attractive proposition to wide sections of the political and military intelligentsia of economically and culturally underdeveloped countries. It is on the other hand highly doubtful whether the Stalinist formula would be useful over large areas of Asia and sub-Saharan Africa,[18] in which conditions of ethnic multiplicity not unlike those of Bohemia and Moravia under the Habsburg empire still obtain. The question therefore arises whether the Renner-Bauer theory, devised for the solution of precisely such contingencies, should not now be revived, brought up-to-date and in a suitably refurbished form applied to those conditions. In such an event, all sorts of Marxist theoreticians,[19] as well as political scientists may before long find themselves engrossed in a Renner-Bauer renaissance of some proportions and at the centre of a greatly renewed interest in theories of multinationalism.

It therefore came as something of a disappointment to note that K. W. Deutsch—who shares much of Renner's and Bauer's multinational background and intellectual outlook—should have rejected the Renner-Bauer formula for a positive approach to the multinational problem so decisively, if only implicitly, in his work on *Nationalism and Social Communication,*[20] first published in 1953. The effect of Deutsch's concentration on flows of transactions and means of communication on his perception of the problem of nationalism was to blur the distinctions between the various criteria so elaborately established by Marxists and neo-Marxists alike over a long time, and to submerge the phenomenon within the field of cybernetics.[21] Appreciating that Deutsch had long-term goals in mind in focussing on a rigidly functional definition of nationhood, it ought nonetheless to be pointed out that his neglect of the multinational, as distinct from the purely national problem, is all the more difficult to understand since his thesis that nationalism is associated with the mass mobilisation of precommercial, preindustrial peasant peoples[22] tied in neatly with Bauer's.

Taking the world of the early 1950s as his oyster, Deutsch concluded that not until the incident of industrialisation begins to spread its effects evenly around the globe can "insistence on national separateness and economic and political barriers" be expected to abate.[23] In this respect his thesis was in striking affinity with Kautsky's, which had insisted—against Renner and Bauer—that the attainment of national independence of the peoples composing the multinational empires existing at the time was the absolute prerequisite for eventual inter-national integration.[24]

Plausible in the historical context of attempts at developing scientifically oriented theories of nationalism in the early 1950s, Deutsch's thesis must on no account be accepted as unconditionally valid a quarter of a century later, when it can be seen to have dangerously underestimated the size of the multinational problem and, even more gravely, the length of the time-span involved in the processes analysed by him. In postulating a solution by way of a redistribution of what he called "capital equipment" over the world's backward regions, Deutsch was taking a very long-term view indeed: "Tying the mobilized populations into national communities and social classes has tended to separate peoples from each other for a time; but it made them fundamentally more alike, and taught many of them to adjust to new and changing patterns of communication."[25] Deutsch thus glossed in lofty fashion over the massive problems of multinational differentiation and conflict in the course of the industrialisation of the "unhistorical" stretches of the underdeveloped part of the globe.

These problems were clearly perceived nearly half a century before Deutsch by Otto Bauer. It would seem certain, therefore, that Deutsch's thesis is due for a substantial revision if it is to fit the multinational realities of the underdeveloped sector of today's world.

NOTES

1. As Herder remarked: "The fatherlands do not make war on each other; only the governments."

2. In Germany it was the brothers Grimm, and in Britain Sir Walter Scott who indirectly were teaching people the value of folk-songs, ballads, and primitive tales.

3. See E. Adler, *Herder und die deutsche Aufklärung.* Zürich: Europa-Verlag, 1970.

4. Similar views had been expressed less emphatically by Rousseau. See C. E. Vaughan (ed.), *Political Writings of Rousseau*, Vol. II, *Project Corse* (1915), p. 319.

5. See Alexander Herzen, *My Past Thoughts* (edited and abridged by D. Mac-Donald). London: Chatto and Windus, 1974.

6. See H. Kohn, "Dostoyevsky's nationalism," 6 *Journal of the History of Ideas* (1945), pp. 385-398.

7. Lord Acton, "Nationalism," *Home and Foreign Review* (July 1862).

8. While unable to deny its existence, Engels despised Russian culture, as indeed did most Russian intellectuals of the nineteenth century.

9. In 1880 an unsigned article, purportedly from Kautsky's pen, appeared in the Zürich paper *Sozialdemokrat,* which advocated the decentralisation of the structure of the party along national lines, thus allowing the German-speaking section to work for an *Anschluss* with Germany. The party was duly thus decentralised in 1887.

10. See Rosa Luxemburg, *Die industrielle Entwicklung Polens.* Leipzig: Heidrich, 1895.

11. Karl Renner (1870 - 1950); Otto Bauer (1881 - 1938). Bauer was born in Vienna, but spent most of his youth in Moravia. Karl Kautsky was an Austrian also but was to spend most of his life in Germany.

12. Otto Bauer, *Die Sozialdemokratie und die Nationalitätenfrage.* Vienna: Volks-buchhandlung, 1907, p. 510.

13. Rudolf Springer (synonym of Karl Renner), *Der Kampf der österreichischen Nationen um den Staat.* Vienna: Volksbuchhandlung, 1902.

14. See A. J. P. Taylor, *The Habsburg Monarchy.* London: Hamish Hamilton, 1948, p. 205.

15. Having been reproved by Kautsky for postulating his concept of *Kulturgemein-schaft,* Bauer defended himself by claiming that economic and social, as well as purely cultural considerations were comprised in this concept.

16. Stalin tended to be impressed by the theories of Nikolai Yakovlyevich Marr (1865 - 1934), which dominated Soviet linguistics from 1920 to 1950. From early investigations of Georgian and other Caucasian languages, Marr gathered that language was a phenomenon of social class rather than nationality. He believed that the relation-ship between languages is an indication of the stage of historical evolution that they have reached.

17. J. V. Stalin, *Marksism i voprosy yazikoznaniya.* Moscow: Gospolizdat, 1950.

18. Only a few illustrations can be provided here. For Asia, see A. T. Embree, "Pluralism and national integration: the Indian experience," 1 *Journal of International Affairs* (1973), pp. 41-52; N. L. Snider, "Is national integration necessary? The Malysian case," *ibid.*, pp. 80-89; R. S. Milne, "Patrons, clients and ethnicity; the case of Sarawak and Sabah in Malaysia" *Asian Survey* (October 1973), pp. 891-907; and G. Wheeler, "Language problems in multinational Asian communities," *Asian Affairs* (October 1973), pp. 287-294. For Africa, see A. R. Zolberg, "Tribalism through corrective lenses," *Foreign Affairs* (July 1973), pp. 728-739; W. E. Phipps, "Christianity and nationalism in tropical Africa," 1 *Civilisations* (1972), pp. 92-100; and N. O. Ijere, "Economics and African nationalism," 4 *Civilisations* (1972), pp. 547-562. For a general idea of the ethnic diversity of Africa south of the Sahara, see C. G. Seligman, *Races of Africa.* London: Oxford University Press, 1957, third ed.

19. While there is some evidence of an unfettered debate on the general subject of nationalism among Soviet scholars, the New Left has been making some efforts in this direction also, though neither side seems to have come up so far with any new theories. On the attempts of the Yugoslav New Left, see Professor Milan Kangra, holder of the

chair of ethics in the University of Zagreb, writing in *Praxis,* an independent critical periodical.

20. K. W. Deutsch, *Nationalism and Social Communication: An Inquiry into the Foundations of Nationality.* Cambridge, Mass.: MIT Press, 1953.

21. Ibid., p. 80.

22. As Deutsch admitted, "this is largely a book on research and on methods of research." See ibid., p. 163.

23. Ibid., p. 164.

24. Ibid., p. 191.

25. Ibid., p. 164.

Chapter 9

THE FEDERATIVE PRINCIPLE:

WITHIN AND BEYOND THE STATE

The federative and national principles may be regarded as historically parallel and theoretically compatible attempts to solve the international problem. Early instances of federative thought[1] in recent history may be found in the age of absolutism,[2] when it was considered that, through the pooling of certain functions, the balance of power—a potential source of international conflict—might be brought under control. These expectations could not stand the test of intellectual inquiry. Thus, Jean Bodin, who had explored the possibilities of the federative principle in relation to the concept of sovereignty at the end of the sixteenth century,[3] arrived at negative conclusions, while Samuel Pufendorf, writing in mid-eighteenth century,[4] likewise found the federative principle to be incompatible with sovereignty. Only Hugo Grotius, writing in the first half of the seventeenth century, was mildly optimistic about the capacity of "federal leagues" (something of a tautology) to survive. Though eschewing the use of the term, the Abbé de Saint-Pierre in his *Projet pour rendre la paix perpétuelle en Europe* (1712), in which he put forward the idea of an international "social contract," was the first writer to be positive about the federative principle.

The original meaning of *foedus* (Latin) was an association, and in the context of Greco-Roman antiquity that meant an alliance between states, usually for purposes of war or diplomatic measures short of war. Both the United Provinces of the Netherlands, which was formed during the first half of the seventeenth century—a genuine, though rather loose federation held together by the powerful office of the *Stadtholder* at the top—and the United States of America, in its fully federated form of 1787,[5] had been wartime alliances, albeit among rebel states, enduring into peacetime. It was only in the course of the nineteenth century, and after the convulsions of the Napoleonic period, that the federative principle came to be looked upon consciously as a pacifist resource to be applied on the international level.

Three more or less distinct phases in the development of the federative principle in its pacifist expression can be distinguished during that period. Between 1815 and 1848 Quaker influence emanating from the United States predominated. After 1848 the emphasis shifted from the religious to the political aspect, to be reduced to almost exclusively academic forms of expression after 1871, when a number of international lawyers at first, and political scientists after them, were adopting federalism as a design for the attainment of peace.

To account for the popularity of the federative principle among pacifists during the first phase of this development is easily done by pointing to the powerful precedent of the successful federation of the United States. In Latin America, for instance, the constitution of the United States was widely copied by many of the newly emancipated states. Being mere paper copies, they proved unsuited to the historical context of Latin America at that time. On a wider, international-continental canvas, Simon Bolívar, the liberator of Hispanic South America, sought unsuccessfully to apply the federative principle to save the Hispanic-American wartime unity from disintegrating in the period of independence.[6] In Europe, the Quakers, enthralled by United States federal experience, and their eyes fixed on the German Confederation of 1815 as a suitable nucleus of a European association of states,[7] were canvassing for a federal "United States of Europe."[8] The efforts made by Bolívar and the Quakers could fairly be interpreted as aiming at pacifist, rather than entirely selfish political ends, and in this respect, as differing from the federative solutions dressed up as peace schemes, but intended as political alliances against outsiders, which had been concocted during the age of absolutism.

If revulsion from large-scale war had been the principal reason for promoting federalism in post-Napoleonic Europe, the advent of functionalism—by-product of the burgeoning industrial revolution—provided the fresh federative impulse in the middle of that century. However, the functional-federal movement was to lose its strength when the Franco-Prussian War of 1870 introduced a new era in international relations in which military technology was eclipsing economic development as prime mover.[9] While the prospects of federalising Europe in those circumstances were remote, the need for the prevention of international conflict was greater than ever. Consequently, pacifists turned to the short-term expedient by way of disarmament of achieving détente and commissions of conciliation.

As a result the federalist movement in its quasi-political form collapsed and political federalism remained dead for at least three generations. Federalism as an intellectual tool in the hands of pacifist-minded academics was born, as lawyers and political scientists took their turn in attempting to solve the mounting international problems of the first half of the twentieth century. Today the federal principle is regarded as a potential solvent of international economic problems, giving rise to a variety of theories vaguely reminiscent of the ideas put forward by the functional-federalists of the mid-nineteenth century.[10]

The Moderates

In the early phases of the French Revolution, the federative principle was espoused by the ruling Girondin party, who saw in it a practical guarantee of the continuance of that revolutionary cohesion between the regions of France which had made possible the recruitment of revolutionary armies. Abstract federal principle, as broached by Montesquieu earlier in the century, appears not to have been involved.[11] The Jacobins, on the other hand—who succeeded the Girondins—were centralisers par excellence committed to effective majority rule as expounded in the writings of Rousseau, for whom federalism was a potentially corroding device. Jacobin excesses made the post-Napoleonic moderates of the Left think of federalism as a counterweight to centralisation. They saw their views confirmed by the advent to power in the France of Napoleon III.

Extending the Girondist principle of federal cooperation to the European continental setting, but viewing it primarily in functional terms, Saint-Simon expressed the hope that, once established on the European continent, functional federalism would triumph the world over.[12] Victor Considérant (1808 - 1893), originally a Saint-Simonian, who later began to subscribe to the ideas of Fourier on political organisation,[13] was to see in the common interest of the international business class and banking community a pacifying element favourable to a European federation.[14] Alexis de Tocqueville similarly expressed himself in favour of federalism.[15]

Further encouragement came from across the Channel, where Richard Cobden threw the weight of economic liberalist thought of the laisser faire school behind pacifist federalism, claiming that economic interdependence would prevent international discord and suggesting in 1842 that free trade agitation be made part of the federalist effort. Impressed by the example of the United States constitution, J. S. Mill maintained hopefully that, as a general principle, the similarity of conditions in several countries should ease the path towards federation.[16] Nationalist leaders of the moderate Left, like Mazzini and Garibaldi, were willing to lend their support also.

Several congresses were held by this amalgam of idealist federalists between 1848 and 1871. In his opening address to the First Congress of the Friends of Peace, held in Paris in 1849, Victor Hugo, the celebrated French writer, called for a "United States of Europe." The enthusiasm was there, but the weakness of the movement lay in its overbroad political base, which would not allow concrete agreement to be reached on matters of political strategy. As cleavages were appearing between the religious, the functionalist, and the nationalist elements—with the latter two stressing the importance of spontaneity, to the detriment of careful planning—the movement began to stall.

The Anarchists

In Britain, William Godwin (1756 - 1836), parson, friend of the poet Shelley and general philosopher, looked upon the state as an institution whereby privileged groups—"officers of the army, the navy, ambassadors and negotiators, all the train of artifices that has been invented to hold other nations at bay, to penetrate their secrets, to traverse their machinations, to form alliances and counter-alliances"—impose sacrifices on the people. Its demise, Godwin was convinced, would result in a world of small, autonomous units that would be peaceful.[17]

In Russia the federative idea made its appearance also. Despite his later excesses of radicalism, Michael Bakunin (1814 - 1876) was part of the early romantic-idealist stream of European nationalism. But his basic sentiment was Pan-Slav and therefore supranational, and this made him see in the federative principle a suitable means for the supranational organisation of Pan-Slavism, as well as an instrument for raising revolution in Russia. Bakunin's scheme for a Pan-Slav federation—contained in his *Appeal to the Slavs* made at the Pan-Slav conference in Moscow in 1848—was given a lukewarm reception by the Western Slavs, who sensed a Russian intrigue.[18] It was also mercilessly flayed by Engels, then still resident in Germany.

Marx and Engels were convinced Jacobins, willing to consider departures from the centralist principle of organisation only after the safe establishment of revolution in a number of countries. Until such time, they would denounce the concept of an international federation as a bourgeois fraud. As Engels forcefully put it in 1849: "We have often called attention to the . . . sentimental fantasies of universal brotherhood of peoples, of a European Federal

Republic and eternal world peace . . . [which are] nothing but disguises for the boundless perplexity and inactivity of the spokesmen of the time."

This was plain enough language and perhaps a not altogether undeserved judgment on the majority of advocates of international federation during the first half of the nineteenth century. It was a criticism that could not so sweepingly be made of Joseph-Pierre Proudhon (1809 - 1865), leading exponent of the federative principle, who proved willing to revise his views in the light of newly emerging facts. Petit-bourgeois in social origin and supicious of large-scale organisation, Proudhon was a localist rather than a nationalist, his social philosophy reflecting the interests of a remnant class of craftsmen rather than those of the growing factory proletariat. Passing gradually from utopia to realism in his assessment of the federative principle, Proudhon remained suspicious to the end of the nationalism, as well as of the centralism, of the Jacobins, with their reliance on state power. To counteract these, he favoured the establishment on a world scale of political and economic associations on decentralist-functionalist lines based on a welter of voluntarily concluded contracts to accomplish common purposes at various levels of activity.[19] Some of these associations would be of an ad hoc, others of a permanent nature, but in each case the vital aspect of the matter was to be the social relationship created by the contract, and not the institutions and the law involved. As he put it with precision: "Federation . . . is a convention whereby one or several heads of family, or several communities *(communautés)*, or states, are obligated reciprocally and equally towards one another for one or several particular objects, whose burden is then the special and exclusive duty of the delegates to the federation."[20] Ultimately, Proudhon visualised a world which was "an association of associations of associations."

Proudhon's great importance in the field of international relations consists in the way in which he passed through distinct phases of thought from favouring (a) global utopian association, then to (b) international functional federalism, and finally to (c) international political confederalism, spanning the crucial decades of the middle of the nineteenth century. During his utopian-associative phase, Proudhon proved to be a staunch opponent of the idea of interstate federalism, even of a functional kind. His gradual conversion from associative functionalism towards a species of political confederalism, and from abstract principle to realistic pragmatism was therefore all the more startling. As Proudhon had to admit in 1862: "I started as an anarchist in 1840, but my critique of government ultimately led me to believe in federation as a necessary basis of the law of nations in Europe, and later for all States." In 1849, however, he was still scoffing at the underlying purposes of the Paris pacifist-federalist congress of that year. In 1851, in *L'idée générale de la Révolution au XIXe siècle,* he stated his associative-functionalist thesis in the firm belief of having laid the theoretical basis of a desirable world organisation: both regional and federal interstate order were dismissed out-right as means of achieving that ultimate aim.

Soon, however, his confidence began to wane, giving way to a sense of doubt. Impressed by the growing strength of nationalist sentiment and shocked by the severity of the Franco-Austrian war of 1859, Proudhon abandoned his former optimism and set out to reexamine the problem of world order in a systematic manner. Thus, *La Guerre et la paix* (1859), closely followed by *Du principe fédératif (1863)*, both betrayed his earnest endeavour to forge instruments for the prevention of war and a concern with international relations on the interstate level which was to loom as large in his mind as the promotion of what he considered the authentic ideals of the French Revolution (betrayed by the Jacobins) had done in his earlier work. Now willing to accept federalism as the handmaiden of functionalism, Proudhon proposed the creation of customs unions and the setting up of joint public works, both isolated from unwelcome state interference, on an international scale and on a federal-functional basis.[21] Proudhon was seeking ways of making the federative principle, as defined by him, the chief means of regulating an equitable distribution of power in Europe, so that it might act as the main guarantor of peace. The concept of equilibrium, alongside that of voluntary contract, was central to Proudhon's schemes. An equitable balance of power in Europe had to be so devised as to ensure freedom as well as peace. The existing balance of power in Europe was seen by him as being tragically threatened by the disrupting tendencies of nationalism, whether of the centralist-integral type, as in Germany and Italy, or the centrifugal-separatist kind, as evidenced by Kossuth's brand of Magyar nationalism in Hungary. As for freedom, that was much safer within a federal framework, such as the one devised for Switzerland in 1849.[22] For that reason alone he would have liked to see the emerging Italian nation-state adopt a federal constituion also.

Perceiving the frightening nature of the new destructiveness of which war was capable in the mid-nineteenth century,[23] Proudhon found himself more and more taking stock of the problem of power in international relations and appreciating the purely political element in the search for peace. The world could no longer afford to wait leisurely for the full maturing and application of his earlier utopian schemes of global associative functionalism. Short-term measures were called for as a matter of urgency in order to prevent further wars. Making due allowances for the prevailing realities in the distribution of power in Europe, Proudhon showed himself anxious in *Du principe fédératif (1863)*—his most mature work—to settle for a rough compromise between the libertarian and authoritarian principles by recommending the formation of confederations by consent, provided (a) there was constitutional restriction to republics or representative monarchies, and (b) that unitary states as well as the big powers were to be excluded. He ruled out an all-embracing European combination on the grounds that it would reduce small states to serfdom vis-à-vis the big powers (a concern already noted by Rousseau), but a grouping of regional federations (Italian, Danubian, Scandinavian, Rhenanian, and Swiss)[24] was acceptable because capable of checking those big powers. To ensure freedom, federation had to be set within the context of wide decentralisation and autonomies, of cities, for example. The general idea was that an association of states should be given fewer functions and powers as its size and scope expanded. Thus returning to his erstwhile conceptions, Proudhon advocated more respect for local traditions in his native France, exhorting his countrymen in 1861 "to make a dozen federated republics" to make France "as young as she was in 1793."[25]

It can readily be seen that in his search for international harmony Proudhon produced a subtle blend of the functional principle of cooperation, the political principle of federation and the international principle of confederation, making the maximum use at all levels of the associative principle he had managed to salvage from his original thought. The closest some of Proudhon's ideas have come to being revived in the twentieth century was in G. D. H. Cole's "guild socialism," which envisaged a proliferation of producers' associations as a realistic Fabian alternative to the principle of centralised bureaucracy championed by the Webbs. Some of them have also found a reflection in the fourth constitution of the Federal Socialist Republic of Yugoslavia in 1974.[26] It is clear, however, that the latter two were meant to solve problems on the intrastate level only, without adopting Proudhon's conception of multiple equilibrium at a variety of levels capable, at least in theory, of preventing interstate conflict.

Pyotr Alexeyevich Kropotkin (1842 - 1921)—Russian nobleman, natural scientist, and convert to anarchism—in an age when Darwinism was the dominant line of thought in the social sciences, maintained that cooperation rather than conflict was the chief factor in the evolution of species. He harked back to the Proudhonian idea of the cooperative association as the basis of civilised existence through mutual aid to check the rise of the coercive bureaucratic state.[27] Kropotkin's teachings would have been of no consequence in the realm of international relations, had he not regarded the war of 1914 as a revolutionary struggle in which the cooperative principle— which he saw, somewhat mistakenly, as governing the life of Slav and Latin peoples—was pitted against a Germany representing the centralising principle in both its Prussian militarist and Jacobin Marxist forms, the very incarnation of authoritarianism. On the other hand, he saw the supposed Slav-Latin cooperative communes as the nucleus of a new libertarian order.

The Academics

It was not long before the general sense of realism, which had affected the thinking of Proudhon from the late 1850s onwards, was also invading the federalist movement as a whole, discouraging further attempts on the part of enthusiasts to promote their aims uncritically through concerted political action. Held in 1867 under Garibaldi's chairmanship, the second Paris Congress of the Friends of Peace revealed numerous political rifts, but the final blow was the Franco-Prussian war of 1870, which must have convinced the federalists that states could not, by political action, be persuaded to curb their own power to the extent demanded by federal schemes of international association. It was at this point that the federal idea, still upheld as potentially beneficial to international relations, was taken up by some academics, and in particular by a handful of lawyers and political scientists.[28] In the late 1870s, when the dust had settled on the Franco-Prussian war, a purely academic debate was triggered off on the subject of federalism as a means of ensuring international peace and security. Thus, J. Lorimer, professor of international law at Edinburgh university, got off to a good start in 1877 by producing a paper on "The final problem of international law," published in the *Revue de droit international*, in which, for the first time, juridical precision was lent to the idea of a European federation, albeit a loose one.[29] But already the derivative character of early academic theorising on international federalism was becoming evident when a year later, in 1878, J. K. Bluntschli, a Swiss lawyer who had made a remarkable contribution to the arbitral solution of the *Alabama* case a few years before,[30] criticized Lorimer in a hard-hitting article[31] for copying United States constitutional federalism against a European background requiring a different approach. Bluntschli's thesis was open to similar objections, since his model of a European union showed close affinities with the history of the Swiss constitution before 1848, in which the confederal pattern predominated.

Taken out of the political arena and being increasingly overshadowed by the movement towards world disarmament and international arbitration, the federalist debate among academics continued, somewhat sluggishly, until 1914. Almost completely eclipsed by the First World War and its aftermath, it only resumed in the 1930s when growing fear occasioned by the rise of the Nazis in Germany gave it new life. In Britain the London-based New Commonwealth Institute was founded in 1932. It was presided over by Lord David Davies, chairman of the League of Nations Union, with Professor Ernst Jaeckh of the Berlin Hochschule für Politik as the moving spirit on the German side.[32] Dr. G. Schwarzenberger, who was made secretary of the Institute's research bureau in 1934, was charged with exploring ways and means of reforming the League of Nations, with special reference to the inclusion in its structure of an international equity tribunal and an international police force. Realising that this could not be accomplished without application of the federative principle, Schwarzenberger, familiar with Proudhon's writings on the subject, was instrumental in giving some of the Institute's publications a marked federative emphasis.[33]

The Second World War not only interrupted this development, but brought new perspectives to bear on the whole field of the study of international relations. Disenchantment with the overelaboration of single remedies for the ills of international society had gone some way, and what was demanded was no longer a concentration on a single idea, in however scholarly a manner, but a broadly based critical approach towards the subject in its entirety.

The only time that federalism sprang to life again after 1945 was when, to smooth the path toward general decolonisation, it was applied to bring together formerly dependent territories on the eve of their independence.[34] Thus, in Britain a distinguished Cambridge constitutional lawyer, Sir Ivor Jennings, was the intellect behind seemingly ingenious schemes of political federation,[35] and before long similar efforts were to be set afoot in France. The result of these tragically misconceived attempts was that, after a short while, the former British and French colonial empires lay strewn with the corpses of unworkable federations. Once again the federative principle, so attractive in its pristine theoretical form, had proved a fallacy in practice. It stood discredited as a device to solve international problems, and was to be supplanted by an uninspiring but moderately workable confederalism on the one hand, and by a new supranational functionalism on the other.

Regeneration?

The federative principle may be in the doldrums today, but it would be rash to write it off altogether. For it is not inconceivable that if and when a climate is beginning to prevail in which the bases of large-scale industrial civilisation are increasingly questioned, the federative principle might undergo a revival within the underdeveloped stretches of the world, where the options of development are still wide open. It was Arnold Toynbee who posed anew the leading question at the Tenth Delos Symposium held in Greece in 1972 as to what the right size and organisation of the ideal human community should be, and what should be its relation with the world community.[36]

One consequence of this might be a seeking towards a regeneration of rural cultures the world over—they are now on the point of collapse—through a synthesis of values with urban civilisation. Large-scale centralisation of public activities might, in those circumstances, be discarded in favour of federations of various rallying points, such as the communities of the *mir* in Tsarist Russia, the *zadruga* in medieval Serbia, the *ejido* in Mexico, or the *ayllu* in Indo-Peru, to mention but a few community forms taken at random from traditional agrarian societies, capable of serving as nuclei of such federations. The range of adaptations, variations and mutations of the federative principle would in those circumstances be almost limitless.

NOTES

1. The term "federative" is used here in preference to the more up-to-date "federal" because it is only recently that semantic distinctions have begun to be made between various types of associations in the legal and social sciences.

2. See above.

3. See J. Bodin, *Six Livres de la République*. Paris: Puys, 1576.

4. See S. Pufendorf, *Gründlicher Bericht von dem Zustande des Heiligen Reichs Teutscher Nation* (1667), Leipzig ed. 1715.

5. For further theoretical illumination on both of these, see *The Federalist Papers* composed by Alexander Hamilton, James Madison, and John Hay in the late 1780s, the most thorough discussion of the federative principle hitherto conducted.

6. On this point, see H. Valladão, *Démocratisation et Socialisation du droit international*. Paris: Sirey, 1962.

7. G. Benecke, *Society and Politics in Germany, 1500 - 1750* (London: Routledge and Kegan Paul, 1974) takes an unfashionably fair view of the confederalism of the Empire of that period, which was the forerunner of the German Confederation of 1815.

8. A clear distinction must at all times be made between the term "confederation" (denoting a loose association of political units) and that of "federation" (a tight, and—once formed—indissoluble one).

Saint-Simon, addressing himself to the parliaments of France and Britain in 1814, referred to thirteenth-century Europe as "a confederate society united through common institutions." The reference should, however, be seen against the feudal background of that Europe. See K. Taylor (ed.), *Henri Saint-Simon, 1760 - 1825*. London: Croom Helm, 1975, p. 131.

9. It is possible that the civil war waged between the federal troops of the North and the confederates of the South in the United States between 1861 and 1865 contributed towards the cooling of enthusiasm in the federal movement.

10. See A. J. R. Groom and P. Taylor (eds.), *Functionalism*. London: Hodder and Stoughton, 1975.

11. The reference here is to Montesquieu's *L'Esprit des lois*. Geneva: Vernet, 1748.

12. Henri de Saint-Simon, *De la Réorganisation de la Societé Européenne ou de la necessité et des moyens de rassembler les peuples de l'Europe en un seul corps politique en conversant a chacun son indépendance nationale* (October 1814). Translated in G. Ionescu (ed.), *The Political Thought of Saint-Simon*. London: Oxford University Press, 1976, pp. 83-98.

13. Charles Fourier (1772 - 1837), favoured the creation of *phalanstères*, comprehensive agrarian-industrial cooperatives on a voluntary basis. On this point, see V. Considérant, *Exposition du système de Fourier*. Paris: Librairie societaire, 1845.

14. V. Considérant, *De la politique générale et du rôle de la France en Europe*. Paris: Bureau de la Phalange, 1850.

15. See J. P. Mayer, *Alexis de Tocqueville*. Paris: Gallimard, 1948.

16. J. S. Mill, *Considerations on Representative Government*. London: Parker, 1845.

17. W. Godwin, *Enquiry concerning Political Justice and its Influence on Morals and Happiness*. London: Robinson, 1798, 2 vols., pp. 191-195.

18. On this point, see F. Fadner, *Seventy Years of Pan-Slavism in Russia*. Washington: Georgetown University Press, 1962; M. A. Bakounine, *Gosudarstvennost i anarkhiya*. Leiden: International Institute of Social History, 1967; B. P. Hepner, *Bakounine et le panslavisme révolutionnaire*. Paris: Riviere, 1950; and E. H. Carr, *Michael Bakunin*. London: Macmillan, 1937.

Russia was not officially represented at the 1848 congress. After the Second World War the idea of East European federation could be turned against Russia. Witness the meeting between Tito and Dimitrov at Bled in 1947. See also H.J. Hoppe, "Georgi Dimitrow wieder aktuell," *Osteuropa* (February 1974), pp. 127-137.

19. See Proudhon's *L'Idée générale de la révolution au XIXe siècle.* Paris: Garnier frères, 1851. Proudhon uses the terms "federatif" and "confederal," and "convention" and "contract" without legal precision, relying on the element of spontaneous association to qualify those terms. In his contracts, federalism emerges as being based on voluntary not on mandatory authority, however close the ties created by the contracting parties.

20. Proudhon, *Du principe fédératif.* Paris: Dentu, 1863, p. 73.

21. This idea was no doubt inspired by Fourier's movement for the establishment of public workshops in France.

22. This idea found expression in Proudhon's *De la justice dans la Révolution et dans l'Eglise.* Paris: Garnier frères, 1858.

23. Henri Dunant's Red Cross idea was similarly conceived in the light of the carnage perpetrated on the battlefield of Solferino in 1859.

24. Proudhon objected to the German Confederation of 1815 on account of its princely character.

25. On Proudhon's European schemes, see, for example, M. Amoudruz, *Proudhon et l'Europe.* Paris: Montchrestien, 1945.

26. To make the Yugoslav system work, there is an elaborate network of "basic associations of associated labour," as each self-managing unit is called, in some ways reminiscent of Fourierist and Proudhonist notions.

27. See P. A. Kropotkin, *Mutual Aid.* Harmondsworth: Penguin, 1939; and *The State: Its Historic Role.* London: "Freedom" Office, 1898.

28. Political science in most continental countries has until recently formed part and parcel of the academic training of lawyers.

Both the International Law Association (original name: The Association for the Reform and Codification of the Law of Nations) and the Institut de droit international, were founded in 1873. On the former, see M. Bos (ed.), *The Present State of International Law and Other Essays: Centenary Publication of the International Law Association.* Kluwer: Deventer, 1973. On the latter, see Institut de droit international, *Livre du Centenaire 1873 - 1973.* Basle: Karger, 1973.

29. See, for instance, C. Frantz, *Der Föderalismus, als das leitende Prinzip für die soziale, staatliche und internationale Organisation.* Mainz: Kirchheim, 1879.

30. See A. Cook, *The Alabama Claims.* New York: Cornell University Press, 1976.

31. Blüntschli was teaching at Heidelberg University at the time. His paper, "Die Organisation des europäischen Staatsvereins," was published in the Swiss periodical *Die Gegenwart* (1878). For his "völkerrechtliche Briefe," see ibid., (1876). See also C. Frantz, op. cit.

32. Lord Davies' first major work was *The Problem of the Twentieth Century.* London: Benn, 1930. Jaeckh was eventually to emigrate to the United States.

33. See, for instance, D. Davies, *Nearing the Abyss.* London: Constable, 1936; *A Federated Europe.* London: Gollancz, 1940; and chapters on federalism in two of his subsequent books: *Facing the Future: Letters to John Citizen.* London: Staples, 1942, Ch. 5, pp. 39-47; and *The Seven Pillars of Peace.* London: Longmans, 1945, Ch. 9, pp. 113-125.

Discussion of the federative principle also went on in the two Institute periodicals, *The New Commonwealth Quarterly* and *Union.*

Attempts to rekindle interest in the federative principle were also made in the United States. See Clarence K. Streit, *Union Now: Proposal for a Federal Union of the Democracies of the North Atlantic*. London: Right Book Club, 1939.

34. Many leaders of nationalist movements in those territories were as eager as their retiring colonial masters in embracing the federal conception.

35. See Sir Ivor Jennings, *The Commonwealth in Asia*. Oxford: Clarendon Press, 1949, especially Ch. VII, pp. 82-108; *The Characteristics of the Indian Constitution*. Madras: Madras University Press, 1953; and *The British Commonwealth of Nations*. London: Hutchinson, 4th ed., 1961.

36. See *The Times*, July 11, 1972.

Chapter 10

THE CONFEDERATIVE PRINCIPLE:

FROM UTOPIA TO REALISM

As a means of associating sovereign states for purposes of preventing conflict among them, the idea of federation was no longer seen as feasible towards the end of the nineteenth century. However, tensions between states grew, rendering the need for détente more urgent than ever. In this way a stimulus was provided for exploring the potentialities of a system of compulsory arbitration, an idea which was to acquire some popularity after the successful outcome of the *Alabama* arbitration between Britain and the United States in 1872.[1] With the gradual realisation that such a system was impossible to enforce in the absence of a structure of international government tight enough to resemble an interstate federation, the search began for a less far-reaching solution embodying a type of international association less rigid than federalism, requiring merely the voluntary coordination of measures to prevent conflict. Such a type was ready at hand in the shape of the confederative principle.

Genesis of the League of Nations

The problem, though under discussion, was not being attacked with any real vigour until the outbreak of the First World War highlighted its extreme urgency in dramatic fashion. Britain provided the lead in thought along confederative lines, when the Fabian Society commissioned the novelist Leonard Woolf to compose a report which, as it happened, contained the germs of what was eventually to be the League of Nations idea, and which, it was hoped, could be submitted to ministers and civil servants as a blueprint for eventual use. When the report was ignored, it was published in 1915 under the short and challenging title, *International Government*. The British government and civil service eventually accepted these and similar proposals as the basis for talks on an international peace-keeping organisation after the war. The end-product of these endeavours was the League of Nations. It was G. Lowes Dickinson who probably coined the term "League of Nations;"[2] H. H. Brailsford, socialist writer and pamphleteer, was also instrumental.[3] A League of Nations Society was founded in 1915.

Early inspiration towards the creation of a distinctly confederal association had come from W. A. Phillips, later Professor of Modern History at the University of Dublin, whose work on *The Confederation of Europe: A Study of the European Alliance, 1813 - 1823 as an Experiment in the International Organisation of Peace* was published in London by Longmans in 1914.

The democratic Left in Britain was divided. On one side were to be found the unconditional pacifists, like Herbert Morrison, Ramsay Macdonald, and Fenner Brockway, who preferred imprisonment to giving support to the war; but on the other side was the bulk of its intellectuals who were in favour of the war provided that, in H. G. Wells' words, it was "a war to end war," which imposed a moral duty to work out detailed schemes for a lasting peace. When Lord Eversley suggested that such a war must be a drawn-out one and might not end where its proponents expected, Wells replied furiously that this was "pseudo-sage intellectual laziness" and "easy dread of prematurity."[4]

President Woodrow Wilson of the United States consciously relied for inspiration on the example of British writers and statesmen, and had frequent intimate exchanges with Britain's radicals.[5] His famous call for "peace without victory" symbolised the sort of settlement which he and his British associates had in mind for the future stability of world order.

As the end of the war drew near, the idea of a League began to assume concrete forms, and it was evident that it would be based on what were in essence radical political notions of currently prevailing Anglo-Saxon character. Chief among these was the idea of widely representative government, enthusiastically espoused by President Wilson, who considered that only democracies were capable of sustaining a viable peace organisation.[6]

The idea of widely representative government was to be buttressed by the force of public opinion. As one influential British writer was to put it: "When public opinion is properly instructed, and when the time is given for passions to cool, it is more likely to favour peace than do the secret operations of diplomacy,"[7] and his words were echoed by Lord Robert Cecil, one of the chief architects of the League, who informed the House of Commons in 1919 that public opinion was "the great weapon we rely upon . . . and if we are wrong about it, then the whole thing is wrong."[8] In 1923, C. K. Webster (later Sir Charles Webster) stated categorically on the occasion of his inaugural lecture that "diplomacy must cease to be secret, and international affairs must be discussed in open debate with the same frankness as domestic."[9] Such ideas closely resembled eighteenth-century optimism regarding the power of rationality in international relations. Thus, Sir Alfred Zimmern was able to maintain as late as 1936 that "the principal cause of our troubles is not moral but intellectual,"[10] while Sir Norman Angell was convinced that to prevent war all that was needed was an intelligent exposition to those in power that war did not pay.[11]

The League system would have to be supported by a system of sanctions for which the major powers would be primarily responsible. Already during the first decade of the century, notions of this kind had been entertained by T. J. Lawrence, Reader in International Law at the University of Bristol, who was thinking of the world powers as the nucleus of a concert of the world.[12] This is not the place for a detailed analysis of the soundness of the League in theory and practice in relation to its peacekeeping task. It is enough to show that an influential body of opinion was fast growing up in Britain, and to a lesser extent in the United States also, committed to the success of the confederative principle as exemplified in the institution of the League of Nations.

The Upholders of the League Idea

Once the war was over and the League safely launched on the basis of the confederative principle, an inquest was undertaken as to what had caused the war in the first place. A painstaking investigation of the German archives was conducted under Karl Kautsky's editorship, yielding a series of volumes of documents, *Die grosse Politik der europäischen Kabinette,* and was matched by equally determined attempts on the part of British historians.[13]

Though there were differences of opinion among the upholders of the League of Nations idea, the commitment to its success was broadly based in Britain, and rather less so in the United States. In the former, it covered a wide spectrum of political opinion, ranging from Lord Robert Cecil on the conservative Right to Konni Zilliacus,[14] head of the Information Section of the League, on the Left. It included the first two incumbents of the newly created Woodrow Wilson Chair of International Politics at the University College of Wales at Aberystwyth, the holder of the Sir Ernest Cassell Chair of International Relations (part-time) at the University of London at the London School of Economics, Philip Noël-Baker, and the occupant of the Montagu Burton Chair of International Relations (full-time) at the same place, C.A.W. Manning.[15]

The principal spokesman of the League and what it stood for was Arnold Toynbee, classical scholar of renown and director of the newly created British (later Royal) Institute of International Affairs,[16] who made his views known through the Institute's annual *Survey of International Affairs*. Prominent also in defence of the League was Lord David Davies, Liberal Member of Parliament, whose enthusiasm for the League was matched by a zeal for certain supplementary reforms of the League.[17]

The upholders of the League idea tended to connect the new system of international relations with political and cultural values cherished in the Anglo-Saxon world, though not all of them would have gone as far as Lord Davies, who "considered that there was no basic difference between the principles which should apply to the ordering of international relationships and those upon which rested the stable and civilised qualities of Western Europe and the United States."[18] Those who did consider that Anglo-Saxon values should underpin the League system could justifiably be regarded as what some of their critics came to call the "utopians."

Realism in the Ascendancy

Early criticism of the 1919 system was concentrated on single aspects. Thus, its economic side was subjected to a famous attack almost at once,[19] while voices were raised in favour of an early revision of some of the burdensome conditions imposed on Germany in particular. The very bases of the system, and the structure of the League which had been superimposed on them, in large part escaped weighty criticism until history itself was taking considerable liberties with both. Then, and only then, in the course of the deep crisis of the 1930s, was a movement of criticism building up. A ferocious attack on the "utopians" was eventually launched by E. H. Carr in 1939,[20] which sowed many of the seeds from which the "realists" subsequently planted an academic school of international relations in opposition to the "utopians" of old and, later, in opposition to the idealist approach to world politics taken in the diplomatic practice of the United States, especially in the years between 1941 and 1947, in which faith in the United Nations was running high.

In contrast to the utopian-idealist school, the realists tended to develop theories concerned with "understanding the world, not with changing it," as one commentator put it aptly in inverting a famous dictum by Karl Marx,[21] relying for their validity mainly on historical precedent in the field of state practice, rather than the opinions or doctrines pronounced by individual writers of the past, which tended to be largely, though not entirely, discounted.

The critical build-up in the 1930s was begun by Reinhold Niebuhr (1892 - 1971), erstwhile supporter of Wilsonian idealism, of German-United States background, who opposed the prevailing trend of idealism in his two seminal works, *Man and Immoral Society* (1932) and *An Interpretation of Christian Ethics* (1935). Feeling that in their social relations, men exhibit an egoistic passion so pronounced that it could be harmonised with the interests of society only by being neutralised, and by harnessing its energies in the service of society, Niebuhr was among the first to give the term "realism" a contextual meaning. To him, it was the intellectual readiness to take into account all factors which are incompatible with established norms as currently interpreted. Applying his realism, so defined, to the sphere of international relations, Niebuhr recognised the force of state interest, but was concerned that an exclusive preoccupation with it would lead to uncontrolled moral cynicism. To prevent this from happening, he pinned his hope on those whose loyalties transcended the state, and who would consequently exercise a moderating influence on the way in which state interest was conceived.[22]

Niebuhr's influence on the formation of realist thought is undoubted, reflected and acknowledged as it is in subsequent works by Carr, Schwarzenberger, and Morgenthau, though it ought to be recognised that the resounding triumph of realism owes most to the historical context within which it was shaping. The rhythm of publications with a realist slant after 1929 would bear this out.[23]

Though the ferocity of Carr's onslaught on the "utopian" upholders of the 1919 system is abated in his relatively moderate conclusions, and though, as the subtitle of his work—*An Introduction to the Study of International Relations*—suggests, it was frankly didactic in intention, he set about his task with iconoclastic gusto. It is true that Toynbee, hitherto a tower of strength of the utopian camp, but disgusted with the poor showing of the League of Nations over the Ethiopian crisis, had deserted the utopian fold in 1936, his desperately moral strictures of Mussolini of that year representing his swansong to utopia. However, Carr's attack was directed against utopian principles mainly, and only occasionally *ad homines*.

A regular member of the British diplomatic service until 1936, when he was appointed to the Woodrow Wilson Chair of International Politics at Cardiff, Carr's writings show the main influences on his mind to have been those of realism, as defined by Niebuhr, of positivism, as developed by Mannheim,[24] and of Marxism.[25] While the purely intellectual influences show most clearly in his analysis, the conventional wisdom he acquired during his diplomatic career is reflected mainly in his conclusions. It is, however, the former, and not the latter, that has caused intellectual ferment.

The 'Harmony of Interests'

Carr thought he could spot the weaknesses of the League of Nations best by focussing his critique on the ideology which underlay it. The gravamen of his strictures concerned the notion of the "harmony of interests" which, according to Carr, formed the backbone of utopianism and implied that under Allied management all would work out well eventually for all parties involved—victors as well as vanquished—and that therefore all states had an equal stake in the maintenance of peace.

Carr's analogy of the functions of the idea of the "harmony of interests" was culled from economic science. Suitable for a society of small producers of roughly equal power, it was out of tune when applied to the realities of large-scale capitalist enterprise. In the latter, the idea of the "harmony of interests" served to protect the favoured position of the powerful, thus ensuring the sanctification of the status quo. On the plane of international relations, Carr insisted, prevailing theories of morality reflected the interest of dominant states, or dominant groups of states. It was profoundly misleading, therefore, to represent the struggle between "satisfied" and "dissatisfied" powers after 1919 as one between morality and power.

"Utopia" was defined by Carr as the product of aspiration, not of analysis. Conceding that the desire to prevent war was legitimate, he warned that, if strong enough, such desires could get the better of the intellect, leading to a diminished sense of appreciation of reality. Referring to the ideologists of the peace settlements of 1919, Carr remarked that in those circumstances thoughtful criticism capable of shaking the original assumptions of its upholders was resented.

However, Carr's most scathing attack was reserved for "social Darwinism," which, he claimed, was inherent in the notion of the "harmony of interests" as applied by the utopians to the settlements of 1919, since it assumed an identification of the whole with the good of the fittest. The only difference between Hitler, most determined challenger of the international order of 1919, and its upholders was that the former's criterion of fitness was physical, whereas the latter's was moral. The results were identical.

As for the League of Nations, Carr's main thrust of criticism of the "metaphysicians of Geneva" was directed against their twin beliefs that public opinion was the voice of reason, and that it was bound to prevail. In agreement with some thinkers on international relations during the age of Enlightenment, he was suspicious of the outwardly attractive idea of world government on the ground that it could lead to tyranny. He did not believe that peaceful change could be brought about either through the political organs of the League of Nations or by way of judicial interpretation by the Permanent Court of International Justice at The Hague, and attacked those who claimed that the perpetual improvement and perfection of international institutions opened a safe way to peace.

Having delivered himself of his attacks, Carr suggested that the proper antidote, though not a clear-cut alternative to utopianism of the kind criticised by him, was realism. Leaning on Niebuhr's definition, Carr saw realism as consisting in (a) the acceptance of facts, and (b) the analysis of their causes and consequences, sounding a warning, for good measure, against the pitfalls of determinism based on existing facts.

In spite of the sharpness of his attack, Carr must be regarded as a moderate critic of the upholders of the 1919 settlement. He had perhaps the two parts he had played in his life in mind when he made the observation that, as intellectuals tended to be drawn to utopia, bureaucrats were suspicious of it. In relation to the utopians of 1919 Carr adopted the stance of revisionist, rather than revolutionist, since he showed no intentions of overturning their basic assumptions altogether. His intention was therapeutic, not—as would seem at first glance—destructive. As he explained, international morality was an amalgam of both expediency and ethics. To yield good results, the diplomatic conduct of international relations had therefore to be based on reasonableness, a halfway-house between utopia and realism. He would not commit himself beyond this perspective by laying down the standards by which such reasonableness could be assessed. To prove his point, he invoked Hitler's foreign policy. What was wrong with it was not that it was inimical to the peace settlements of 1919, but merely that the Nazis were pushing their opposition to unreasonable lengths. Carr was a supporter of the Munich agreement of 1938.

Carr's objectivity, if only revealed implicitly in respect of universal values, is marked. Though still acquiescing in the existence of the colonial system, he showed an open mind towards the values of Marxism-Leninism as proclaimed in the Soviet Union at the time, and was to dedicate the best part of his later years to the disinterested study of the history of the Soviet Union.[26] This would preclude any presumption that an Anglo-centric outlook may be attributed to the term "reasonableness" as used by him in the present context.

Though on the surface no more than a powerful historical-sociological critique of the international system created in 1919, Carr's *Twenty Years Crisis* carried definite theoretical implications. It became a manual for all self-styled realists, was swiftly accepted as a text, and has never since been ignored.

High Realism

Less polemical both in tone and intent, and attempting a comprehensive analysis of the nature and functions of international society, G. Schwarzenberger's *Power Politics* of 1941[27] was subtitled *An Introduction to the Study of International Relations and Post-War Planning* and explicitly theoretical. The subtitle was changed in the 1951 edition to *A Study of International Society* and in 1964 to *A Study of World Society,* reflecting the author's altering emphasis.

As research secretary in Lord Davies' New Commonwealth Institute, founded in 1934, and in that capacity instructed to devise ways and means by which an international equity tribunal and an international police force could be added to the League of Nations by way of supplementary reform, Schwarzenberger found himself compelled in the discharge of this duty to undertake a systematic reassessment not only of the structure of the League but also of the basic premises on which it rested. Concluding ultimately that neither an equity tribunal nor a police force could be made to function effectively within a confederal structure like that of the League, he was led to expand his findings into a regular treatise on international relations. Benefiting from insights already provided by Niebuhr and Carr, Schwarzenberger maintained that power was the crucial element in international relations, that its ingredients were many, and that those wielding power in international society preferred normally to achieve their ends by posing the threat of effective sanctions, without the actual use of physical power.

Beyond that, Schwarzenberger's contribution to existing thought on international relations was threefold. In the first place, he introduced the basic sociological distinction between "community" and "society" into the prevailing typology of associations. Originally impressed by Pufendorf's critique of the confederal structure of the Holy Roman Empire,[28] he found a ready-made formula in F. Toennies' dichotomy of *Gemeinshaft* and *Gesellschaft* to guide him.[29] Thus armed, Schwarzenberger embarked on a fully consistent critique of the confederal principle, his main point being that confederal structures tend to provide contraptions within which international relations continue to be conducted on the customary basis of "power politics." Confederalism generated the typical phenomenon of "power politics in disguise," as he called it. The import of the basic taxonomical distinction of "community" and "society" into the field of international relations was of lasting value, as it enabled thinkers to visualise the organisation of international society on various levels of political integration. In the second place, he noted Karl Marx's observation of a trend towards progressive centralisation in the world economy and applied it to international society. Herbert Spencer had developed a similar idea, arguing that while the increasing size of societies made for larger wars, the reduced number of independent units made for the occasioning of fewer ones.[30]

Finally, in affinity with typologies created by Max Weber, the German sociologist whose thought had made a deep impression on him, Schwarzen-

berger made sets of political patterns in international relations available for
selection to practitioners in the field in such a way that each pattern was
logically related to a corresponding level of international integration. In this
way he tried to show that ultimately it was possible for politicians and
statesmen to get round the acerbities of power politics. Claiming by this
token that power politics was not unavoidable in international relations, he
preferred to be described as "relativist" rather than "realist" in his approach
towards that subject.[31]

The palm of being the purest as well as the most self-conscious apostle of
realism must surely go to H. J. Morgenthau, whose *Politics among Nations*
was first published in 1948.[32] Benefiting from Schwarzenberger's work,[33]
and expressly disclaiming any intention of fashioning a formal theory of
international relations, Morgenthau, to a much higher degree than either Carr
or Schwarzenberger, shared Niebuhr's sceptical view of human nature, to
which he ascribed "bio-psychological drives by which . . . society is created."[34] There was a corresponding striving for power which characterised all
politics. These were radical assumptions to make, and only marginally softened by his qualification that the "revolt against power is as universal as the
aspiration for power itself"—a reservation made in distinctly low key.[35]

International politics, according to Morgenthau, was a function of interest,
defined in terms of power.[36] There was no essential difference between
domestic and international relations, since the attainment of power on either
level was the immediate objective, whatever the long-term goals might be.[37]
The bulk of power in international society resided in its members, the states,
and the drive towards further power in that social context had therefore to
express itself through the states on an interstate basis. Morgenthau's heavy
emphasis on the concept of interest evokes Edmund Burke's injunction to
states "not to sit like judges, to act with perfect impartiality, to the exclusion
of all ideas of self. Their first duty was to take care of themselves."[38]

As regards the function of international institutions, Morgenthau was
sceptical as to their effectiveness in the field of collective security, judicial
settlement or peaceful change. Moral principles he conceded to be existing in
international relations, but felt they must be circumscribed by the limits
drawn by reality. As to the future, Morgenthau distinguished between the
two states of "peace" and "permanent" peace, in the manner of Kant. The
former is attainable through diplomatic accommodation[39] springing from
prudence, which he defines as "the weighing of the consequences of alternative political actions." Prudence is "the supreme virtue in politics"[40] and
its exercise in international politics requires a high grade of statesmanship
applied in a spirit of moderation.[41] Morgenthau placed little hope in the
ability of devices like the "balance of power," international law or the force
of world opinion to maintain peace. "Permanent peace," he held in a

somewhat circular argument—is dependent on the creation of a world state[42] which, however, had to be preceded by the development of a world community,[43] which, according to him, could only result from a prolonged period of diplomatic accommodation.

The directness of Morgenthau's arguments, and the outspokenness of his views, as well as the crispness of his style, account for much of his success. However, this success, which was both instant and striking, requires a historical gloss to be fully appreciated. Three closely connected factors were responsible for it: (a) a sudden and profound aversion towards the idealism reflected in the Wilson-Roosevelt approach to international politics; (b) the outbreak of the "Cold War"; and (c) the new status of the United States as the strongest power in the world. Morgenthau's severe realism suited the prevailing mood in the United States for at least a decade and a half, and was reflected in a stream of publications in the realist mould on the subject of international relations.[44] However, before too long, and while still in its prime, the realist interpretation of international relations was to find a set of critics of an entirely new type.

NOTES

1. See A. Cook, *The Alabama Claims*. New York: Cornell University Press, 1975; and J. B. Scott, *The Hague Conventions and Declarations of 1899 and 1907*. Baltimore: Johns Hopkins, 1909.

2. See L. W. Martin, *Peace without Victory: Woodrow Wilson and the British Radicals*. London: Kennikat, 1958, p. 62.

3. H. N. Brailsford, *The War of Steel and Gold: A Study of the Armed Peace*. London: Bell, 1914. For a German contribution, see W. Schücking, "Die Organisation der Welt," in P. Laband, *Staatsrechtliche Abhandlungen*. Leipzig: 1908, Vol. 1.

4. L. W. Martin, op. cit., p. 50.

5. See L. W. Martin, op. cit., pp. 13 and 129.

6. See Gilbert Murray, *The League of Nations and the Democratic Idea*. London: Oxford University Press, 1918; and A. Wolfers and L. W. Martin (eds.), *The Anglo-American Tradition in Foreign Affairs*. New Haven, Conn.: Yale University Press, 1956, pp. 275-279.

7. J. Bryce, *Proposals for the Prevention of Future Wars*. London: Allen and Unwin, 1917, p. 4.

8. House of Commons, *Parliamentary Debates*, O.R., 21 July, 1919, p. 992.

9. C. K. Webster, *The Study of International Politics: Inaugural*. Cardiff: The University of Wales Press Board, 1923, p. 25.

10. Sir Alfred Zimmern, "The problem of collective security," in Qu. Wright (ed.), *Neutrality and Collective Security*. Chicago: University of Chicago Press, 1936, pp. 3-29. See also by the same author, *Learning and Leadership*. London: Oxford University Press, 1928.

11. Sir Norman Angell, *The Great Illusion*. London: Heinemann, 1910.

12. See C. Holbraad, *The Concert of Europe*. London: Longmans, 1970, pp. 190-191.

13. See G. P. Gooch and H. W. Temperley, *British Documents on the Origins of the War, 1898 - 1914*. London: H.M.S.O., 1928; and G. P. Gooch, *History of Modern Europe, 1878 - 1919*. London: Cassell, 1923.

14. See K. Zilliacus, "The nature of working of the League of Nations," in Geneva Institute of International Relations, *Problems of Peace*. London: Oxford University Press, 1929, pp. 1-18.

15. See Sir Alfred Zimmern, *Capitalism and International Relations*. Oxford: Ruskin College, 1917; and *The Study of International Relations*. Oxford: Clarendon Press, 1931.

On Sir Charles Webster's "burning zeal for the League," see S. T. Bindoff and G. N. Clark, "Charles Kingsley Webster, 1886 - 1961," in British Academy, *Proceedings*. London: Oxford University Press, 1962, Vol. 2, p. 434.

16. A. J. Toynbee, *The World after the Peace Conference: Being an Epilogue to the History of the Peace Conference of Paris (ed. by H. W. Temperley), and a Prologue to the 'Survey of International Affairs'*. London: Royal Institute of International Affairs, 1925.

17. On these points, see also B. Porter (ed.), *The Aberystwyth Papers: International Politics 1919 - 1969*. London: Oxford University Press, 1972. See also L. W. Martin, *Peace without Victory: Woodrow Wilson and the British Liberals*. New Haven, Conn.: Yale University Press, 1958.

18. B. Porter (ed.), op. cit., p. 88.

19. J. M. Keynes, *The Economic Consequences of the Peace*. London: Macmillan, 1919.

20. E. H. Carr, *The Twenty Years Crisis 1919 - 1939: An Introduction to the Study of International Relations*. London: Macmillan, 1939.

21. J. Frankel, *Contemporary International Relations Theory and the Behaviour of States*. London: Oxford University Press, 1973, p. 22.

22. See C. W. Kegley and R. W. Bretall (eds.), *Reinhold Niebuhr*. New York: Macmillan, 1956.

23. R. L. Buell, *International Relations*. New York: Holt, 1929; R. B. Mowat, *The European States System: A Study of International Relations*. London: Oxford University Press, 1929; F. H. Simonds and B. Emery, *The Great Powers in World Politics*. New York: American Book, 1935; and F. L. Schuman, *International Politics*. New York: McGraw-Hill, 1933.

24. K. Mannheim's *Ideology and Utopia,* first published in German in 1929, had its first English language edition in 1936.

25. During one stage in his diplomatic career Carr was stationed in Riga (Latvia), an excellent post of observation of the Soviet Union.

26. See E. H. Carr, *A History of Soviet Russia* (several volumes). London: Macmillan, 1950–.

27. G. Schwarzenberger, *Power Politics*. London: Cape, 1941. The 1951 and 1964 editions were produced in London by Stevens.

28. S. Pufendorf, *Gruendlicher Bericht von dem Zustande des Heiligen Reichs teutscher Nation*. Leipzig: 1667.

29. F. Toennies, *Gemeinschaft und Gesellschaft* (originally published in Leipzig in 1887; Republished Berlin: Curtius, 1926).

The taxonomical distinction of "community" and "society" had been made earlier by Sir Henry Maine in his treatise on primitive law based on observations made in the East, and also by the Dutchman, C. van Vollenhoven, in the course of his research work on Indonesian society and law. See Sir Henry Maine, *Village Communities in the East and West.* London: Murray, 1871; and C. van Vollenhoven, *De Drie treden van het volkenrecht.* Gravenhage: Nijhoff, 1918.

30. H. Spencer, *Man versus the State.* London: Williams and Norgate, 1885, p. 45.

31. Subsequent editions of *Power Politics* comprised a comparative analysis of the League of Nations and the United Nations.

32. H. J. Morgenthau, *Politics among Nations.* New York: Alfred A. Knopf, 1948.

33. See his warm review of *Power Politics* in 36 *American Journal of International Law* (1942), pp. 351-352.

34. See p. 34 of the 1973 edition, which I have used for present purposes.

35. Ibid., p. 225.

36. Ibid., p. 5.

37. Ibid., p. 27.

38. *Parliamentary History,* Vol. 30, p. 433, as cited in A. Wolfers and L. W. Martin (eds.), *The Anglo-American Tradition in Foreign Affairs.* New Haven, Conn.: Yale University Press, 1956, p. 112.

39. Morgenthau, op. cit., Chs. 31 and 32.

40. Ibid., p. 11.

41. Edmund Burke remarked of the "rules and definitions of prudence" that they "can rarely be exact, never universal." See *A Regicide Peace,* Vol. 5, pp. 241-243, as quoted in A. Wolfers and L. W. Martin (eds.), op. cit., p. 117.

42. Morgenthau, op. cit., p. 549.

43. Ibid., p. 497.

44. Examples of this kind of literature are as following: W. Friedmann, *An Introduction to World Politics.* London: Macmillan, 1952; T. Kalijarvi and associates, *Modern World Politics.* New York: Thomas Y. Crowell, 1953; F. L. Schuman, *International Politics.* London: McGraw-Hill, 1953, 2nd ed.; R. Strausz-Hupé and S. T. Possony, *International Relations.* New York: McGraw-Hill, 1954; C. P. Schleicher, *Introduction to International Relations.* New York: Bailey & Swinfen, 1954; N. J. Padelford and G. A. Lincoln, *International Politics.* New York: Macmillan, 1954; M. Ball and H. B. Killough, *International Relations.* London: Stevens, 1956; C. I. Lerche, *Principles of International Politics.* New York: Oxford University Press, 1956; and V. van Dyke, *International Politics.* New York: Appleton-Century-Crofts, 1957.

Raymond Aron's *Peace and War: A Theory of International Relations*—first published in its original French text by Calmann-Lévy in Paris in 1962, and in an English translation by Doubleday in New York in 1966—while grand in format and impressive in structure, basically constitutes a commentary in which a realist philosophy is implicit.

Chapter 11

REVOLUTIONISM:

WORLD STATE AND WORLD REVOLUTION

Previous chapters have examined propositions made by various writers towards the reform of the system of international relations. This chapter will deal with those authors who considered the international system to be workable only after a thorough transformation, brought about by revolutionary means. The category of writers adopting this attitude has been called "revolutionist,"[1] and though it contains anarchist writers, the main contributors have been Marxists.[2]

A Marxist Theory of World Revolution

Classical Marxism held that, viewed in historical perspective, world society tended towards integration on an increasingly large scale—an assumption derived from Marxist analyses of the capitalist system, as well as from Jacobin centralism inherited from the French Revolution. Given its basic premises, classical Marxist reasoning could not be faulted on logical grounds: capitalism was cosmopolitan in character, as was the bourgeoisie, its progenitor; and so was the proletariat, its victim. Capitalism knew no frontier: the globe itself was its sphere of activity.

Originally, Engels had deduced from a comparative analysis of the English Revolution of the seventeenth and the French Revolution of the eighteenth century that a bourgeois stage was inescapable in the revolutionary process, and a necessary prerequisite, in conditions of preindustrial economic development, for proceeding to the next and final stage of revolution—proletarian revolution in conditions of advanced industrialisation. From 1844 onwards, in conditions of rudimentary industrialisation as then prevailing in Germany, Marx was questioning the practicability of isolating the bourgeois stage of revolution. The revolutionary impulse once given, the increasingly numerous proletariat would be drawn into the revolutionary process immediately. The revolution could not stop halfway, but had to run its full course, and to that extent it would be "permanent."[3] At no point did either Marx or Engels doubt the universal character of the revolutionary process.[4] Lack of a clear-cut Marxian pronouncement was thereafter to give rise to major inter-Marxist polemics concerning the relative evenness or unevenness of the actual geographical incident of revolution on a world scale.

"Socialism in One Country"

In 1847 Engels was still able to write: "Can the proletarian revolution take place in one country? The answer is no. . . . The Communist revolution therefore will not be merely national but will take place simultaneously in all civilised countries."[5] Given its premises, this was a logical enough deduction to make. However, the vision of a neatly homogeneous capitalist system expanding without pause on a world scale came to be increasingly questioned as the century wore on. Modifying their original model accordingly, Marxists were more and more prepared to concede that revolution might, within individual countries, occur piecemeal. As Engels was to write to Kautsky in Vienna on 12 September, 1882: "Once Europe is reorganised, and North America, that will furnish such colossal power and such an example that the semi-civilised countries will of themselves follow in their wake; economic needs, if anything, will see to that. But as to what social and political phases these countries will then have to pass through before they likewise arrive at socialist organisation, I think we today can advance only rather idle hypotheses."[6] However, at one time during the early 1870s Engels was convinced that Russia was on the eve of a revolution.[7]

The new version raised new problems. If revolution happened in one or a few countries only, would it be able to maintain itself within a system of capitalism which was, by definition, worldwide? Marx seemed to think not.[8] On the national as well as the international level, it seemed to him, revolution had to be permanent in order to be successful. It was a German Marxist, Georg von Vollmar, who in 1879 raised the prospect of the "uneven development" of capitalism giving rise to the phenomenon of "the isolated Socialist State."[9] No conclusion seems to have been drawn from this discovery until the problem raised itself in practice in a dramatic manner in 1917.

Neither Marx nor Engels had ever believed in the construction of ready-made utopias, resting content with advocating the application of the philosophy of dialectical materialism to any one historical situation. When the Bolsheviks seized power in 1917, therefore, they were unable to fall back on any specific systems theory of international relations to assist them in finding their bearings in a turbulent international situation. This was the time to regret their previous immediate preoccupation with the nature of relations between capitalist states in the age of imperialism, and their remarkable failure to theorise about international relations between (a) capitalist and Socialist countries, and (b) among Socialist countries.

The Bolshevik Revolution had given rise to hopes of a revolution at least on a European scale,[10] but these were dimmed when the Red Army was defeated in front of Warsaw in 1920, and were given up for the time being when an attempted Communist rising in Germany failed in October 1923. The intervening five years were to stimulate extended debates as to what would happen to the Russian Revolution if similar revolutions were to occur in the rest of Europe.

Predisposed to regard Communist revolution as an essentially international movement, the Bolsheviks were inclined to have no connection with any kind of particularism.[11] Believing that the nation-state had had its day, they continued to place great emphasis on the interdependence of the world's economies. The revolution could not be confined to one country, as its repercussions would be felt throughout the capitalist system. The implication was that, having broken out in one country, the revolution would have to be a permanent one until such time as the entire capitalist system had been revolutionised on a world scale. This was not a matter of choice but a question of survival. A revolutionary government existing in isolation would be as little able or willing to prevent this as—in conditions of early industrialisation—the bourgeoisie could have restrained the proletariat from carrying the revolutionary process to its logical conclusion. The concept of "permanent revolution" represented an extension from the domestic to the international dimension of the concept of continuous revolution.

When the test came in 1917, Trotsky, imbued with Eurocentric notions of progress which can be traced back to Saint-Simon, was convinced that the revolution would perish in backward Russia unless aided by fellow-revolutionary states in the industrialised West. To him revolution in the West was a necessity, not just a pious hope. Preobrazhensky, similarly, thought there was no way out for Soviet Russia but world revolution. It is not quite clear whether Trotsky was thinking in terms of mere physical survival, attended by an inability to carry out the political mission of the revolution or whether he considered the revolutionary government itself to be doomed.[12]

Bukharin's ideas on the subject were more concrete, since he regarded world revolution (in fact: revolution in industrialised Western Europe, for a start) as the source of "reinforcements" for the beleaguered Soviet economy. "The victory of the Western proletariat will make it possible to heal in a planned way the economic wounds of Russia with highly developed West European technologies [tekhniki]. The economic backwardness of Russia will be offset by the high technical level of Europe."[13] Eight years later he was more optimistic, maintaining that far from being disrupted by its own contradictions, the Soviet Union could survive in isolation, having to fear only a combined imperialist assault which would not provoke spontaneous risings in support of the Soviet Union in other countries.[14]

It is only by comprehending the extent of revolutionary expectations cherished by the Bolsheviks between 1917 and 1923 that any sense can be attributed to Trotsky's remark on being appointed the first People's Commisar for Foreign Affairs in 1917 according to which he would "publish a few revolutionary proclamations and then close shop." In 1919, with short-lived Soviet régimes in power in Hungary and Bavaria, his optimism knew no bounds: "Today Moscow is the centre of the Third International. Tomorrow ... the centre will shift westward, to Berlin, Paris, London."[15] It was only after 1923 that, disappointed in his expectations in Western Europe, he began—very much as a second best—to look for fresh revolutionary opportunities in the East. The theory of the permanent revolution nonetheless stayed with him until the end of his life.

Lenin, while sharing Trotsky's views on this subject to some extent, preserved a pragmatic independence. The supreme pragmatist, however, turned out to be Stalin who, in the autumn of 1924 and following the revolutionary failure in Western Europe, formulated his theory of "socialism in one country" within the context of a general debate on the merits of intensive industrialisation of the Soviet economy.[16] At the same time Stalin began to cite the half-forgotten Georg Vollmar on the subject of the "isolated Socialist state" and to invoke Lenin's law of the unevenness of capitalist development (also first expounded by Vollmar) in order to infer, with apparently sound logic, a corresponding law of uneven revolution. Stalin said: "All we Marxists, beginning with Marx and Engels, maintained the view that the victory of socialism in one country was impossible; and that in order for socialism to win, simultaneous revolutions were necessary in a series of countries, at least in the more developed, civilised ones," adding for good measure that "the difference between Lenin and Engels" was the "difference between two historical periods."

Stalin now set forth a different message: it was possible for the Soviet economy to be self-sufficient and consequently for the Soviet revolution to survive on its own. To give theoretical support to this notion, he developed the concept of the "two world economies," capitalist and Socialist, which carried the distinct implication that the latter was capable, in however isolated a condition, of surviving. This thesis he defended until his death in 1953. Yet, in so far as the emphasis of the class struggle would have to be transferred from the intragroup to the interstate plane, Stalin's thesis raised anew the old unresolved problem of the levels of analysis. The concept of "proletarian internationalism," originally meaning international Socialist solidarity, was now being redefined to mean the "unreserved, unhesitating and unconditional" defence of the Soviet Union, the basis of the world revolutionary movement. The tables had been neatly turned on Trotsky: the world revolution depended on the survival of the Soviet Union—not the other way round. Stalin's world revolution depended above all on the successful self-assertion of the Soviet Union in an international environment of power politics. Trotsky was quick—some would say overquick—in denouncing this idea as "petit-bourgeois."

The problem of the levels of analysis had been solved: the interstate dimension of world revolution was to be dominant. Soviet power politics—not necessarily intrinsically aggressive—rather than social revolution was to be the prime factor of world revolutionary progress for the time being. Implicit in this notion was the idea that the world strategic balance might shift eventually in favour of the Soviet Union, as was indeed forecast by Lenin who had envisaged the "transformation of the dictatorship [of the proletariat] from a national ... into an international one ... in at least several advanced countries capable of exerting decisive influence on world politics."[17]

The "Transitory" Period

So long as the Bolshevik régime was able to maintain itself, the world was on the move from capitalism towards communism, in theory at least—for it was never denied that a combined world capitalist onslaught was capable of destroying that régime. Soviet leaders never ceased being acutely aware of this historical perspective, and it was in this context that the concept of the "transitory period" acquired great theoretical significance in Bolshevik thought on international relations.

Lenin himself was the first to coin the term "transitory period."[18] Subsequently a number of leading Bolsheviks wrote books on the subject: Trotsky discussed the cultural aspects while Preobrazhensky and Bukharin explored its economic sides.[19] The closest any Bolshevik writer got to developing a comprehensive academic theory of international relations was E. V. Korovin, who examined the "transitory period" in the light of postrevolutionary international law.[20]

Korovin was an international lawyer who had completed his academic training under the Tsarist régime, lending his support to the Bolshevik government from the start. However, his work inevitably reflects the presence of contemporary and considerable pressures of external circumstances, which somewhat detracts from the pure academic quality that his work might have had if attempted solely in the abstract before the Revolution. In the circumstances, Korovin could not help being somewhat inhibited in the expression of his views by the practical diplomatic requirements of the Soviet Union.

The part of Korovin's work dealing with the substance of international law of the "transitory period"—namely the principles of law governing relations between Communist and capitalist states—forms the core of his work. Its main points can be summed up as follows: (a) as a system, international law is "pluralistic" and not universal in scope, being composed of several interlocking circles of states on a geopolitical basis. These are: inter-Communist; Communist-capitalist; inter-American; and capitalist-colonial; (b) as regards the crucial relationship between Communist and capitalist states, this must be constructed, from its inception, through highly formalised consensual engagements of a mutually binding character; and (c) the body of international customary law, built up between states over the centuries—while no doubt continuing to be valid in governing the relations between non-Communist states—must, as a basis of international law, be repudiated root and branch by Communist states.

Stripped of its ideological overtones, Korovin's view of international law was a reaffirmation of the classical doctrine of sovereignty which would not lightly presume departures from it except on the basis of strictly formal engagements ad hoc. It reflected the isolation of the Soviet Union in an international environment patently hostile, and could be construed as implying the existence of conditions of siege during the "transitory period." As such it did not go unchallenged within the Soviet Union, whose leadership was making strenuous efforts at the time to come to terms with capitalist countries. Notions smacking of "permanent revolution," such as those implicit in Korovin's international law of the "transitory period," were not helpful in those circumstances. As the theory of "socialism in one country" came to be more widely shared as the prevailing norm, legal counsel in the People's Commissariat of Foreign Affairs began to take exception to a model of international law supposed to govern relations between capitalist and Communist states which, if acted upon, would render the isolation of the Soviet Union virtually certain.[21] The principal objection here was to Korovin's uncompromising rejection of the principles of international customary law, the very basis of traditional international law, to which non-Communist states were firmly committed.

Here was a difference of opinion between pure theorist and pure pragmatist, or at least between on the one hand a scheme of international law of the "transitory period" elaborated within the wider theory of "permanent revolution," and on the other, one dictated by the necessities of "socialism in one country" under conditions of prolonged capitalist encirclement of the "isolated Socialist state" first mentioned by Vollmar in 1879.

Though for many years a wide range of approaches within the subject of international law was tolerated, the scholar who was to gain official Soviet favour in the theory of international law in the mid-1920s was E. B. Pashukanis,[22] whose model of "commodity-exchange" dominated Marxist jurisprudence in the Soviet Union, and certainly Soviet teaching in international law until 1935.[23] It is certain that after that date exigencies of Soviet diplomatic practice totally determined the character of prevailing theories of international law.

Revolutionist Theories of War

On November 19, 1792 the French National Convention had made a solid promise to come to the aid of all peoples "who are seeking to recover their liberty," an idea which in the practice of Revolutionary France was interpreted as, *in extremis,* involving the opening of hostilities against oppressor countries. Clearly, wars waged on those grounds were regarded by France's revolutionary government as just. The rationale underlying French policy on this point was the notion of the indivisibility of world revolution—French eighteenth-century style[24]—and might be regarded as being akin to the theory of "permanent revolution" championed by certain Bolshevik leaders after 1917.

The French Revolution exerted a powerful influence on Bolshevik thinking on the subject of the justice or injustice of war, and Lenin attempted a classification of interstate conflicts with the object of constructing an operationally useful theory of war.[25] In reviewing the history of war in recent times, he encountered certain difficulties since Tsarism had stood "side by side with civilised, comparatively democratic countries . . . in Europe between 1815 and 1905." In its theories of imperialism, neo-Marxism had worked out a plausible thesis of the inevitability of war between capitalist states.[26] Between 1915 and 1916, Lenin broached the entirely new subject of the nature of war between capitalist and Socialist states. When the Revolution came in Russia, the Bolsheviks—still without a theory of war between capitalist and Communist countries—tried to end the war, and in their famous decree "On peace" of November 8, 1917, committed themselves to the general view that declared aggressive war was "the greatest crime against mankind." When the German armies, with whom the Russian armies were in direct contact, refused to respond to their call, Bukharin put forward the notion of a "revolutionary war," which differed profoundly from Lenin's stratagem of the previous two years, which had postulated the transformation of the imperialist into a revolutionary war. What Lenin had in mind was a state of general confusion capable of being turned into a revolutionary situation, rather than war between a formerly capitalist state turned Socialist and its capitalist opponent facing it across the frontline. Unlike Bukharin, Lenin had no illusions as to the ability of the Bolsheviks to subvert the victorious German imperial forces by engendering a revolutionary spirit among them. Lenin's views ultimately prevailed over Bukharin's, leading to the conclusion of the Peace Treaty of Brest-Litovsk with imperial Germany in March 1918.

As the Bolsheviks were to discover before long, the matter of determining the question of the justice or injustice of war was no less difficult in post-revolutionary conditions than it had been during the nineteenth century. For, while it was axiomatic that any defensive war waged by Communist states was always just, the same could not necessarily be said of wars undertaken by the Soviet Union coming to the aid of other Communist states or simply for the purpose of spreading Communist revolution. It was only towards the end of 1924—and with the advent of the theory of socialism in one country—that official Soviet opinion settled down to the view that only defensive wars qualified as just ones. In the meantime, a bewildering variety of views was being expressed, with Lenin maintaining that any war in which a Communist state was involved was just, regardless of how such a war had begun. It was "not the defensive or offensive character of war, but the interests of the international proletarian movement" which, according to him, determined the matter.

Lenin's view was broad enough to accommodate a theory of Communist offensive war suited to conditions prevailing in Eastern Europe after the collapse of imperial Germany, which had left a gaping power vacuum on the Western flank of Soviet Russia. At this stage the political notions of permanent revolution began to mingle with concepts of Napoleonic offensive strategy acquired by certain high-ranking Red Army officers at Tsarist military academies. Chief among these officers was M. N. Tukhachevsky who also envisaged the creation of an international general staff to conduct the military aspects of world revolution.[27] His views were shared by Bukharin and Preobrazhensky,[28] who—harking back to the Jacobin phase of the French Revolution—considered that Communist states had a basic right to grant armed assistance to those Communist forces who, in the course of seizing power, had not yet obtained control of the bourgeoisie.[29] Preobrazhensky was most outspoken of all in envisaging "an aggressive Socialist war, launched by Russia against the capitalist West with the support of the European proletariat"[30] in the event of the revolution failing in the materially advanced states. Trotsky, progenitor of the theory of permanent revolution, steadfastly opposed such ideas.[31]

There was, however, one aspect of war on which Bolshevik theory has remained silent, and that concerned the possibility of conflict, open or covert, among Communist states within a nexus of power politics. Irrespective of the constitutional shape of international Communist society of the future—whether universal, regional or sectoral—it has to this day remained an article of faith that such conflict must be the result of a lapse, permanent or merely temporary, of Communist principles. Consequently inter-Communist conflict has tended to be accompanied by mutual ideological denunciations.

Ironically, the very success of Communist revolution in the underdeveloped regions of the world has tended to create such divisions. The pattern of steadily deteriorating Sino-Soviet relations would suggest that the system of power politics, which has operated among non-Communist states, will not stop short of the sphere of inter-Communist relations, especially if—as seems not unlikely—countries of the size and importance of India, for example, should go Communist in the future. This is not to suggest that this is inevitable, but rather that inter-Communist relations are far from immune from the usual pitfalls of power politics.[32]

Several problems have so far been raised to which Communist theory of international relations has not provided an answer. What, for instance, is the relationship of, on the one hand, between the use of power, and on the other the genesis of revolutionary situations? Can revolutionary situations be created, and if so, at what level? Above all, what is the function of state power in the world revolutionary process in the nuclear age?

The present state of Communist theory can only be vaguely inferred from Communist state practice which imposes an emphasis on three strategic elements, listed in descending order of priorities as follows: (1) the world Communist system of states; (2) antiimperialist movements in the underdeveloped regions of the world; and (3) the working class movement in the developed regions of the world. There are certain affinities here with the elements outlined in Korovin's theory of international law and relations, as modified in the course of the period of socialism in one country; but the overwhelming weight of emphasis will almost certainly continue to rest on the world Communist system of states, with the working class movement in the developed countries at an increasingly heavy discount, as it continues to favour gradualism and reformism over revolutionism.

Peaceful Coexistence

The theory of the inevitability of interimperialist rivalry and self-disruption formed part and parcel of the neo-Marxist explanation of imperialism and was taken over in toto by Soviet political theory. Already in 1915, however, Lenin had warned that the victory of socialism in any one country would provoke plots among capitalist states directed against that country, aggravating the danger of a counterrevolutionary war. Soviet theory subsequently maintained that—unlike interimperialist conflict, which sprang from the very nature of capitalism in its monopolistic stage—armed conflict between capitalist and Communist states was not inevitable, but avoidable. In those circumstances more or less prolonged periods of "peaceful coexistence," *mirnoye sosovshchustvovaniye* (in Russian),[33] would occur in the "transitory period" from capitalism to socialism.

As a concept, peaceful coexistence was not prominent in Soviet pronouncements before the end of the Second World War. In 1947 Zhdanov revived the model of the "two camps" (the Communist camp now greatly expanded) unalterably opposed to one another. Stalin modified it in 1952 to the extent of confining the stresses allegedly existing between the "two camps" to the imperialist camp entirely, thereby lending his authority to the view that war among capitalist states was still inevitable, but that the capitalist and Communist systems in their relations with each other were perfectly capable of restricting their competitive urges to the economic sector. This competition could be conducted under conditions of peaceful coexistence.

Khrushchev in turn expanded the term to a point at which it became the hub of his foreign policy. Time and again after 1956 the Soviet leader expressly denied the need for world war as a preliminary for the establishment of communism, insisting that the Communist camp had everything to gain from keeping the peace, not only between Communist and capitalist states, but even among capitalist states themselves. Peace had become an end in itself in neo-Communist theory, and had to be sought in complete disregard of the differing social and economic systems prevailing in various parts of the world.[34]

This remarkable shift of emphasis reflected a growing concern with the effects of nuclear conflict, which could not be effectively isolated or controlled. And where Communists in the past would have regarded wars among non-Communist states in a spirit of ethical indifference, nuclear war was now looked upon as absurd by any standards. Since any conventional conflict might escalate into a nuclear war, such conflicts were also regarded with growing disfavour, which accounts for the marked lack of enthusiasm displayed by the Soviet leadership for ambitious "Bakuninist" schemes to launch *guerrillas* in various parts of the underdeveloped regions of the world.[35]

Pressed to its logical conclusion, the trend towards coexistence, taken beyond the sphere of military security, would issue in convergence between the two systems. And although a theory of convergence has been advanced by writers in the West, it has consistently been repudiated by revolutionists.[36]

World Communist Order: The Political Image

Classical Marxism postulated a stateless world communism as its ultimate objective, but remained silent as to the exact manner in which states would be made to fade out in the penultimate stage.[37] That stage was still very distant indeed when the Bolsheviks seized control in Russia. Unlike nineteenth-century anarchism—with its conception of spontaneously formed and mutually overlapping associations on a world scale—the Bolsheviks had perforce to look upon the state as their highest available form of political organization, though, in all fairness to them it ought to be said that under internationally less turbulent conditions the *sovyety*[38] (Soviet = council) might conceivably have been used as trans-boundary links between states at below state level. Such a course would, however, have gone directly against the strongly entrenched Jacobin tradition which Bolshevik thought inherited from classical Marxism.

Engels' opposition to the principle of federalism as an interstate link is well known, although he might have changed his mind when faced with the real prospect of a federation specifically Socialist in content. Marx would have gone no further than rather vaguely envisaging loose ties of a confederal kind among Socialist states. Karl Kautsky's ideas on the subject were qualified by his insistence that only national states should be eligible for taking part in schemes of international integration.[39] Karl Renner, on the contrary, tried to preserve multinational states precisely because in his eyes they formed the ideal basis of further macrostructures. Neither of those two men insisted on imposing the condition of the adoption of socialism as an essential prerequisite.

Lenin would have none of this indiscriminate internationalism. In 1918 he saw the not too distant prospect of a World Federation of Socialist Republics as the only permissible international framework of a "harmonious socialist society." Yet, the transition from ingrained Jacobinism to semidecentralised federalism as the basic form of a large-scale organisation of Socialist states came less easily to some Bolsheviks than to others. Trotsky was not untypical of the former. Perceiving centralising tendencies in all parts of the world economy in 1915, he confidently concluded that interstate frontiers would become obsolete. Two years later, he called for the formation of a federal type of Socialist United States of Europe, and in 1923 he indulged in a neo-Saint-Simonian vision in which such a European federation would ultimately wrest control of the world economy from United States capital and establish a Federation of Socialist Peoples of the World.[40]

Loth at first, like Trotsky and Stalin, to part with Jacobin centralism, Lenin was compelled before long to yield to short-term considerations of expediency in giving in to federalism. Impressed by the stubborn nationalist particularism of the Poles in the war of 1920 - 21, he admitted that existing cultural diversities had to be taken into account and organisational stereotypes avoided in thinking about future international Communist organisation.[41] Originally inclined to think like Lenin in these matters, Stalin—by then richly experienced in his capacity of People's Commissar for Nationalities—suggested in 1920 that even a federal connection between existing Socialist units was feasible only in cases where there existed a previous historical basis, as, for instance, in the former Russian empire, and that a structure on confederal lines was more in accord with cultural realities when it came to constructing communism on a world scale. The Georgian realist failed to get his way, and consequently the furthest his Bolshevik colleagues could be prevailed upon to depart from the hallowed Jacobin principle of centralism was to adopt the federalist pattern.

Neither Trotsky nor Stalin was at any point prepared to pursue the subject of cultural diversity to its logical conclusion by recommending polycentric patterns of international Communist control. This idea had to wait until forced upon world Communist attention during the severe inter-Communist crisis in Eastern Europe in 1956, when it was taken up publicly by Palmiro Togliatti, leader of the Italian Communist party.

Glimpses of the future could be caught in the constitution of the Russian Soviet Federal Socialist Republic proclaimed in 1918 which expressly stated "the victory of socialism in all countries" to be its ultimate aim. It was only after the collapse of imperial Germany in that year that the Bolsheviks were compelled to consider the nature of constitutional ties between the newly formed RSFSR and the various Communist states which were confidently expected to arise in the rest of Eastern, and possibly Central Europe. Any number of schemes were examined, but the final answer was provided in the constitution of the Union of Soviet Socialist Republics which, ratified on December 30, 1922, was described by Stalin as "the prototype of a future World Soviet Socialist Republic." Admission was to be open to all future Soviet republics, but its general tone was different from its purely Russian predecessor in being the product of lawyers rather than of politicians.[42]

On the academic level E. V. Korovin included an analysis of the constitution of the USSR in his book on the international law of the "transitory period" in which period, true to Lenin's final word on the subject, federalism was accepted as a desirable mode of association among Communist states. Careful not to commit himself irrevocably to the ultimate form of inter-Communist association, Korovin did hint that the necessarily ephemeral law of the "transitory period" would have to expand eventually into full "inter-Soviet" law of "world dimensions." The unitary principle of Jacobin centralism was, for the time being, kept in reserve.

World Communist Order: The Economic Image

The ideal of international Socialist economic order is based on the overall principle of "mutual aid," a term first employed by Kropotkin, the Russian anarchist, and would rest on three conditions: (1) equality of welfare; (2) full mobility of the factors of production; and (3) the perfect matching of production to existing material resources. The motto, "From each according to his ability; to each according to his contribution," under conditions of economic scarcity would eventually give way to the motto, "From each according to his ability; to each according to his needs," under economic conditions of plenty.

The Bolsheviks took over these precepts from classical Marxism. On the first lap to communism, their two principal economic spokesmen, Bukharin and Preobrazhensky[43]—believing firmly in the victory of western Europe's proletariat and taking for granted the ensuing advent of international Communist solidarity—looked forward to a fruitful, and to the weak Soviet economy vital exchange of Soviet raw materials for Western manufactures. As the Western-oriented Trotsky was to observe in 1922, "a genuine advance in the construction of a Socialist economy in Russia" was possible only after the victory of the proletariat "in the most important countries of Europe." In the same year Preobrazhensky considered that the rationalisation of international trade could not be accomplished while the world remained politically divided.[44]

In 1920 Lenin optimistically visualised a world Communist economy of the future regulated "according to one common plan." For this purpose Yu. Pyatakov, People's Commissar of Finance, wished to see the immediate creation of a world council of economy, not unlike the international general staff envisaged in the military sphere by Tukhachevsky. Perhaps G. S. Strumilin, a present-day Soviet economist, was casting his mind unusually far ahead, by Soviet standards, in drawing his own image of world communist economic order. Writing in the Soviet periodical *Novy Mir,* known for occasionally expressing nonconformist views, in 1960, Strumilin predicted that "The communes, which exercise all the functions of production and consumption, coordinating their cooperative labour efforts, will be united by a single, centralised plan of action in a progressively expanding measure—from the regional level to the national and thence to the international level, culminating in a world federation of countries and peoples. Such a federation is conceived by Marxists to be a purely economic, nonpolitical organisation."[45]

In the post-1945 period, E. S. Varga, long regarded as Stalin's foremost councillor in international economic matters, put forward the thesis of the continued resilience of capitalism in the West,[46] only to be disowned by

Stalin in 1952, who thought the capitalist world would crumble under the weight of its own contradictions. It was interesting to see Stalin's logical extension of the notion of the economic viability of "socialism in one country" to that of the world Socialist system of states, and curious to see his diagnosis of the internal contradictions of Western capitalism confirmed fourteen years later by Ernest Mandel, a Belgian academic economist committed to Trotskyist Communism.[47] It was ironical that Varga's eventual successor at the Moscow Institute for World Economy and International Relations, Nikolai Inozentsev, should have repeated Varga's thesis emphatically in a realistic report submitted in 1975 to the central committee of the Soviet Communist party, in which he strongly denied the possibility of a deep-going crisis in the capitalist system. On the contrary, for no less than the next three decades, Inozentsev could only hold out prospects of continued technological progress and the same rate of economic growth as during the past two decades.[48]

After 1952 inter-Communist economic relations went curiously unmatched by any theoretical contributions that could have further illuminated or supplemented what had been written or said previously. Numerous works on the Council of Mutual Economic Aid (COMECON) deal, almost without exception, with the purely empirical and technical aspects of that institution,[49] leaving wide open some of the basic problems of inter-Communist economic relations still prevailing. Perhaps it would be worth drawing attention to Rumania's insistence on economic sovereignty within COMECON, as its economy is, to some degree, closing in order to establish a wider economic base, before reentering the process of full-scale international specialisation within that body. Implicit in its policy is a distinctly mercantilist reasoning which equates economic with political power, marking out Rumania's preoccupations as ultimately political. Meanwhile, COMECON's underlying structural design betrays a confederal pattern which seems out of character with the original intentions of the framers of the constitutional principles of the constitutions of the RSFSR of 1918 and that of the USSR of 1922, but in accord with what Stalin had considered practicable in those years.[50]

Present Trends

Soviet practice has to a large extent supplanted original Communist theories of a revolutionist kind, so far as the field of international relations is concerned. With pragmatic demands for "coexistence" and even for a limited amount of collaboration with the rest of the world in certain fields, Soviet theory of international relations has had to adjust, more or less awkwardly, from time to time to satisfy these demands, losing some of its revolutionism in the process. This had had the curious, though largely unintended effect of detracting from the forcefulness and credibility with which the classical Marxian concept of the class struggle had been applied on the international level in past periods.

Within the political framework of Soviet-dominated Eastern Europe, the experiences of Hungary (1956) and Czechoslovakia (1968) have shown that in the field of foreign policy and defence, as well as in the realm of basic internal order, the so-called 'Brezhnev Doctrine' has to be accepted as law.[51] On the academic level, a fresh look was taken at the subject of international relations by the Institute for the Study of the United States, where A. Gromyko, Jr. and Dr. Khozin have been pondering problems of conflict theory and the international control of the environment. Yet, there seem to be limits beyond which the pragmatic trend in Soviet theory of international relations must not be taken. F. M. Burlatsky had to find this out when he tried to set up a special section on international relations within the Institute of Concrete (empirical) Research. The section was disbanded in 1971.[52] In the sphere of international law it seems now to be realised that in a shifting world situation it would be unwise to allow single scholars to dominate the field any longer. As a result, the writing of textbooks has been made a collective task.

NOTES

1. See M. Wight, "Why there is no international theory," in H. Butterfield and M. Wight (eds.), *Diplomatic Investigations*. London: Allen and Unwin, 1966, pp. 17-34.

2. Anarchist writers, with their preoccupation with problems of association, fit in better in the chapter on the federative principle. See above.

3. On that point, see E. H. Carr, *The Bolshevik Revolution. 1917 - 1923*, Vol. 1. London: Macmillan, 1950, pp. 12-13. For an interesting present-day thesis concerning a country undergoing industrialisation, see Y. Tsedenbal, "Towards socialism, by-passing capitalism," *Far Eastern Affairs* (1975), pp. 7-29.

4. After 1882, and presumably impressed by the rapid forward march of industrialisation in Russia and the simultaneous enfeeblement of the archaic system of Russian autocracy, Marx and Engels thought the revolution might break out in Russia first. Still, they considered that, once started, revolution would ultimately be worldwide in character.

5. F. Engels, *Principles of Communism*. New York: Monthly Review Press, 1847.

6. Letter first published in full in Russian translation in *Marks-Engels Arkhiv*, Nr. 6, (1932).

7. "Kein Zweifel, Russland steht am Vorabend einer Revolution"—Engels, *Internationales aus dem Volksstaat, 1871 - 1875*. Berlin: Vorwärts, 1895, p. 59.

8. Writing in his *Critique of the Gotha Programme* (London: Lawrence, 1933), Marx asked the German Social Democratic Party how it was possible that a national framework could suffice for revolution if it was "itself economically within the frame-

work of the system of States." And though in 1882 Marx expressly considered the possibility of a Russian revolution in isolation, he thought that it would be forced "in sheer economic self-defence" to follow the route of economic development "already traversed by the more advanced countries of the West." See I. Berlin, *Karl Marx*. London: Oxford University Press, Second ed., 1948, p. 258. On Marx in general, see E. H. Carr, *Karl Marx: A Study in Fanaticism*. London: Dent, 1934.

9. On this point, see E. R. Goodman, *The Soviet Design for a World State*. New York: Columbia University Press, 1960, p. 155.

10. Thus, Adolf Joffe, Bolshevik delegate to the peace negotiations with Imperial Germany held at German military headquarters at Brest-Litovsk between 1917 and early 1918, once turned to Count Czernin, Austro-Hungarian foreign minister, remarking with polite hopefulness that "I hope we may be raising the revolution in your country too." See J. W. Wheeler-Bennett, *Brest Litovsk: The Forgotten Peace*. New York: Morrow, 1939, p. 113.

11. This was certainly the view expressed by a group of Bolshevik intellectuals in their Stockholm exile in 1915 and echoed by Trotsky a year later.

12. According to the latest research, Trotsky believed in the possibility of a survival of the Soviet government. See R. B. Day, *Leon Trotsky and the Politics of Economic Isolation*. London: Cambridge University Press, 1973.

13. *Sotsial-Demokrat*, November 9, 1917.

14. See S. Heitman, *Put k sotsializmu v Rossii*. New York: Free Press, 1970. See also N. I. Bukharin, *Capitalist Stabilisation and Proletarian Revolution*. Moscow: Executive Committee of the Comintern, 1926.

15. L. Trotsky, *Sochineniya*, Vol. 13, pp. 14-30. See also Bukharin's "Teoriya permanentnoi revolutsii," a review article of Trotsky's book, *The Lessons of October*, in *Za Leninizm*. Leningrad: Gosizdat, 1925. See also Trotsky, *Permanentnaya Revolutsia*. Berlin: Izdatelstvo "Granit," 1930; and *Voina i Revolutsia*. Petrograd: Gosizdat, 1922.

16. It was perhaps the eloquent pleas made by the eminent Bolshevik economist, E. A. Preobrazhensky, in favour of self-sustained industrialisation that induced Stalin to do so. See Preobrazhensky, *Novaya Ekonomika*. Moscow: Gosizdat, 1926.

17. See *Polnoye sobranie sochineniya*, Vol. 41, p. 165.

18. Lenin, ibid., Vol. 26, pp. 311-312.

19. E. A. Preobrazhensky, *Itogi Genueskoy konferentsii i khozvyastvennye perspektivy Evropi*. Moscow: Gosizdat, 1922; N.I. Bukharin, *Ekonomika perekhodnovo perioda*. Moscow: Gosizdat, 1920; and L. Trotsky, *Sochineniya* (1925 - 1927), Vol. 21: *Kultura perekhodnovo vremeni*.

20. E. A. Korovin, *Mezhdunarodnoye pravo perekhodnovo vremeni*. Moscow: Gosizdat, 1923.

21. On this point, see E. H. Carr, *A History of Soviet Russia: Socialism in One Country, 1924 - 1926*, Vol. 3 (1964), pp. 8-9.

22. For a seminal paper on this subject, see W. E. Butler, "Soviet international legal education: the Pashukanis syllabus," 2 *Review of Socialist Law* (1976), pp. 79-102.

23. See Pashukanis' paper in *Entsiklopediya gosudarstva i prava* (1925 - 1926).

24. See R. Schnur, "Weltfriedensidee und Weltbürgerkrieg, 1791 - 1792," *Der Staat* (1963), pp. 329-341.

25. See Lenin, *Polnoye sobranie sochineniya*, Vol. 49, pp. 369-370. See especially ibid., Vol. 26, pp. 311-312: "The great French Revolution opened a new era in the history of mankind. From that time to the Paris Commune, from 1789 to 1871, wars of a bourgeois-progressive, national-liberation character constituted one type of war."

26. As Lenin wrote, "Capitalism has moved from the progressive to the reactionary stage and has developed productive forces to a degree forcing mankind either to move to

socialism or suffer for years, even decades, armed conflicts among the "great" powers for the artificial preservation of capitalism by means of colonies, monopolies, privileges and national oppressions of various types." *Polnoye solbranie sochineniya,* Vol. 26, p. 314.

27. See Tukhachevsky's lectures on "Revolution from the outside," reprinted in his book *Voina Klassov. Stati 1919 - 1920.* Moscow: Gosizdat, 1921.

28. *ABC of Communism.*

29. In April 1975 the resumption of hostilities by North Vietnamese forces was explained in terms of a breach by South Vietnam of the Paris Agreement of 1973: while the annexation of fresh areas by the South Vietnamese Provisional Revolutionary Government was justified in terms of "punishing the aggressor." See *Neue Zürcher Zeitung,* April 8, 1975.

30. See Preobrazhensky, *Ot NYEPa k sotsializmu.* Moscow: Gosizdat, 1922, p. 120.

31. I. Deutscher, *Prophet Unarmed: Leon Trotsky, 1921 - 1929.* London: Oxford University Press, 1970. Deutscher claims Trotsky opposed both the aggressive phase of the war against Poland in 1920 and the conquest of Menshevik Georgia in 1921.

32. On this point, see G. Lütkens, "Das Kriegsproblem und die marxistische Theorie," 49 *Archiv für Sozialwissenschaft und Sozialpolitik* (1922), pp. 467-515.

33. At the Genoa conference on the world economy in 1922, G. Chicherin, Soviet foreign minister, used the term *mirnoye sozhitelstvo.*

34. In this respect the Communist theory of war has reverted to the basic assumptions made during the latter years of the second Socialist International, in which the desire to prevent war was extended from the working to the ruling classes of the world. On this point, see G. Haupt, *Socialism and the Great War.* Oxford: Clarendon Press, 1972. In the sphere of international law, the line was being taken under Khrushchev that the Soviet Union had had its share in shaping a new type of international law, and that the deep antithesis stressed by Korovin no longer existed to nearly the same extent.

35. On this point, see F. Parkinson, *Latin America, the Cold War and the World Powers, 1945 - 1973.* Beverly Hills: Sage Publications, 1974, pp. 215-224.

For a recent Soviet assessment of "peaceful coexistence," see V.B. Yegorov. *Mirnoye Sosovshchustvovaniye i revolyutsionniy protsess.* Moscow: Mezhdunarodniye otnosheniya, 1971. The position appears to have remained unchanged under Khrushchev's successors. See the late E. Varga, leading Hungarian-born Soviet economist, in his essay "The problem of inter-imperialist contradictions and war," in *Politico-Economic Problems of Capitalism.* Moscow: Progress, 1968, who echoes his political leaders in confirming that the chances of inter-capitalist war have declined, since bourgeois statesmen are now aware of the threat inherent in it.

A curiously jarring note was struck by the East German Minister of Defence in May 1976. General Hoffmann, in a lecture delivered to the SED College in East Berlin, criticised "progressive forces in the international peace movement who hold that nuclear war no longer represents a continuation of the policy of the class struggle but merely the nuclear destruction of the world." See *Financial Times,* May 28, 1976. It is possible that General Hoffmann was expressing the views of a certian military section within the Soviet Union.

36. On this point, see W. von Bredow, *Vom Antagonismus zur Konvergenz.* Frankfurt: Metzner, 1972.

37. Engels merely mentioned a "world republic" as the final outcome of all Marxist striving.

38. The soviets first made their appearance during the Revolution of 1905 as a spontaneous revolutionary form of political organization.

39. The theoretical implications of Kautsky's thesis were far-reaching, envisaging as they did the previous disintegration of all multinational structures as a condition for the

subsequent international integration of their constituent parts on a wider basis.

40. On these points, see E. R. Goodman, op. cit.

41. Ibid.

42. The RSFSR was incorporated into the USSR.

43. N. I. Bukharin and E. A. Preobrazhensky, *ABC of Communism* (1920).

44. See Preobrazhensky, *Ot NYEPa k sotsializmu*. Moscow, 1922. It is well to recall, in this connection, that Kropotkin had stated that "a reorganized society will have to abandon the fallacy of nations specialised for the production of either agricultural or manufactured produce." See *Fields, Factories and Workshops*. London: Hutchinson, 1899.

45. Quoted by E. Oberländer, "Communist society as a world order," in B. Landheer, J.H.M.M. Loenen, and F. L. Polak (eds.), *Worldsociety*. The Hague: Martinus Nijhoff, 1971, pp. 115-126, at p. 125.

46. See E. S. Varga, *Osnovnye voprosy ekonomiki i politiki imperializma posle vtoroi mirovoi voini*. Moscow: Gosudarstvenny izdatelstvo politicheskoy literatury, 1951.

47. E. Mandel, *Europe versus America? Contradictions of Imperialism*. London: Merlin, 1968. The French original appeared in 1966.

48. *Der Spiegel*, October 6, 1975.

49. See, for instance, P. Kalensky, "Mezhdunarodnoye khozvyastvennye organisatsii stran-chlenov SEV. Voprosy pravovogo regulirovaniya," *Sovyetskoye Gosudarstvo i Pravo* (1975), Nr. 9, pp. 103-109.

50. G. Ginsburgs, "The constitutional foundations of the 'Socialist Commonwealth,'" 27 *Yearbook of World Affairs* (1973), pp. 173-210.

51. G. Ginsburgs, "Socialist internationalism and state sovereignty," ibid., Vol. 25 (1971), pp. 39-55; and I. Lapenna, "The Soviet concept of 'Socialist' international law," ibid., Vol. 29 (1974), pp. 242-264.

52. See J. Goormaghtigh, "International relations as a field of study in the Soviet Union," 28 *Yearbook of World Affairs* (1974), pp. 250-261.

Chapter 12

SCIENTISM:

TOWARDS A SYNTHESIS?

The term "scientism"—often employed pejoratively by those who disbelieve outright in the validity of the scientific method applied to social questions—is used in this chapter in a strictly descriptive and ethically neutral way to avoid the clumsy expression "social scientific," an awkward translation from the German compound adjective *gesellschaftswissenschaftlich.* No disparagement whatever is intended.

The scientific spirit has been afoot since the Renaissance, but truly spectacular progress in the field of technology was not achieved before the twentieth century. It was not until the twentieth century either that the scientific spirit could make a deep impact on philosophy. The present century has witnessed the rationalisation of philosophy, showing itself in (a) its break-up into a number of social sciences, each undergoing further specialisation within its own boundaries; (b) the growing professionalisation and organisation of those engaged in philosophical activity; and (c) a shift of method away from reflection towards quantification.

Thought on international relations could not remain unaffected by these powerful trends in philosophy, especially after the gigantic scientific achievement in splitting the atom during the Second World War, and the appearance of the nuclear device in military technology. After 1945 science operated on a scale which was as boundless as it was unprecedented, especially in the

United States, making the gravitational pull of the scientific method on the social sciences in those circumstances irresistible. While to be welcomed in principle, this development raised a number of problems whose meaning was only gradually recognised. Of these, perhaps the thorniest and most unresolved remains the one relating to the extent to which the natural sciences should serve as a model to be followed by social science. It was the well-known German philosopher G. W. Leibniz (1646 - 1716) who first pointed out the essential difference between the laws of nature and the laws of mathematics. The temptation of mimicry carried in its train the danger of false analogies. These pitfalls are still not being altogether avoided by those staking their hopes of a solution to international problems on the application of scientific techniques adopted from the natural sciences.

The greatest potential danger to the field of study of international relations comes from the uncritical rejection of traditional philosophy and history, resulting in the growing separation of the social sciences from the mainstream of the humanities. As the late Professor M. Ginsberg put it in 1962 in his address to the British Association for the Advancement of Science, a belief in the problem-solving powers of science is the only ideology that is still riding high.[1] Wittgenstein before him had signalled the impending retreat of philosophy into inaccessible technicality. The trend towards what one may call the scientist philosophy has since been amply confirmed and analysed by Martin Heidegger (1889 - 1976) and other outstanding philosophical minds, and criticised by the politically oriented school of social scientists, of which Jürgen Habermas (b. 1929) is the leading light.[2] A whole new school of philosophers has been exclusively preoccupied with rethinking the task of philosophy in the light of the advent of the sciences.[3]

Two Sources of Scientism

The scientist strand in current theories of international relations derives its strength from natural and historical sources, of which only the former may be welcomed without reservations, as will be shown.

THE NATURAL SOURCE

The classical economists from Adam Smith onwards obtained their view of the social system from Newtonian mechanics, while Marshall and Veblen, in Britain and the United States respectively, tried to introduce newer concepts from biology. The trend was followed in the rest of the social sciences, and has led to attempts to unify these sciences under the comprehensive umbrella of a general theory. The latter is symbolised by general systems theory—with its notions of the steady state (homeostasis) and self-exhaustion (entropy), which has been looked upon as the conceptual framework linking all science, including the social sciences. In spite of its name, general systems theory is an aspiration, much more than a theory in the strictly scientific sense, and a programme pointing in the direction in which contemporary philosophy of science is moving.[4] It is, so to speak, the structural image of that philosophy.

The claims made on behalf of general systems theory vary in their magnitude, the extravagant ones representing the residue still of the vogue of linguistics, which had its heyday in the 1950s. In the field of international relations, the claim has been put forward that general systems theory is capable of (a) rendering scientist ambitions manageable, and (b) maintaining a global perspective.[5] The latter claim amounts to a tautology, since by definition the discipline of international relations has had a global perspective from the beginning. Somewhat big and unsubstantiated is the claim made by J. W. Burton that "General Systems Analysis is more and more integrating the study of international politics with the study of politics generally, and the study of world society with the study of any society and with separate aspects of it."[6] Epitomising the danger that a fascination with this concept may promote it to an end in itself, instead of a means to an end, is C. F. Weizsäcker's facile claim that general systems theory may help one to view international relations in terms of "global internal policy" *(Weltinnenpolitik).*[7] It is still too early to arrive at firm conclusions regarding the usefulness of general systems theory in international relations. Searching critiques of recent origin would suggest, however, that it is limited, since it appears to lack predictive capacity.[8] It also encourages the bad habit of calling in the aid of metaphors where rigorous analysis is faltering.

Another set of theories adopted from current technology for application in the social sciences has been communications theory, with its three branches (a) cybernetics, (b) information theory, and (c) sign-behaviour. Communications theory, defined as that branch of science dealing with flows of goods, persons, and messages across borders, was applied by K. W. Deutsch to the field of international relations as a gauge to assess the strength of the social fabric of communities. As such it proved a valuable technical aid in research.[9] His attempts to apply cybernetics have, however, been less fortunate. Cybernetic methods have been applied with great success in the field of engineering, where monistic, and not, as in international society, pluralistic systems apply—a striking instance of the danger of mimicry in the social sciences.[10] However, the notion of "feedback," properly explored on an empirical basis, might prove fruitful in the field of international relations in the long run.

The Advent of Behaviouralism

TOWARDS EPISTEMOLOGY

The apparent finality of the somewhat melancholic conclusions reached by some realists seemed strikingly at odds with the bright vistas opened up before mankind by science and technology. As for revolutionist expectations, it could plausibly be argued that the progress to economic strength and military power by the Soviet Union was due to the application of modern technology, rather than to any inherent virtues of communism. Considerations of this nature no doubt help to explain the strength of the reaction when it came in the shape of the behavioural approach to international relations.[11]

The two Ford Foundations reports of 1949 and 1952 were the first to use the term "behaviouralism" by way of a challenging synonym for scientism. Yet, the historical form assumed by behaviouralism differed essentially from scientism. Whereas the latter represented an innate tendency in general philosophy towards rationalisation, behaviouralism was to superimpose itself on scientism as an outgrowth, tending to divert scientism from its preordained path. Behaviouralism was a temporary influence on the wider, scientist approach to international relations, and was to fade away eventually. It may, in retrospect, be seen as having contained the seeds of its own destruction from its inception.

The essence of behaviouralism, as indeed of all behaviour, was learning, and from that point of view behaviouralism evinced a tautological tendency from the beginning. Rejecting introspection in favour of prediction and control, rather than understanding, behaviouralism was a variation of behaviourism, a doctrine of reducing concepts to publicly observable behaviour. Yet, it seemed to hold out real promise, especially when contrasted with the predeterminism of some realists and the remoteness of the revolutionist approach. As such it recommended itself to theorists probing for an opening in the sphere of international relations. Where the theorists of realism had relied on a few simple concepts, and the revolutionists on a single, compact doctrine, the behaviouralists shared the common epistemological assumption that the complex data of the field could be explained by reference to a single theory—a general theory,[12] sometimes referred to, and confused with, a conceptual framework.[13] In this they were to some extent encouraged by the prospect of bringing about a "revolution" in the social sciences, a notion of some power after the publication in 1962 of T. S. Kuhn's *Structure of Scientific Revolutions,* in which scientific progress was attractively portrayed as the product of a number of revolutionary "paradigms."[14] Taking in their stride the entire range of the social sciences, yet—try as they might—failing to find a single focus of comprehension, the behaviouralists soon came to regard the cohesion of the social sciences as an end in itself.

To overcome the daunting problem of comprehensiveness, some behaviouralists developed an obsession with problems of methodology, finding themselves immobilised in a morass of epistemology.[15] More rigorous and flexible in its methods was the quantitative-mathematical-statistical approach adopted by certain behaviouralists who disdained sweeping theorisation in favour of close empirical pursuits. Though fascinated by computer technology, J. D. Singer in the United States showed a willingness to experiment with the inductive method.[16] In Britain, M. B. Nicholson, directing the Richardson Institute, has been struggling valiantly with the problem of establishing the proper logical framework within which to accommodate mathematical precision in the explanation and, ultimately, prediction of international behaviour, without being able to escape the pull of epistemology altogether.[17]

What was shown clearly in the context of the behavioural method was the extreme degree of vulnerability of international relations. As Quincy Wright warned as early as 1955, the discipline of international relations has developed synthetically, and this has militated against its unity.[18] Originally conceived as performing coordinating, integrating and even synthesising functions, international relations has proved prone to dissolve, a tendency made manifest under the impact of amorphous behaviouralism. The question is whether international relations is the proper field in which to develop a scientific methodology for explaining and predicting social phenomena.[19] The outcome has been the decentralisation of the discipline of international relations to a point of disorientation, involving the loss of its identity as a distinct field of study. The connection between behaviouralism and international relations has become tenuous.

The prospect of catching up with the natural sciences led to the habit of model building on the basis of metaphors.[20] All abstract words have originated from concrete ones by process of analogy, and this has proved fruitful in the sciences. In the field of international relations there has occurred under the influence of behaviouralism a pairing of euphoria with metaphoria that has inhibited progress, since metaphors borrowed from a concrete stage in the evolution of the natural sciences are inappropriate when applied to international phenomena which have not reached a comparable stage.[21]

As Kelman noted, the new behavioural approach to international relations had developed "close ties with political science."[22] There also arose the promising but sickly child of perceptual studies, born in a work by K. E. Boulding.[23] While Professor Boulding managed to put his finger on a crucial problem in international relations, it has unfortunately not proved possible to develop perceptual studies to a degree of maturity in which they could be useful to international relations.[24] Dedring's critical comment in this respect is worth quoting in extenso: "It is next to impossible to abolish the wide range of causes and factors that make for the distortions and errors in our images of the world. This is especially grave in the severely complicated circumstances surrounding the way governments and states view each other and devise their measures accordingly."[25]

TOWARDS "VALUE FREEDOM"

The manner in which behaviouralists applied scientism to the field of international relations is now recognised to have been hasty. There are, however, some sociological and historical circumstances which may help to account for this haste.

"Value freedom" was an article of faith in all scientism, and impartial investigation would have been impossible without at least an approximation to it. However, as well as keeping out unwarranted political interference, the concept of "value freedom" could be deployed to evade civic responsibility in face of a determined political onslaught. It was this aspect of "value freedom" which may have affected the development of thought in the field of international relations. Significant in this respect was the breath-taking turn-around in political values induced by the diplomatic exigencies of the Cold War after 1945. This produced a climate of confusion and equivocation which stood in brutal contrast to the comforting political certainties cherished during two world wars. Ambiguity and disorientation were marked features of the world's new political landscape after 1945. Worst of all for international relations, what Carlyle said most historians omitted from their account of the French Revolution—"the haggard element of fear"—was making its presence felt, as United States government agencies and the intellectuals associated with them came under fierce attack from various sides.[26]

The academic community in the United States was taken completely by surprise by the ruthless abandon with which old political values were now being jettisoned, and though the main thrust of the attack was directed against government agencies, the academic world was to be deeply affected in a variety of ways. There can no longer be any doubt that vulnerable intellectuals were terrorised and hounded out of jobs on suspicion of Communist leanings. With political value judgements thus inhibited and academic styles cramped, "value-free" scientism seemed the only way of ensuring immunity from noxious political probings of this kind.[27] An atmosphere of this kind may well have served to promote a somewhat remote and arid behaviouralism, though basically the latter had independent roots in the deeper soil of scientism. The detailing of these portentous historical developments would seem essential if the behaviouralist syndrome is to be grasped in all its manifestations. Three episodes made up the sequence of events: the *Amerasia* affair; the Korean War; and the Oppenheimer case.

The *Amerasia* case was described as "one of the weirdest in the history of United States criminal jurisprudence."[28] It involved the suspicion of subversive influences at work in the offices of *Amerasia,* a periodical founded in the 1930s to promote the better understanding of Asian affairs in the United States. Suspicion was first cast on members of its staff in 1945, even before the end of the Second World War in Europe. It was not before 1950 that proceedings were dropped, leaving a cloud of suspicion behind. In 1951 the Institute of Pacific Relations, a highly respectable body, had its files seized in the wake of the *Amerasia* affair. Actions like these caused a tremendous stir and consternation in the academic community.

Things came to a head during the Korean War (1950 - 1953) when Senator Joseph McCarthy conducted his destructive investigations which tended to split opinion in practically all political circles and institutions. McCarthy focussed general discontents on such specific symbols of the establishment as intellectuals and diplomats.[29] Guilt by association was frequently assumed in this atmosphere of suspicion, as attacks were launched by right-wing groups on political scientists.[30] Hand in hand with these happenings went the politicization of United States private institutions performing research in the field of international relations.[31]

The case of Professor Robert Oppenheimer may be regarded as the highwater-mark of the McCarthy era "in which non-conformity had become synonymous with treason in the minds of far too many people."[32] A respected leader of the scientific and intellectual community and director of the Institute of Advanced Study at Princeton, he was "not penalized for any criminal offence. He was found technically guilty of behaviour which the United States at the peak of the cold war was not ready to tolerate in someone entrusted with any national secrets. For this he was removed from the public scene."[33]

Eventually McCarthyism was discredited. But the damage was done. The intellectual community remained inhibited, not to say intimidated, and it was in an atmosphere of this nature that demands for a "value-free" science were pushed hard, and accepted more widely than would have been the case in normal circumstances.

The Postbehavioural Restoration: Behaviouralism Indicted

Just as the advent of behaviouralism had to some extent been a function of the Cold War, so its decline was related to the demise of the latter.

In the field of international relations, the "Copernican revolution," anticipated by Stanley Hoffmann in 1959, had failed to materialise.[34] In 1969 at the latest it was realised that the so-called "behavioural revolution" had failed also. Just as the Meiji Restoration of 1868 in Japan was in reality a revolution, so the "postbehavioural revolution" of 1969 was in reality a restoration. The circumstantial evidence would suggest that the manner in which behaviouralism was abandoned in that year owes something to the turn of military fortunes in Vietnam. Indictments of behaviouralism began to be made in 1968, when the charge of "scholasticism" was levelled.[35] More detailed in form and severe in nature were the charges listed in a scholarly article published in the following year. According to these, behaviouralism was guilty of (a) cultivating theory at the expense of philosophy; (b) engaging in data collection at the expense of analysis; and (c) practising quantification at the expense of meaning.[36] A year later, in 1970, two political scientists operating in the field of international relations pilloried behaviouralism on the grounds that its "output of the 1960s has been disappointing, not just by traditional standards, but in terms of scientific criteria."[37] In 1971 Holsti noted that "the major preoccupations of theorists during the past decade have been to explore specific problems, to form hypotheses or generalizations explaining limited ranges of phenomena, and, particularly, to obtain data to test those hypotheses."[38]

THE FANTASY: "RELEVANCE" AND "ACTION"

The pseudo-drama of the 'postbehavioural revolution' was acted out at a meeting of the American Political Science Association in 1969, with Professor D. Easton proclaiming the end of the "behavioural revolution" and the coming of the "postbehavioural revolution," complete with battle-cry of "relevance" and "action." The "postbehavioural revolution" was to be "future-oriented."[39] Professor Easton coolly asserted that it was "better to be vague than non-relevantly precise."[40] He announced gravely that "mankind today is working under the pressure of time. Time is no longer on our side."[41] He pitched mercilessly into "the heart of behavioral inquiry" which, according to him, was "abstraction and analysis, and this serves to conceal the brute realities of politics."[42] He admitted that there had been "technical excesses of research."[43] However, "research about and constructive development of values" were "indistiguishable parts of the study of politics."[44] And, just to show that, as a "postbehavioural revolutionary," he was not one to believe in half-measures, he advocated the "politicization of the professions," a process which was "inescapable as well as desirable."[45] With behaviouralism blazing bright on its funeral-pyre, Professor Easton's blessing was bestowed on the new faith of "postbehaviouralism."

THE REALITY: RETURN TO NORMALCY

In reality, all that was happening after the political sobering and academic debehaviouralization was that political science returned from the wilderness to the traditional comforts of civilisation. Instead of attaching blame where it belonged, namely to the hasty endeavours of the behaviouralists to pull away as fast and hard as they could from philosophy and history in order, so they believed, to catch up with the natural sciences, the fault was sought in lack of "relevance." As the old pretensions to "value freedom" were discarded, the studied apoliticism of behaviouralism crumbled. Thus, by distinguishing between "negative" and "positive" peace, J. Galtung showed how little international relations could be separated from political philosophy,[46] while J. D. Singer was to call eventually for a balance between utopia and "short-run intermediate steps," a somewhat inelegant euphemism for the pragmatic approach.[47] After the vicissitudes of behaviouralism, normalisation was at last becoming the order of the day in the study of international relations in the mid-1970s.

Conflict Resolution

Intergroup analysis is one field in which important progress has been initiated and further energies might still be valuably concentrated. Any achievements so far reached have resulted significantly from reliance on analytical techniques established well before the advent of the "behaviouralist" and "postbehaviouralist revolutions." Pursued singlemindedly and systematically, the resolution of conflicts on the intergroup plane can be turned into a potentially useful discipline. However, after an upsurge of enthusiasm in the mid-1960s, interest in the field subsided, and, in spite of some attempts to keep interest alive in the United States, shows no sign of a real revival.

One of the reasons for the flagging interest in the subject has been a questioning of its alleged basic premise—the attainment of a world free of conflict. Thus, Professor F. S. Northedge expressed grave doubts about the value of the concept of what he terms "conflict-free millennium,"[48] while similar misgivings on that score were voiced in the course of a public debate on the subject conducted in Western Germany recently.[49] The point is worth raising, but should not be used to impede further research and experimentation in this area, especially since (a) the positive dialectical functions of conflict, as elaborated by Simmel, Coser, and others[50]—and already explicit in Hegel and Marx—have been widely, if sometimes ambivalently accepted by practically all scholars active in the field; and (b) since no such extravagant claims towards the attainment of a "conflict-free millennium" have ever been put forward.

THE TRADITIONAL APPROACH TOWARDS INTER-GROUP CONFLICT

In tackling the problem of inter-group conflict the assumption has been made that traditional modes of resolving conflict on that plane—whether diplomatic or judicial in nature—have been only marginally successful. While underrating the potency of the diplomatic process, scholars in this field are justifiably sceptical in regard to the judicial mode of settling interstate and intercommunal disputes.[51] International lawyers would readily agree that the rate of submission of cases to international judicial institutions has been pitifully low, in spite of the ready availability of machinery both elaborate and expensive, when compared with the number of actual disputes arising.[52]

Novel Approaches

In the belief that techniques borrowed from the fields of psychoanalysis and group dynamics might yield better results, attempts have recently been made in new directions. Their genesis is worth detailing here, as some of their successes would seem to justify cautious optimism. Three stages may be discerned: (a) individual psychoanalysis; (b) intragroup therapy; and finally, (c) intergroup therapy.

INDIVIDUAL PSYCHOANALYSIS

Though there has been a considerable variety of approaches within the psychoanalytical profession—of which the differences between the Freudian, Jungian, and Adlerian schools furnish the classical case—there is general agreement that the psychoanalytical method is basically concerned with bringing about changes in perception and alterations in attitudes where unadjusted perception and the persistence of rigid attitudes have led to failure of function resulting in nervous, biological and social disturbance. It was Freud's merit to have gone beyond the hypnotic technique of analysis to "free association," and to have hit upon the concept of "transference" of affections as the centre of the psychoanalytical process. "Free association" served to tease out of the patient the problems to be analysed, whereas "transference" was used as a means of relieving him of his nervous tensions.

What is most relevant in the context of the search for suitable techniques applicable to intergroup conflict is the nature of the psychoanalytical method. This is—as O. Fenichel, its leading exponent, remarks—"to expose dangers not objectively present,"[53] by analysing resistances to investigation.

Beyond recommending that the "right analytical atmosphere" of relaxation be established,[54] Fenichel quotes Sandor Ferenczi, Freud's protegé and close collaborator, as stressing the point that psychoanalysis is primarily an affective, and less an intellectual process.[55] Equally relevant to our present purposes is the insistence by both Glover and Sharpe[56] that psychoanalysis is an art likely to succeed not through abundant intellectual knowledge on the part of the analyst so much as by way of the deep analysis of the therapist himself, as well as of the patient.

The great value to the social sciences of the psychoanalytical technique was freely attested to by Clyde Kluckhohn, leading anthropologist in the United States, who confirmed that the writings of psychoanalysts were providing the anthropologist with a theory of "human nature in the raw."[5][7] At the same time, and in happy complementation, Gestalt psychology, always empirically oriented, developed the parallel discipline of group dynamics,[58] permitting a confluence to take place between it and psychoanalysis, the full potential of which has still not been fathomed.[59] The scientific study of the behaviour and structure of groups, and ultimately the attempted resolution of conflicts arising within and between them, would have been impossible without the prior development of those two disciplines in the course of the twentieth century.[60]

INTRAGROUP THERAPY

Intragroup therapy had its origins in the United States as early as the beginning of the twentieth century,[61] but because of the commanding position attained by individual psychoanalysis lay largely dormant until the Second World War, when it was beginning to be employed as a less costly alternative to the latter.[62] At Harvard, E. V. Semrad set up seminars of medical students and young social scientists who observed their own reactions as a group,[63] while in Britain S. H. Foulkes proceeded on the assumption that release of tensions within a group, and ultimately within the members composing that group, could only be accomplished through psychological insights achieved under the supervision of a therapist in charge of the group. Foulkes considered the task of the superviser of the group as being roughly analogous to that of a "conductor" of an orchestra, rather than that of a guide leading his patients in the right direction. He was to be the nodal point of communications within the group. As Foulkes observed, "the therapist confines himself entirely to interpretations,"[64] leaving as much work as possible to be done by the patients themselves.

Recognising to an increasing extent the central strategic role of the "conductor" of the group, Foulkes in his last work dealt extensively with his requisite qualifications, a matter regarded by him as of direct concern to the success of the entire exercise of intragroup analysis.[65] Here the question of the "conductor's" motivation assumed an eminent place. Foulkes expressly warned against the danger of irrelevant motives on his part. In particular, Foulkes insisted, he must not be "overweighed with motives such as 'helping other people' because this is too often based on deep-seated individual motivations—even unresolved conflicts." Again, "his interest should be of a mere detached, sublimated kind, similar to that of a scientist or artist." He should have an "active and open mind," and be accustomed to leading a full life without necessarily having to be a "gregarious socialite." Unsuited as "conductors" are those with "undue therapeutic ambitions" incapable of showing patience, as well as those "who think they have a mission to fulfill." It is to be noted that, though Foulkes—echoing Fenichel—considered that the group therapist, like the psychoanalyst, had to keep abreast of the social sciences and the arts in general, apart from his special priorities, "a basic familiarity with the most important aspects in these respects might suffice." The therapist need not be a specialist in any of those disciplines. What was absolutely essential in the fully trained "conductor" was "group-analytical experience and training."[66]

Comparing the function of the group therapist with that of the psycho-analyst, Foulkes—who, according to W. Schindler based his approach on Kurt Lewin's field theory, rather than on classical Freudian psychoanalysis—noted that, while there were certain similarities, there also existed essential differences. The group therapist had at all times to be self-conscious of the fact that he was operating within a group nexus. While he had to attempt to set up within the patients composing the group the wish to change and be changed, he was not allowed to "wish to change the patient" to his own image. Insights could not be imposed, but had to spring spontaneously from the *Erlebnis,* i.e., the active experience leading to the insight. As W. Schind-ler,[67] of Freudian-Stekelian background, put it: "The therapist is not only to be seen as a conductor acting from the outside, but has to look upon the members of the group as co-therapists."[68]

INTERGROUP THERAPY

Small scale. New problems pose themselves once the therapeutic process is taken to the intergroup level. The chief task on the intragroup level of analysis was to solve the neurotic problems of individuals making up the group by "conducted" collective effort. On the intergroup level, on the other hand, it is groups of individuals, whether small groups—such as rival gangs of boys in a holiday camp—or large groups, such as states or ethnic communities, that are the object of the exercise.

It is not surprising that a beginning in intergroup analysis should have been made with small units. Between 1949 and 1962 M. Sherif and his associates in the United States made steady contributions in this sphere. What made Sherif's experiments distinct from mere "gaming" were his strenuous attempts to get as close to reality as possible in the study of intergroup relations. This he first achieved in the Robber's Cave experiment, so-called because of the name of the holiday site chosen for two groups of schoolboys unaware that they were the object of close observation. This was indeed a marked advance on previous work of this sort, in which students and social scientists had to play roles assigned to them within the framework of traditional gaming, and which consequently lacked the air of unselfconscious-ness and spontaneity displayed during the Robber's Cave experiment. Thus, it was Sherif's merit to have taken the decisive step from simulation to reality, from which others were to profit later.[69]

Large scale. However, as W. Schindler rightly observed, scepticism is in place as regards experiments with "large groups," represented collectively as groups, rather than individually through their appointed representatives.[70] It was the latter approach which was adopted by J. W. Burton in London and by the so-called Fermeda "workshop" in Northern Italy in the mid-1960s in promotion of realistic intergroup therapy. The difference from Sherif's approach was remarkable, as the London and Fermeda experiments dealt with real international conflict, and not just with real groups whose encounter had been contrived for purposes of observation only. Where Sherif had confined himself to observation, the London and Fermeda workshops attempted to set in motion the process of conflict resolution.[71]

In an interesting paper, Burton elaborated on his technique, explaining that his model was the clinical case study method that had "proved so valuable in the analysis of individual and small group conflicts" and was so helpful in generating data which could subsequently be used in the development of theory. His chosen methods, he affirmed, bore close resemblance to those applied in psychoanalysis.[72] Burton summed up his method as one of "controlled communication." This was valid on the assumption that international conflict was a function of neurotic disturbances within an intergroup context, even though the duly appointed representatives of these large groups were men and women chosen, inter alia, for their emotional stability.[73] By helping to establish lines of communications between these, Burton was hoping to create the conditions in which the neurotic elements could be identified and eventually dissolved, clearing the way for a final settlement by the parties themselves. As he put it, "controlled communication is a further step ... away" not only "from third-party decision-making and towards direct negotiation between the parties," but also from "simulation" in "quasi-laboratory conditions," as well as from "gaming," "a particular form of simulation, the game being constructed to suit the special needs of some enquiry."[74]

The London and Fermeda experiments were conducted under conditions of relaxed privacy and absolute confidentiality. While the identity of the parties in Burton's London experiments was carefully concealed, those in the UNITAR-backed Fermeda experiment were disclosed as representatives of Somalia, Kenya, and Ethiopia, countries then locked in frontier disputes. Among the many characteristics which the two experiments had in common was the desire not only to prepare the ground for definite settlements of the conflicts in question, but also to add to the general body of theory existing in the sphere of international relations. As will be shown subsequently, the simultaneous pursuit of these two objectives may have been among the flaws which prevented these experiments from achieving full success.

THE LONDON AND FERMEDA EXPERIMENTS: A CRITIQUE

The setting within which intergroup therapy has to be attempted is far more complex than that on lower levels of association, posing a correspondingly greater number of technical problems.

Since direct intergroup analysis is impracticable where large groups are concerned, therapy has to be conducted through their representatives. This gives rise to a dual problem of communication. There are, first of all, the lines of communication between the groups concerned and their delegates in the experiment, and, secondly, there are the lines of communication connecting the delegates themselves, which run via the "mediary."[75] But while, within this setting—as Kelman reminded us—the "mediary" may induce the parties to relent towards each other, he is quite unable to control the processes of communication between the delegates and their principals.[76]

There is also the agonising dilemma that the closer the participant is to the decision-making processes of the principal, the more valuable his participation in the exercise on account of the great authenticity of his submissions; but the less likely is he to depart from the line taken by his principal, and vice versa.[77] In theory this dilemma could be overcome in cases in which the principals are so eager to seek resolution as to take the initiative in requesting the setting up of a workshop of this kind. The difficulty here, however, is that in practice they would use all channels open to them, finding little difficulty in making contact. They would not have to be induced to do so in the first place.[78]

There is also the problem of duration. All the experiments conducted on the intergroup level have been—measured by the normal time-span of psychoanalysis—of extremely short duration, extending over no more than two or three weeks, even where "follow up" procedures were expressly envisaged.[79] However, the length of time to be devoted to therapy on the intergroup level—if it is to have the slightest chance of success—must in hard cases, and there is general agreement that only hard cases are relevant, be measured in many months, if not several years.[80] Experiments of this length would require the accrediting of special, more or less permanent diplomatic representatives. And while perfectly sensible once the practical utility of the exercise is recognised, they may or may not be feasible now, or at any time.

Beyond that, there are also criticisms of substance which can be made of the two experiments, and if these tend, on the whole, to bear more heavily on the London than the Fermeda workshops, this is due to the greater ambition displayed in the former. Specifically, three points of criticism may be made, relating to (a) the overestimation of the factor of communication; (b) a corresponding underestimation of the therapeutic technique; and, closely connected with the two former points, (c) the predominance in practice of the didactic over the analytical element.

(a) *The factor of communication*

While it is true, as Burton states,[81] that "conflict and ineffective communication are causally related," they are not the only aspects of the problem, since, even where effective communication exists, methods other than that of the establishment of communication may have to be employed to achieve the desirable results. Underlying the Burtonian hypothesis that "conflicts of interest are subjective"[82] is the neo-Benthamite notion of the "harmony of interests," which, while irrefutable on grounds of pure logic, is of questionable historical validity.[83] But, as Freud noted, many persons seem so attached to their libido that they cannot be detached from it however clearly their objective interests may be exposed to them.[84]

(b) *Underestimation of the therapeutic technique*

Central to a general critique of the London and Fermeda experiments is the matter of the technique employed. While there is general agreement as to the informal atmosphere and relaxed relationships which must prevail during such experiments, the precise role and function of the "mediary"—whether he be a single person or a panel of experts—as evidenced during the two experiments under discussion— gives rise to controversy, as a gap seems to have developed between theory and practice. It may suffice at the moment to recall Burton's two basic propositions in this respect; namely, that (a) the "mediary's" role is "not to persuade . . . or judge the reasonableness of argument" put forward by the parties in dispute, and (b) that it must be his objective to promote "reperception" of the trauma, or, as Foulkes would have called it within the intragroup context, to provoke the *Erlebnis*.[85]

(c) *Predominance of the didactic over the analytic*

In practice, the two experiments proceeded in a manner inconsistent with their stated intentions as to technique. For, as Burton stated explicitly, the "third party," as he refers to the "mediary," is "to explain conflict" in terms of academic theories.[86] This represents a decisive break with the psychoanalytical technique, which—as Ferenczi pointed out—was of primarily affective rather than intellectual nature.

Once this problem is broached, the question of the degree of "activeness"—as distinct from "participation"—of the "mediary" raises itself. In this respect the organisers of the Fermeda experiment were quite explicit, as occasional intervention was regarded by them as an accepted routine of "sensitivity training" (also referred to as "T-group theory"), itself a variant of the classical psychoanalytical technique. As T. A. Wickes, one of the Fermeda "trainers" (as the "mediaries" were referred to), remarked: "From time to time throughout a workshop, staff members present more structured experiences that help the participants better to conceptualise and understand many of their experiences in the T-Group. These may range from formal lectures through movies or other audiovisual devices to the role playing of specific relevant situations or the practising of skills that will be of use in the immediate and distant future."[88] As Doob pointed out, however, the "games" part of the Fermeda experiment was only employed as part of clarification by demonstration, not as part of the central therapeutic technique.[89] In this important qualification he could rely on Ferenczi, who considered "shaking up" as a permissible intervention on the part of the analyst where there has developed a blockage.[90]

Originally willing to accept psychotherapeutic techniques as congenial to the exercise,[91] Burton raised high expectations as to the eventual perfection of a method whereby inductive processes of theory-building would emerge from empirical bases. In practice he proceeded deductively. Far too much emphasis was placed by him on the "academic framework,"[92] whereas, as he had set out clearly in his preface, "the purpose of controlled communication" was "to provide a clinical framework, and a means by which an applied science of international relations can develop."[93] It by no means followed as axiomatic that "the academic framework, contrived for purposes of research" could be "perceived by those who have responded as fashioning a new tool for use by parties seeking a resolution of conflict."[94] For, though it is true that "the research worker and the practitioner are often one and the same person,"[95] data have to be generated in the course of the experiment, and the direction of their flow has to be basically from practice into theory, and not the other way round. As Ferenczi noted, progress was to be expected "not from the statistical turnover of many, but from the intensive exploration of individual cases," though he seems to have overstressed the point.[96]

Having stressed the function of casework in the development of theory, Burton appears to have gone back on his thesis by insisting that "the parties are helped, not by the third party as such but by the use of ordinary academic tools of analysis."[97] The sound, inductive method based on casework originally envisaged by Burton was rejected in practice, the clinical aspect being relegated to a secondary place in favour of the thesis that experiments must be based on "a set of propositions drawn from the theoretical literature that seemed to be relevant."[98] The reference here was to theories of international relations, and not to psychoanalytical theory.

Here lies the centre of the controversy: too strong an academic-intellectual conviction may be inconsistent with sound psychotherapeutic practice since it would tend to narrow the range of choices, and thereby to preempt the solutions open to the parties in dispute. As Reik, one of the interwar pioneers of the psychoanalytical method, once noted, too much knowledge can be harmful to the analyst because it might lead him to misapply his knowledge and to hamper his intuition.[99] It is true that Fenichel thought he was going too far,[100] but his criticism was made in the context of individual psychoanalysis where it was probably appropriate. Reik's strictures seem, however, most apt when seen in the perspective of intergroup therapy. As Kelman was to remark, "the social scientists [on the panel of "mediaries" in the London workshop] used conflict theory and other theoretical concepts as a psychotherapist might use personality theory."[101] However, the deployment of personality theory in psychotherapy is a legitimate pursuit since it was the product of patient casework over a long period of time. The theory of international relations, as developed by Burton and others, however ingenious in design, has remained largely untested; partly because it has come up with propositions that are not easily testable in practice. It would not therefore be permissible to apply it in a manner suggesting that it had undergone the process of testing. According to Kelman, the social scientists involved in the London experiment contributed by applying the functional theory of conflict resolution.[102] Whether the latter raises a presumption of irrefutability is a highly contentious issue, and the use of the theory in the way described, to the exclusion of most others, would seem to hinder, rather than to promote the casework method. This is not to say that the London experiment was useless on that count, merely to suggest that inconsistencies in the application of techniques may have been an important factor in the modest impact made.

CONFUSION OF OBJECTIVES

It is eminently desirable to build up a body of theory based on results obtained from the case method. However, this must be the last, and not the first step in a series of steps to be taken. As Kelman maintains, attention should at all times be focussed on the substantive issues of the conflict, since problem-solving workshops of this kind should not be equated with sensitivity training.[103] While inclined to overestimate the distance that separates these two objectives, Kelman is probably right in principle. The first duty must be to help the parties in conflict, the contribution towards theory having meanwhile to be relegated to a secondary place. The temptation to use the parties as guinea-pigs[104] in order to develop or perfect a theory of international relations must be resisted at almost all costs if the case is to be conducted in earnest, and not as part of an exercise in mere "simulation" or "gaming."

It is the latter two techniques, and not therapy, which offer the proper testing ground for academic theories.[105] The decisive step so far as intergroup conflict and its resolution is concerned, is from simulation to therapy, with the latter tending to import affective and displace intellectual techniques. The choice seems clear: if it is the further development of academic theories of international relations that is intended, then the proper procedure is to apply techniques developed in the social sciences; if, however, the primary objective is to resolve intergroup conflict, then the corresponding technique must be psychotherapy.

INTERGROUP THERAPY AND THE FUNCTION OF THE "MEDIARY"

Once the primacy of the psychotherapeutic technique in the resolution of intergroup conflict has been established, attention must once more be focussed on the role and function of the "mediary," whether a single individual or a collectivity. In his capacity of catalyst, his foremost concern must be to bring latent conflict out into the open, thereby clarifying the issues for the benefit of the parties to the dispute. In pursuit of this goal, his greatest asset is therapeutic skill, and not mastery of preconceived theories.

It is at this point that special consideration should be given to the question of the qualifications of the "mediary." The conclusion drawn by Burton that persons versed in the theory of "systems behaviour and systems response to the environment" are specially qualified to identify with all parties to a dispute[106] can be dismissed out of hand as totally lacking in empirical basis. The bulk of psychological science turns on the functions of the subconscious mind and the motivations located there. To lift the latter out of their obscure depths into the shallow but crystal-clear waters of the conscious mind requires above all else the application of psychotherapeutic skills. One of the chief attributes of the latter is the ability to break down subconscious resistances. This the analyst may achieve by means of transferring certain feelings from the patient to himself. However, in attempting this, the analyst must, in Ferenczi's words, "at the same time consistently control his own attitude towards the patient, and, when necessary, correct it"[107] to avoid what Freud called "counter-transference" taking place from the analyst to the patient.[108] Freud, Ferenczi, and generations of psychoanalysts of all schools after them have since been at one in agreeing that the risk of "counter-transference" of irrational thoughts in this manner can be minimised, though never be entirely eliminated, by the therapist's own intensive psychoanalysis.[109] It would seem, therefore, that before he attempts to act as "mediary" within the difficult and highly complex framework of intergroup therapy, the completion of intensive psychoanalysis on the part of the therapist would represent an essential requirement. There can be few countries in the Westernised world in which psychoanalysts are licenced to practice without having undergone this preliminary training, even where full medical qualifications may be dispensed with. It seems strange, therefore, that Foulkes, in dealing with intragroup therapy, should touch on this matter rather lightly, and downright astonishing that Burton, Doob, and Kelman—concerned with the resolution of intergroup conflict—should remain altogether silent on this supremely important aspect of their endeavours.

How can a "mediary," by whatever name he may be referred to ("conductor," "trainer," "controller," etc.), be expected to accomplish the task of uncovering hidden motives on the part of the disputants without having first gone through the hard discipline of psychoanalysis in order to recognise his own subconscious motivations? The latter are bound to come into play at some stage in the proceedings. If he is not thus qualified, he will run the grave risk of carrying his unrecognised subconscious motivations into the process of intergroup analysis, thus complicating rather than facilitating his own task.

INTERGROUP THERAPY: THE PROSPECTS

The pioneers of the London and Fermeda experiments made the mistake of attempting to do too much by seeking to bridge the gap between the intellectual and affective elements in intergroup analysis, as it were, prematurely, and by failing to get their technical priorities right. It would have been surprising if no mistakes had been committed in the pioneering stage. There is, however, no reason why, given the right technical priorities, intergroup therapy should not in the long, perhaps very long run, be as successful as individual psychoanalysis and intragroup therapy have been before it. As R. E. Walton, Professor of Business Administration at Harvard University, and one of the "trainers" during the Fermeda experiment, aptly put it, "the method simply has too much potential not to be used again."[110] Exercising his usual caution, Freud once stated that neurotic patients cannot be guarded against future conflict, they can only have their present ones resolved.[111] Much progress, especially in the field of social psychology, has been made since then, and such scepticism would no longer be entirely in place today. It is difficult to dissent from Burton's view, therefore, that the general method of intergroup analysis is capable of serving prophylactic, as well as therapeutic functions.[112]

There is a good case to be made for the energetic resumption of "workshop" experiments on a reformed basis.[113] If allowed to develop along lines of psychotherapeutic casework, the "workshop" technique can be made to succeed provided it ensures intellectual returns in the shape of testable propositions which will eventually be capable of being fitted into the wider framework of the theory of international relations. But one could go further than that in making positive recommendations in respect to the training of intergroup therapists. Seeing the potential of the technique, university undergraduates opting to major in the subject of international relations should be made to undergo gentle psychotherapy under proper professional supervision as part of their degree requirements. This "integrated" therapeutic training would enable them to qualify as "mediaries" with highly specialised knowledge of all aspects of intergroup relations, and perform a valuable role in international society.

Towards a Synthesis?

In so far as a grand synthesis has not been achieved and as disillusionment with behaviouralism has led to a certain apathy, the danger of a disintegration of the discipline of international relations as an integral field of study is great. T. de Reuck gave it expression in noting resignedly that "some of us see . . . an unending programme for all time, and not one for which final conclusions will ever emerge."[114] Since its aphilosophical and ahistorical bias has been the undoing of behaviouralism, the remedy seems close at hand: the reconnection of philosophy and history—still the two queens of the social sciences—with the mainstream of scientist endeavour. As one scholar working in the field of international relations remarked perceptively: "Scientific approaches may uncover previously neglected factors to be examined, but they must be examined through the use of traditional historical research."[115] Thus data gathering and theorising, the two legitimate pursuits of scientism, must be performed in accord with philosophical method and be the subjects of empirical analysis. The present state of scientism is still suffering from its prolonged contamination by behaviouralism. What is the way out?

Burton is most positive that general systems theory is the means to achieve an "integrated system of thought."[116] However, M. H. Banks had to admit that the application of general systems theory to international relations was "a task of staggering proportions," and that there was "much dispute within the international relations discipline on how to set about it."[117] The difficulty with general systems theory is that it is a device for facilitating perception, not a tool of analysis.

Professor R. Morgan came closer to a constructive solution by listing four aspects which will be important in a resuscitated discipline of international relations: (a) the progressive integration of strategic studies into the general conspectus of international studies; (b) the declining emphasis of quantification; (c) the growing interest in futurological models; and (d) the sense of a need for theorists to exchange the abstract for the real world.[118] Indeed, efforts have been made in recent years to break out in new directions. Of these, three seem prima facie eligible and should therefore be sympathetically reviewed.

Futurology. It has been argued that the real task of philosophy in the age of science and technology is to engage in futurology, rather than pure, deductively based prediction.[119] Futurology is a discipline which attempts to make forecasts (a) on the basis of discernible trends which can be projected into the future; and (b) by prognosis, relying largely on intuitive guesses as to the shape of the future.

That peering into the future is absolutely essential at all times is a commonplace. What is not so widely appreciated is that present-day technology requires ever longer terms of planning and projection. In so far as futurology can answer that demand, it can be useful. Ultimately, however, it merely extends the time-scale of present methods of analysis and, as such, is largely a mechanical exercise.[120]

As regards projection, only one trend can at present be confidently identified as continuing indefinitely into the future, and that is worldwide rationalisation, with its two by-products, organisation and bureaucratisation.[121] Max Weber's law of the inevitable growth and irreversibility of bureaucracy, whether by socialist revolution or by the forces of the market, seems not to have lost any of its validity.[122]

Prognosis, on the other hand, has to rely on intuition and presupposes the existence of basic assumptions which cannot be made without philosophical aids. Futurology, at best an exercise in probabilism,[123] is therefore an inadequate tool for dealing with the wider problems of international relations.

Ecology. This discipline, which has had a long existence, recently sprang into prominence in the measure to which the long-term consequences of the exploitative practices and destructive tendencies of science- and technology-oriented civilisation are being recognised. Directing its criticism at the cult of industrial efficiency, with its smug assumptions of material progress, the world ecological movement has, however, proved unable to work out a comprehensive philosophy of its own.

Re-ligion. International relations tends to broach problems of ontology bordering on the philosophy of religion. It is a mistake to regard all re-ligion (here deliberately spelt with a hyphen) as of theistic content, since the word is derived from the Latin *religere,* which meant to rely. This is its proper sense.

Impatience was the order of the day during the decade of the behaviouralist illusion, and this gave rise to arrogance on more than one occasion. As M. B. Nicholson, director of the Richardson Institute in London, and erstwhile sympathiser with behaviouralism, wrote recently in a survey of the work performed by his institute: "The claims made . . . have frequently been extravagant, and humility was not, perhaps, the most conspicuous quality displayed."[124] Disenchantment with behaviouralism has brought with it a nascent tendency in world society to seek a fresh moral orientation. This has led to critiques of present world culture. Reinhold Niebuhr expressed the view that the conviction that science is "the profoundest, because it is the latest fruit of culture" is an illusion. High technology, being bred by, and in turn breeding highly disciplined, organised, but above all conforming societies, came in for criticism from the New Left, particularly H. Marcuse. The late György Lukàcs' great popularity in recent years can be accounted for in this way.

Equally stringent have been the indirect criticisms of contemporary world culture pointing to the lack of connection between science and faith. Before the First World War, Max Weber noted that there was no bridge between science and faith.[125] After the First World War, L. Wittgenstein delivered his message that science tells us nothing we really want to know.[126] After the Second World War, Professor A. Toynbee produced a monumental argument for the thesis that there is a transcendental meaning to history. He displayed a tendency to link man's history with man's nature and ultimate destiny, bringing a mystical element to bear on his ruminations.[127]

To remedy this state of affairs, E. Bloch, Marxist with Kantian inclinations, insisted in his main work on the positive functions of utopia, and came close to advocating the transformation of the concept of hope into an ontological category.[128] The debate among Marxists about the respective merits of positivist scientism and Kantian normative theory has never ceased, as was recently noted by the Polish Marxist philosopher, L. Kolakowski.[129]

A rather less sanguine note was struck in the existentialism of M. Heidegger (1889 - 1976) who, while acknowledging the limited scope of philosophy, nonetheless held out the possibility of a return to metaphysics in divine form.[130] Existentialism may be regarded as the philosophy appropriate to scientism. Thus, E. Husserl (1859 - 1938), Heidegger's mentor, claimed to have established the notion of "pure science."[131] It is interesting to note, however, that he was careful in confining himself to "European" science, leaving open the possibility of a philosophical revival inspired from extra-European sources. This view seems to have been shared by his disciple Heidegger, who saw the only alternative to scientism-existentialism in atavistic wisdom and traditions.[132]

More concretely, the Anglo-German philologist F. M. Müller announced as early as 1870 the "science of religion," which would be made up eclectically from the findings of the comparative study of religions.[133] The Ninth Congress for the History of Religions held in Tokyo in 1958 stated that "scientific enquiry has discovered more and more the close relationship existing among outwardly differing religions."[134] Finally, the controversial German Protestant theologian, R. Bultmann (1884 - 1976), relying heavily on existentialist premises, believed in a demythologised Christianity.[135]

During the behavioural era the ghost of philosophy seems to have been given up for the flesh-and-bones of science. Has the spirit of science then driven out gods and demons alike? If it has, then there is an acute danger of a separation in the sphere of thought in international relations between creative reflection and systematic enquiry. Yet, the antithesis between philosophy and science is a false one. It is a pleonasm to say that philosophy is scientific, since the concept of philosophy implies the notion of science. "For us," said the logical philosopher W. V. O. Quine (b. 1908), "philosophy of science is philosophy enough."[136]

Philosophy allowed itself too easily to be displaced by pure scientism, as one after the other of the social sciences hived itself off its stem. A science of international relations in the strictly formal sense does not exist; not—Heaven knows!—for lack of trying, but because the necessary preconditions were lacking. This former behaviouralists are now pondering, as they reassess their false directions of the past. Some of their statements have the air of confessions about them. Thus, R. J. Rummel considered that the most pressing problem was to pay attention "to the most fundamental philosophical questions, the most central issues about the nature of man and society, and our ultimate ethical dilemmas."[137] "To ignore metaphysics," he averred, "is to leave unquestioned the foundation of our social knowledge, our ethics and our epistemology. It is to adopt subconsciously a teleology and to accept one's starting point, one's perspective or faith."[138] Instinctively, some scholars have turned to natural law in a search for universal values extracted from scientific experience.[139] However, as Professor H. Bull has warned, "there is no such thing as a science of end or values that can establish that one course of action is objectively more right or just than another."[140]

Today we are interdisciplinarians all, and to be a sound scientist one has to be a polymath. There is nothing wrong in an approach to international relations based on scientism. Yet, until the techniques of scientism have been refined beyond recognition, it would be extremely unwise to cut off scientism from historical enquiry and to eschew conventional wisdom (which is never static) in favour of scientist preferences altogether. Too often, during the behavioural predominance in international relations, the rejection of conventional wisdom has been tantamount to the rejection of all wisdom.

All social sciences have undergone and are undergoing change. The problem in international relations is not that of which approach is to dominate, but what is the most suitable framework for their accommodation. Some former behaviouralists are now ready to admit that. Thus, C. A. McClelland has called for the creation of a "single, all-encompassing ordering idea."[141] It is suggested here that an up-to-date version of history is capable of answering that need. Dedring raised the possibility of a "dynamic understanding of peace, which implies that we have to incorporate the element of constant transformation into our image of the world peace order."[142]

Those are steps in the right direction, away from the barren ahistoricism of the behaviouralists. Historians have long ago taken steps to meet scientism halfway. In his inaugural lectures at the Collège de France in 1933, Lucien Febvre argued ("Examen de conscience d'une histoire et d'un historien") that, just as linguistics, a new science, emerged from comparative philology, so a new kind of history will emerge from the global study of historical wholes.[143] Here, then, is a field of history of an open-ended kind awaiting fertilisation.[144]

At first sight it would seem that history is a discipline that is, almost by definition, past-oriented. Yet, quite apart from Lord Halifax's apt remark in the seventeenth century that "the best qualification of a prophet is to have a good memory," historical method has not stood still since Ranke's days. The most imaginative history written today is the one that has assimilated what is best in the social sciences and refined its methods accordingly.[145] Some misunderstandings still exist on that score. Thus, T. de Reuck argued that "So far as present conflicts are concerned, it is not what actually happened in the past that may be central and crucial to their understanding, but rather what people now believe to have happened."[146] The main flaw in that argument is that it is historians who make interpretations of the past possible, affecting current attitudes directly thereby.

The late Professor M. Wight seems to have gone too far the other way in asserting that historical literature "does the same job [as social science] — provides a common explanation of phenomena; but it does the job with more judiciousness and modesty,"[147] as he came close to claiming a degree of exclusiveness for the historical method which is unwarranted.

J. W. Burton maintained that "diplomacy involves the study of all aspects of world civilization which bear upon relations between the independent states which comprise world society; every event, development, change in attitude or external appearance of change which takes place within a state and which affects the behaviour of other states, falls within the study of diplomacy."[148]

Choosing the New Framework

Several attempts have been made to choose a framework capable of holding the disciplined study of international relations together. The least satisfactory ones are those which, taking the line of least trouble, lumped together all enquiries relating to international relations under the convenient but misleading rubric of "international studies." Beyond providing clear empirical evidence of the continuing confluence of the social sciences concerned with international relations, it offers us nothing.[149] If anything, it confirms the centrifugal tendencies at work under the unitary surface, as evidenced in the rising number of symposia produced at the expense of thoughtful synthesis. Among scholars in Britain, C. A. W. Manning has called for a new focus within a "social cosmology,"[150] while G. Schwarzenberger and J. W. Burton have chosen "world society" as their context.[151]

There is a strong case to be made in favour of a critical, all-embracing "historical cosmology" which would be capable of reducing the complexity of international relations everyone is complaining of[152] by giving it a suitable structure, while, incidentally, answering the requirements of general systems theory.[153] Such a scientifically oriented world history will have to draw its inspiration from the continued vigour of philosophy. There has been a surfeit of misplaced scientism due to mimicry of the natural sciences, and a renewed preoccupation with the concerns of classical scholarship is now badly needed to restore the balance between the sensible world of appearances and the intelligible one open to rational knowledge.

Such a "historical cosmology" must be both multidimensional and open-ended, and have as its long-term object the gaining of a unified picture of the world. It will have to operate on two levels of analysis and be able to direct its sights to past, present and future. One of the consequences of this will be the restoration of the state as one of the basic units of analysis. With the restoration of focus on interstate relations must go the frank recognition that "interest" and "power"—the two divisive elements to be found wherever there are states—must be given their due place. This may be a bitter pill to swallow for such die-hard behaviouralists as have survived the postbehavioural restoration.

Conversely, a transactionist dimension must be included side by side with the interstate perspective, to provide the unifying element in the long run. In effect, it will be a critical functionalism of an open-minded, and not a starry-eyed kind, that alone will be capable of sustaining the transactionist thesis in practice. To perform this task to satisfaction, functionalism will have to pay far more attention than hitherto to institutions, whether of the intergovernmental or of the intercorporate type.

A "historical cosmology" of this nature should be resilient and broad enough to absorb and digest newly emerging trends, such as a theory of bureaucracy,[154] or organisation theory,[155] without generating undue enthusiasms, providing interim answers to the perennial problems of international relations.

NOTES

1. *The Times,* August 31, 1962.

2. See M. Heidegger, *The End of Philosophy.* London: Souvenir Press, 1975; Heidegger, "Die Frage nach der Technik," 3 *Jahrbuch Gestalt und Gedanke* (1954), pp. 70-108.

      On Habermas, see *Zur Logik der Sozialwissenschaften.* Frankfurt: Suhrkamp, 1968, and *Technik und Wissenschaft als Ideologie.* Frankfurt: Suhrkamp, 1968. Even in his most recent work, Habermas refused to renounce his political commitment, while altering its bases somewhat. See *Zur Rekonstruktion des historischen Materialismus.* Frankfurt: Suhrkamp, 1976.

3. The periodicals *Metaphilosophy,* published in Britain; and *Philosophy and Public Affairs,* published in the United States, are wholly devoted to exploring the role of philosophy in a technologically oriented world.

4. See L. von Bertanlanffy, *General Systems Theory*. New York: Braziller, 1963; D. Easton, *A Systems Analysis of Political Life*. New York: John Wiley, 1965; E. Laszlo, *The Systems View of the World*. New York: Braziller, 1972; J. Piaget, *Structuralism*. London: Routledge and Kegan Paul, 1971; and J.W. Sutherland, *A General Systems Philosophy for the Social and Behavioral Sciences*. New York: Braziller, 1973. On the functions of General Systems Theory in international relations, see P.A. Reynolds, *An Introduction to International Relations*. London: Longmans, 1971.

5. See P.A. Reynolds and M.B. Nicholson, "General systems, the international system and Eastonian analysis," 15 *Political Studies* (1967), pp. 12-31.

6. J.W. Burton, *Conflict and Communication: The Use of Controlled Communication in International Relations*. London: Macmillan, 1969, at p. xiv.

7. See J. Dedring, *Recent Advances in Peace and Conflict Research*. Beverly Hills: Sage Publications, 1976, p. 51.

8. See J.J. Weltman, *Systems Theory in International Relations: A study in metaphoric hypertrophy*. Lexington: Lexington Books, 1973; and D. Berlinski, *On Systems Analysis: An Essay Concerning the Limitations of Some Mathematical Methods in the Social Political and Biological Sciences*. Cambridge, Mass.: MIT Press, 1976. See also K.E. Knorr, *On the Cost-Effectiveness Approach to Military Research and Development: A Critique*. Santa Monica: RAND, 1966.

9. See K.W. Deutsch and others, *Political Community and the North Atlantic Area: International organisation in the light of historical experience*. London: Oxford University Press, 1957.

10. K.W. Deutsch, *The Nerves of Government: Models of Political Communication and Control*. New York: Free Press, 1963. He was inspired by Norbert Wiener's *Cybernetics* (Cambridge, Mass.: MIT Press, 1948) and probably also by J.L. Doob's *Stochastic Processes* (New York: John Wiley, 1953).

See also J.D. Steinbruner, *The Cybernetic Theory of Decision: New Dimensions of Political Analysis*. Princeton, N.J.: Princeton University Press, 1974.

11. The behavioural credo in the political sciences was stated by D. Easton, *A Framework for Political Analysis*. Englewood Cliffs, N.J.: Prentice-Hall, 1965, especially pp. 4-15.

12. See J.W. Burton, *International Relations: A General Theory*. London: Cambridge University Press, 1965.

As Easton put it succinctly: "In its ideal and most powerful form, a general theory achieves maximal value when it constitutes a deductive system of thought, so that from a limited number of postulates, assumptions and axioms, a whole body of empirically valid generalisations might be deduced in descending order of specificity." See D. Easton, *A Systems Analysis of Political Life*. New York: John Wiley, 1965, p. 9.

13. One of the finest expositions of the aims and assumptions of behaviouralism in the sphere of international relations was made by M.H. Banks, "Two meanings of theory in the study of international relations," 20 *Yearbook of World Affairs (1966)*, pp. 220-240.

14. T.S. Kuhn, *The Structure of Scientific Revolutions*. Chicago: University of Chicago Press, 1962.

15. See M.J. Levy, "Methodology: means or a field?" in E.H. Fedder (ed.), *Methodological Concerns in International Studies*. St. Louis: University of Missouri, 1970.

16. Witness Singer's impatience with barren deductivism in "The incompleat theorist: insight without evidence," in K.E. Knorr and J.N. Rosenau (eds.), *Contending Approaches to International Politics*. Princeton, N.J.: Princeton University Press, 1969, pp. 62-86, at pp. 77-78. See also Singer (ed.), *Quantitative International Politics: Insights and Evidence*. New York: Free Press, 1968.

17. On the general problem of quantification, see R. Jervis, "The costs of the quantitative study of international relations," in K.E. Knorr and J.N. Rosenau, op. cit., pp. 177-217; and J. Galtung, *Reason and Unreason in the Application of Mathematical Models in Sociology*. Oslo: University of Oslo Institute of Sociology, 1957.

18. As quoted in C.A. McClelland, "On the fourth wave: past and future in the study of international systems," in J.N. Rosenau (ed.), *The Analysis of International Politics*. New York: Free Press, 1972, pp. 15-40.

19. R.K. Merton, *Social Theory and Social Structure* (New York: Free Press, 1949) noted (p. 85) that "twentieth century physics and chemistry are (usually) taken as methodological prototypes or exemplars for twentieth century sociology. These comparisons are inevitably programmatic, rather than realistic. More appropriate methodological demands would result in a gap between methodological aspiration and sociological attainment at once less conspicuous and less invidious."

20. See C.D. Burns, "On the dangers of metaphors in economic thought," in Geneva Institute of International Relations, 5 *Problems of Peace*. London: Oxford University Press, 1929, pp. 87-89.

21. J.J. Weltman, op. cit.

22. H.C. Kelman, *International Behavior. A Social-Psychological Analysis*. New York: Holt, Rinehart and Winston, 1965, p. 3.

23. See K.E. Boulding, *The Image*. Ann Arbor: University of Michigan Press, 1956.

24. For a recent assessment, see J. Harrod, "International relations: perceptions and neo-realism," 31 *Yearbook of World Affairs* (1977), pp. 289-305.

25. Dedring, op. cit.

26. For a personal account from one who suffered in this way, see Lillian Hellman, *Scoundrel Time*. London: Macmillan, 1976. This throws some lurid light on the activities of the House Committee on Un-American Activities, which included Representative R.M. Nixon.

27. On the general phenomenon, see N.W. Polsby, "Towards an explanation of McCarthyism," 8 *Political Studies* (1960), pp. 250-260. See also R.E. Cushman, "Repercussions of foreign affairs on the American tradition of civil liberty: the loyalty tests," 42 *Proceedings of the American Philosophical Society* (1948), pp. 257-263; and D.C. Williams, "The Cold War in America," 21 *Political Quarterly* (1950), pp. 280-287.

28. See E. Latham, *The Communist Controversy in Washington: From the New Deal to McCarthy*. Cambridge, Mass.: Harvard University Press, 1966, p. 203. Numerous references to the *Amerasia* affair are contained in pp. 203-216.

29. See M.P. Rogin, *The Intellectuals and McCarthy: The Radical Specter*. Cambridge, Mass.: MIT Press, 1973, p. 218.

For a presentation of the McCarthyist case, see E.M. Root, *Collectivism in the Campus*. New Jersey: Devin, 1955.

30. See R.M. MacIver, *Academic Freedom in Our Times*. New York: Columbia University Press, 1955, pp. 124-125; also pp. 36 and 154-178. See also R.C. Goldston, *The American Nightmare*. New York: Bobbs-Merrill, 1973, especially pp. 88-93.

31. N.D. Houghton, "The challenge to political scientists in recent American foreign policy: scholarship or indoctrination?" 52 *American Political Science Review* (1958), pp. 678-688.

32. Lord Zuckerman, at p. ix of the preface to P.M. Stern, *The Oppenheimer Case: Security on Trial*. London: Hart-Davis, 1971. See also C. Strout, "The Oppenheimer case: melodrama, tragedy and irony," 40 *Virginia Quarterly Review* (1964), pp. 268-277.

33. Lord Zuckerman, op. cit.

34. S. Hoffmann, "International relations: the long road to theory," 11 *World Politics* (1959), pp. 346-377.

35. A.A. Said, "Recent theories of international relations: an overview," in A.A. Said (ed.), *Theory of International Relations: The crisis of relevance.* Englewood Cliffs, N.J.: Prentice-Hall, 1968, p. 24.

36. F.W. Neal and B.D. Hamlett, "The never-never land of international relations," 13 *International Studies Quarterly* (1969), pp. 281-305, at p. 294.

37. M. Haas and T. L. Becker, in M. Haas and H.S. Kariel (eds.), *Approaches to the Study of Political Science.* San Francisco: Chandler, 1970, pp. 479-504, at p. 447.

38. K.J. Holsti, "Retreat from utopia: international relations theory, 1945-1970," 4 *Canadian Journal of Political Science* (1971), pp. 165-177, at p. 171.

39. D. Easton, "The new revolution in political science," 63 *American Political Science Review* (1969), pp. 1051-1061, at p. 1051.

40. Easton, op. cit., p. 1052.

41. Op. cit., p. 1053.

42. Ibid.

43. Op. cit., p. 1054.

44. Op. cit., p. 1052.

45. Ibid.

46. J. Galtung, "La science et la paix. Historique et perspectives," 1 *Science et paix* (1973), pp. 38-63.

47. Dedring, op. cit., p. 8.

48. See F.S. Northedge, *The International Political System.* London: Faber, 1976, pp. 302-303.

49. On this point, see the recent debate in Düsseldorf between K.H. Biedenkopf, Secretary-General of the Christian Democratic Union, H. Marcuse, the veteran sociologist and intellectual leader of the New Left, and A. Mitscherlich, prominent psychoanalyst, under the chairmanship of Professor K. Sontheimer, political scientist at the University of Munich. For a brief report, see *Der Spiegel,* September 6, 1976. See also the chapter on "A World Without Frustration" (originally composed in 1944) in F.G. Alexander, *The Scope of Psychoanalysis.* New York: Basic Books, 1961, pp. 440-446.

50. See G. Simmel, *Conflict and the Web of Group-Affiliations.* New York; Free Press, 1955; and L.A. Coser, *The Functions of Social Conflict.* London: Routledge and Kegan Paul, 1956. See also R.C. North, H.E. Koch, and D.A. Zinnes, "The integrative functions of conflict", 4 *Journal of Conflict Resolution* (1960), pp. 355-374.

51. See, for instance, F.S. Northedge and M.D. Donelan, *International Disputes: The Political Aspects.* London: Europa, 1971.

52. On the distinction between justiciable and nonjusticiable disputes, see Sir Hersch Lauterpacht, *The Function of Law in the International Community.* Oxford: Clarendon, 1933; D.W. Bowett, *The Law of International Institutions.* London: Stevens, Third ed., 1975; and G. Schwarzenberger, *A Manual of International Law.* London: Stevens, Sixth ed., 1977.

53. O. Fenichel, *Problems of Psychoanalytical Technique.* Albany, N.Y.: The Psychoanalytic Quarterly, 1941, p. 7. See also J. Strachey, "The nature of therapeutic action in psychoanalysis," 15 *International Journal of Psychoanalysis* (1934), pp. 127-160; E. Glover, "Lectures in technique in psycho-analysis," ibid., Vol. 8 (1927), pp. 311-338 and 486-520; ibid., Vol. 9 (1928), pp. 7-46 and 181-218; and E.F. Sharpe, "The technique of psycho-analysis," ibid., Vol. 9 (1930), pp. 251-277 and 361-386; and ibid., Vol. 12 (1931), pp. 24-60.

54. Fenichel, op. cit., p. 19.

55. Ibid., p. 100.

56. Ibid., pp. 108-109.

57. C. Kluckhohn, "Culture and behaviour" in G. Lindzey (ed.), 2 *Handbook of Social Psychology.* Cambridge, Mass.: Addison-Wesley, 1954, pp. 921-976, at p. 964.

58. See K. Lewin, "Frontiers in group dynamics," 1 and 2 *Human Relations* (1947), pp. 5-41 and 143-153; and W. Köhler, *Gestalt Psychology*. New York: Liveright, 1929.

59. D.S. Whitaker and M.A. Lieberman, *Psychotherapy through the Group Process*. New York: Atherton, 1964.

60. For developments in the United States, see E.A. Shils, "The study of the primary group," in D. Lerner and H.D. Lasswell (eds.), *The Policy Sciences*. Stanford: Stanford University Press, 1951, pp. 41-69; and C.H. Cooley, *Social Organization: A Study of the Larger Mind*. New York: Scribner's, 1909.

61. On this point, see T.L. Burrow, "The group method of analysis," 14 *Psychoanalytical Review* (1924), pp. 268-280; and W. Schindler, "Entwicklung der Gruppen-Psychotherapie," 21 *Praxis der Psychotherapie* (1976), pp. 59-67.

62. For a brief review of the origin of the treatment of groups, see M. Rosenbaum and M. Berger (eds.), *Group Psychotherapy and the Group Function*. New York: Basic Books, 1963. See also E.V. Semrad and others, "The field of group therapy," 13 *International Group Therapy* (1963), pp. 352-475; and S.H. Foulkes, *Therapeutic Group Analysis*. London: Allen and Unwin, 1964.

63. E.V. Semrad and J. Arsenian, "The use of group processes in teaching group dynamics," 13 *American Journal of Psychiatry* (1951), pp. 358-363.

64. S.H. Foulkes, op. cit., p. 18.

65. S.H. Foulkes, *Group Analytic Psychotherapy: Methods and Principles*. London: Gordon and Breach, 1975, especially pp. 157-165.

66. On this point, see also S. Thompson and J.H. Kahn, *The Group Process as a Helping Technique*. Oxford: Pergamon, 1970.

67. W. Schindler, op. cit., p. 60.

68. Ibid., p. 64.

69. The earliest experimental work on face-to-face groups was concerned with questions about the efficiency of groups in problem-solving situations. From there, small group experimentation spread out in many directions. See B.E. Collins and H. Guetzkow, *A Social Psychology of Group Processes for Decision-making*. London: Wiley, 1964.

On Sherif's work, see M. Sherif and others, *Intergroup Conflict and Cooperation: The Robber's Cave Experiment*. Oklahoma: University Book Exchange, 1961; M. Sherif (ed.), *Intergroup Relations and Leadership*. New York and London: Wiley, 1962; and M. Sherif, *Group Conflict and Cooperation*. London: Routledge and Kegan Paul, 1966, especially pp. 81-93.

70. W. Schindler, op. cit., p. 65.

71. See J.W. Burton, *Conflict and Communication: The Use of Controlled Communication in International Relations*. London: Macmillan, 1969; and L.W. Doob (ed.), *Resolving Conflict in Africa: The Fermeda Workshop*. New Haven, Conn.: Yale University Press, 1970. For a general appreciation of those two experiments, see H.C. Kelman, "The problem solving workshop," in R.L. Merritt, *Communication in International Politics*. Chicago: University of Illinois Press, 1972, pp. 168-204.

72. J.W. Burton, "The analysis of conflict by casework," 21 *Yearbook of World Affairs* (1967), pp. 20-36.

73. The report on the Fermeda workshop makes a special point in mentioning that only "emotionally stable" Africans were selected. See L.W. Doob (ed.), op. cit., p. 16.

74. Burton, *Conflict and Communication*, pp. 142 and 157.

75. In the present context it would be preferable to call him "mediary," rather than "intermediary" or "mediator" as the latter retain the flavour of traditional processes of conflict resolution. See O.R. Young, *The Intermediaries: Third Parties in International Crises*. Princeton, N.J.: Princeton University Press, 1967.

76. Kelman, op. cit., p. 177, considered that intergroup analysis of the London and Fermeda type are more effectively designed to produce changes in the participants than to feed such changes into the policy process.

77. Ibid., p. 198.

78. Thus, in the case of the Cuban "missile" crisis of 1962, contact was effortlessly established through a United States journalist, John Scali, who happened to be a convenient go-between at that particular moment.

79. Burton, op. cit., pp. 109-110.

80. Thus, one of the African participants in the Fermeda experiment found the pace "agonisingly slow." The report on the Fermeda workshop suggests that many participants considered that substantially more barriers might have been broken down among the parties in dispute if the experiment had had a much longer run. See Doob (ed.), op. cit., p. 46.

81. Ibid., p. 51.

82. Ibid., p. ix.

83. One of the African participants in the Fermeda workshop expressly doubted the validity of the idea of the 'harmony of interests' that seemed to form the central assumption of the experiment. See Doob (ed.), op. cit., pp. 92-93.

84. As quoted in Fenichel, op. cit., p. 120.

85. Burton, op. cit., pp. 45 and 61-62.

86. Ibid.

87. On "sensitivity training," see L.P. Bradford, J.R. Gibb, and K.D. Benne (eds.), *T-Group Theory and Laboratory Methods.* New York: John Wiley, 1964.

88. Doob (ed.), op. cit., p. 27.

89. Ibid., p. 69.

90. Sandor Ferenczi, *Further Contributions to the Theory of Psycho-Analysis.* London: The Hogarth Press, Second ed., 1950, pp. 236-237.

91. Burton, op. cit., pp. 68-9.

92. Ibid., p. 46.

93. Ibid., p. 13.

94. Ibid., pp. 31-32.

95. Ibid., p. 34.

96. Ferenczi, op. cit., p. 124.

97. Burton, op. cit., p. 72.

98. Ibid., p. 5.

99. T. Reik, "New ways of psychoanalytic technique," 14 *International Journal of Psycho-Analysis* (1933), pp. 321-339.

100. Fenichel, op. cit., p. 109.

101. Kelman, op. cit., p. 171.

102. Ibid., pp. 171-172.

103. Ibid., p. 194.

104. Doob (ed.), op. cit., p. 72, cites one participant in the Fermeda experiment who felt that at least some of his coparticipants "did not want to be used as guinea-pigs."

105. See H. Guetzkow, "Some correspondences between simulation and "realities" in international relations," in M.A. Kaplan (ed.), *New Approaches to International Relations,* New York: St. Martin's, 1968, pp. 202-269, at p. 202.

106. Burton, op. cit., p. 64.

107. Ferenczi, op. cit., p. 187.

108. See S. Freud, *Group Psychology and the Analysis of the Ego.* New York: Liverwright, 1949; first published in 1921.

109. Ferenczi, op. cit., p. 187.

110. See Doob (ed.), op. cit., p. 136.

111. Fenichel, op. cit., p. 117.

112. Burton, op. cit., p. 101.

113. On the latest state of affairs in this respect, see H.C. Kelman and S.P. Cohen, "The problem-solving workshop: a social-psychological contribution to the resolution of international conflicts," 13 *Journal of Peace Research* (1976), pp. 79-90.

114. T. de Reuck, *Conflict Resolution Society Bulletin* (March-April 1976).

115. R.B. Finnegan, "International relations: the disputed search for method," 34 *Review of Politics* (1972), pp. 40-66, at p. 50.

116. J.W. Burton, *Systems, States, Diplomacy and Rules.* London: Cambridge University Press, 1968, p. 170.

117. M.H. Banks, "Charles Manning and the concept of 'order,' " in A. James (ed.), *The Bases of International Order.* London: Oxford University Press, 1973, pp. 193-194, 196 and 200.

118. R. Morgan (ed.), *The Study of International Affairs: Essays in Honour of Kenneth Younger.* London: Oxford University Press, 1972.

119. H. Lenk, *Philosophie im technologischen Zeitalter.* Stuttgart: Kohlhammer, 1971.

120. See O.P. Flechtheim, *History and Futurology.* Meisenheim: Hain, 1966. R. Jungk, working in his Institute of Futurology in Vienna, compared it to field theory in physics; Herman Kahn at the Hudson Institute analysed the problem in terms of alternative futures. Another body occupying itself with futurological problems is Professor C.F. Weizsäcker's Max-Planck Institute for the Investigation of Living Conditions in a Scientific-Technological World, at Lake Starnberg in Bavaria.
See also R. Jungk and J. Galtung, *Mankind 2000.* Oslo: Universitetsforlaget, 1967. Since 1967 Professor Flechtheim has been publishing the periodical *Futurum.*

121. See G. Therborn, *Science, Class and Society: On the Formation of Sociology and Historical Materialism.* London: New Left Books, 1976.

122. See also H. Jacoby, *The Bureaucratisation of the World.* London: California University Press, 1976.

123. J.M. Keynes wrote a book on probability. See G.L.S. Shackle, *Keynesian Kaleidics.* Edinburgh: Edinburgh University Press, 1974.

124. M.B. Nicholson, *Conflict Research Society Bulletin,* (March-April 1976).

125. M. Weber, *Wissenschaft als Beruf.* Munich: (3rd ed.) Duncker und Humblot, 1930.

126. L. Wittgenstein, *Tractatus Logico-Philosophicus.* London: Routledge and Kegan Paul, 1949, reissue.

127. A. Toynbee, *A Study of History,* Vol. 12: *Reconsiderations.* London: Oxford University Press, 1961.

128. E. Bloch, *Der Geist der Utopie.* Munich: Duncker and Humblot, 1918; and *Das Prinzip der Hoffnung.* Berlin: Aufbau, 1954.

129. *The Listener,* May 4, 1972.

130. See J. Macquarie, *An Existentialist Theology: A comparison of Heidegger and Bultmann.* London: Pelican, 1973.

131. E. Husserl, "Die Krisis der europäischen Wissenschaften und die transzendentale Phänomenologie," 1 *Philosophia* (1936), pp. 77-176.

132. Heidegger, in an extensive interview published posthumously in *Der Spiegel,* May 31, 1976.

133. See E.J. Sharpe, *Comparative Religion.* London: Duckworth, 1976, p. 76.

134. See R.L. Slater, *World Religions and World Community.* New York: Columbia University Press, 1963.

135. J. Macquarie, op. cit.

136. *The Listener,* April 22, 1976.

137. R.J. Rummel, *Understanding Conflict and War*, Vol. 1. Beverly Hills: Sage Publications, 1975, p. 4.

138. Ibid.

139. J.W. Burton, "Universal values and world politics," 24 *International Journal* (1969), pp. 673-692.

140. H. Bull, "New directions in the theory of international relations," 14 *International Studies* (1975), pp. 277-287, at p. 285. See also Bull, "Order and justice in international society," 19 *Political Studies* (1971), pp. 269-283; R. Linton, "Universal ethical principles: an anthropological view," in R.N. Anshen (ed.), *Moral Principles of Action: Man's Ethical Imperatives.* New York: Harper Mussen, 1952; and A.B. Bozeman, *The Future of Law in a Multicultural World.* Princeton, N.J.: Princeton University Press, 1971.

141. C.A. McClelland, "Field theory and system theory in international relations," in A. Lepawsky, E.H. Buehrig, and H.D. Lasswell (eds.), *The Search for World Order.* New York: Appleton-Century-Crofts, 1971, pp. 371-385, at p. 382.

142. Dedring, op. cit., p. 210.

143. Lucien Febvre, *A New Kind of History and Other Essays,* ed. by P. Burke, New York: Harper and Row, 1973.

144. For a good example of the new type of history, see W.H. McNeil, *A World History.* London: Oxford University Press, 1967.

145. See W.B. Gallie, *Philosophy and the Historical Understanding.* London: Chatto and Windus, 1964.

146. T. de Reuck, *Conflict Research Society Bulletin* (March-April 1976).

147. M. Wight, "Why is there no international theory?" in H. Butterfield and M. Wight (eds.), *Diplomatic Investigations.* London: Allen and Unwin, 1966, pp. 17-34, at p. 32.

148. J.W. Burton, *Systems, States, Diplomacy and Rules.* London: Cambridge University Press, 1968, p. 208.

149. See also F.W. Riggs (ed.), *International Studies: Present Status and Future Prospects.* Philadelphia: American Academy of Political and Social Sciences, 1971.

It is perhaps worth mentioning in this context that Soviet studies have been sensitive to this problem quite early. Witness the name of their prewar periodical devoted to international relations: *Mirovaya ekonomika i mirovaya politika* (World Economics and World Politics).

150. C.A.W. Manning, *The Nature of International Society* (Reissue with a new introduction). London: Macmillan, 1975, Ch. 16: "Social cosmology—its problems, procedures and place," pp. 200-216.

151. G. Schwarzenberger, *Power Politics: A Study of World Society.* London: Stevens, 1964; and J.W. Burton, *Systems, States, Diplomacy and Rules.* London: Cambridge University Press, 1968.

152. R.A. Brody in K.E. Knorr and J.N. Rosenau (eds.), *Contending Approaches to International Politics.* Princeton, N.J.: Princeton University Press, 1969, p. 112.

153. A recent successful attempt to write history in terms of General Systems Theory has been I. Wallerstein, *The Modern World System: Capitalist Agriculture and the Origins of the European World Economy in the Sixteenth Century.* London: Academic Press, 1974.

154. E. Jacques, *A General Theory of Bureaucracy.* London: Heinemann, 1976.

155. B. Lussato, *A Critical Introduction to Organisation Theory.* London: Macmillan, 1976.

BIBLIOGRAPHY

GENERAL
Books
BOZEMAN, A.B., *Politics and Culture in International History* (Princeton, N.J.: Princeton University Press, 1960).

BULL, H., *The Anarchic Society: A Study of Order in World Politics* (London: Macmillan, 1977).

FORSYTH, M.G., and others (eds.), *The Theory of International Relations: Selected Texts* (London: Allen and Unwin, 1970).

LANGE, C.L., *Histoire de l'internationalisme, 1919-1963* (Oslo: Nobel Institute, 3 vols., 1963).

RUSSELL, F.M., *Theories of International Relations* (New York: Appleton-Century, 1936).

RUYSSEN, T., *Les sources doctrinales de l'internationalisme,* 3 vol. (Paris and Grenoble: University of Grenoble, Faculté des Lettres, 1954-1961).

CHAPTER 1
Books
BAINTON, R.H., *Christian Attitudes Towards War and Peace* (Nashville: Abingdon, 1960).

BALDRY, H.C., *The Unity of Mankind in Greek Thought* (Cambridge: Cambridge University Press, 1965).

BARRACLOUGH, G., *The Medieval Papacy* (London: Thames and Hudson, 1968).

BELCH, S.F., *Paulus Vladimiri and His Doctrine Concerning International Law and Politics,* 2 vol. (The Hague: Mouton, 1965).

BENTON, J.F. and BISSON, T.N. (eds.), *Medieval Statecraft and the Perspectives of History* (London: Oxford University Press, 1971).

BERTRANDUS, Petrus, *De origine jurisdictionum* (Paris: Chaudière, 1520).

BROWN, P., *Religion and Society in the Age of Saint Augustine* (London: Faber, 1972).

BROOKE, C.N.L. and others (eds.), *Church and Government in the Middle Ages* (London: Cambridge University Press, 1977).

CADOUX, C.J., *The Early Christian Attitude to War* (London: Allen and Unwin, 1940, original edition, 1919).

DANIEL, N., *The Arabs and Medieval Europe* (London: Longman, 1975).

DEANE, H.A., *The Political and Social Ideas of Saint Augustine* (New York: Columbia University Press, 1963).

D'ENTRÈVES, A.P., *Natural Law* (London: Hutchinson, 1970; 2nd. ed.).

GIERKE, O. von, *Political Theories of the Middle Age* (Cambridge: Cambridge University Press, 1900).

GILSON, É., *Les métamorphoses de la cité de Dieu* (Louvain and Paris: University of Louvain, 1952).

GRIMAL, P., *Hellenism and the Rise of Rome* (London: Weidenfeld and Nicolson, 1968).

JOHNSON, J.T., *Ideology, Reason and the Limitation of War. Religious and Secular Concepts, 1200-1740* (Princeton, N.J.: Princeton University Press, 1975).

JOLOWICZ, H.F., *A Historical Introduction to the Study of Roman Law* (London: Cambridge University Press, 1961).

KHADDURI, M., *War and Peace in the Law of Islam* (Baltimore, M.D.: Johns Hopkins, 1955).

LaPRADELLE, A., *Le Droit des Gens* (Paris: Classics of International Law, 1916).

MATTHEW, D., *The Medieval European Community* (London: Batsford, 1977).

MOODY, E.A., *Studies in Medieval Philosophy, Science and Logic* (London: California University Press, 1975).

MURRAY, G.E.A., *Stoic, Christian and Humanist* (London: Watts, 1940).

PARRY, J.H., *The Age of Reconnaissance* (London: Weidenfeld and Nicolson, 1963).

——— , *The Spanish Theory of Empire in the Sixteenth Century* (Cambridge: Cambridge University Press, 1940).

POLLOCK, Sir Frederick, *The History of the Law of Nations* (Cambridge Modern History, 1910).

SCHULTE, J.F. von, *Geschichte der Quellen und Litteratur des canonischen Rechts*, 3. vols. (Stuttgart: Enke, 1875-1880).

SMALLEY, B., *Historians in the Middle Ages* (London: Thames and Hudson, 1974).

ULLMANN, W., *A Short History of the Papacy in the Middle Ages* (London: Methuen, 1972).

——— , *Medieval Papalism. Theories of the Medieval Papalists* (London: Methuen, 1949).

——— , *Principles of Government and Politics in the Middle Ages* (London: Methuen, 1961).

Articles

McCOLLEY, G., "The twelfth century doctrine of a plurality of worlds," 1 *Annals of Science* (1936), pp. 385-430.

TARN, W.W., "Alexander the Great and the unity of mankind," 19 *Proceedings of the British Academy* (1933), pp. 46-52.

CHAPTER 2

Books

BUTTERFIELD, H., *The Statecraft of Machiavelli* (London: Bell & Sons, 1955).

CALLIÈRES, F. de, *De la manière de négocier avec les souverains* (Brussels, 1716).

CHIARAMONTI, S., *Della ragione di stato* (Florence: Nesti, 1635).

D'ENTRÈVES, A.P., *The Notion of the State* (Oxford: Clarendon Press, 1967).

FIGGIS, J.N., *The Political Aspects of Saint Augustine's "City of God"* (London: Longmans, 1921).

GILBY, T., *Principality and Polity* (London: Longmans, 1958).

GUICCIARDINI, F., *Storia d'Italia* (1537) (Florence: Torretino, 1567).

HALE, J.R. and others (eds.), *Europe in the Late Middle Ages* (London: Faber, 1965).

——— , *Machiavelli and Renaissance Italy* (London: English Universities Press, 1961).

HAMPSHIRE, S., *Spinoza* (London: Faber, 1956).

HINSLEY, F.H., *Sovereignty* (London: Watts, 1966).

HOBBES, T., *Philosophical Rudiments Concerning Government and Society* (London: Royston, 1651).

KAMENKA, E. and NEALE, R.S., *Feudalism, Capitalism and Beyond* (London: Arnold, 1975).

LEFORT, C., *Le travail de l'oeuvre: Machiavel* (Paris: Gallimard, 1973).

LUSINGE, S.di, *Dell'origine, conservazione e decadenza di gli stati* (Ferrara, 1590).

MEINECKE, F., *Die Idee der Staatsräson* (Munich: Oldenbourg, 1929).

―――, *Machiavellism: The Doctrine of Raison d'État and its History* (New Haven, Conn.: Yale University Press, 1957).

MORRALL, J.B., *Political Thought in Medieval Times* (London: Hutchinson, 1958).

PRYNNE, W., *Thomas Campanella: An Italian Friar and Second Machiavel* (London, 1660).

ROHAN, Duc de, *De l'interest des princes et des estats de la chrestienté* (Paris, 1638).

ROWDON, M., *Lorenzo the Magnificent* (London: Weidenfeld and Nicolson, 1974).

SHEA, W.R., *Galileo's Intellectual Revolution* (London: Macmillan, 1972).

VALE, M.G.A., *Charles VII* (London: Methuen, 1974).

WALEY, D.P.L., *The Papal State in the Thirteenth Century* (London: Macmillan, 1961).

WERNHAM, A.G. (ed. and tr.), *B. Spinoza. The Political Works* (Oxford: Clarendon Press, 1958).

Articles

BENOIST, C., "L'Influence des idées de Machiavel," *52 Receuil de Cours* (1925), pp. 131-303.

WALEY, D.P., "The primitivist element in Machiavelli's thought," 31 *Journal of the History of Ideas* (1970), pp. 91-98.

WRIGHT, P.Q., "Grotius and the law of war and peace," 35 *American Journal of International Law* (1941), p. 35.

WOOD, N., "Machiavelli's concept of 'virtù' reconsidered," 15 *Political Studies* (1967), pp. 159-172.

CHAPTER 3

Books

ANCILLON, F., *Tableau des révolutions de système politique de l'Europe depuis la fin du quinzième siècle* (Berlin: Duncker, 1803-1805).

BOLINGBROKE, Viscount, *Works,* Vol. 2 (London: 1754).

BORKENAU, F., *Der Übergang vom feudalen zum bürgerlichen Weltbild: Studien zur Geschichte der Philosophie der Manufakturperiode* (Paris: Alcan, 1934).

BULL, H., *The Anarchical Society: a Study of Order in World Politics* (London: Macmillan, 1977).

BUTTERFIELD, H., *The Origins of Science, 1300-1800* (London: Bell, 1957).

BUTTERFIELD, H. and WIGHT, M. (eds.), *Diplomatic Investigations. Essays in the Theory of International Politics* (London: Allen and Unwin, 1966).

COLEMAN, D.C. (ed.), *Revisions in Mercantilism* (London: Methuen, 1969).

DAVENANT, C., *Essays upon the Balance of Power: the Right of Making War, Peace and Alliances; and Universal Monarchy* (London: Knapton, 1701).

GALTUNG, J., *Notes on the Balance of Power: Problems and Definitions* (Oslo: International Peace Research Institute, 1962).

GENTZ, F., *Fragments on the Balance of Power* (London: Peltier, 1806).

GULICK, E.V., *Europe's Classical Balance of Power* (Ithaca: Cornell University Press, 1955).

HINSLEY, F.H., *Power and the Pursuit of Peace* (London: Cambridge University Press, 1963).

JAMES, A. (ed.), *The Bases of International Order. Essays in Honour of C.A.W. Manning* (London: Oxford University Press, 1973).

KAEBER, E., *Die Idee des europäischen Gleichgewichts in der publizistischen Literatur vom 16. bis zur Mitte des 18. Jahrhunderts* (Berlin: Duncker, 1907).

KAHN, H., BROWN, W., and MARTEL, L., *The Next 200 Years* (New York: Associated Business Programs, 1977).

KAHN, H., *On Thermonuclear War* (Princeton, N.J.: Princeton University Press, 1961).

KAPLAN, M.A., *System and Process in International Politics* (New York: John Wiley, 1957).
KISSINGER, H.A., *A World Restored* (Boston: Houghton Mifflin, 1957).
——— , *Nuclear Weapons and Foreign Policy* (New York: Harper and Row, 1957).
LECKIE, G.F., *An Historical Research into the Nature of the Balance of Power in Europe* (London: Taylor and Hessey, 1817).
LIJPART, A. (ed.), *World Politics* (Boston: Allyn and Bacon, 1966).
McNEILLY, F.S., *The Anatomy of Leviathan* (London: Macmillan, 1968).
NEUMANN, J. von, and MORGENSTERN, O., *The Theory of Games and Economic Behavior* (Princeton, N.J.: Princeton University Press, 1944).
OGG, D. (ed.), *Sully's Grand Design of Henry IV of 1611* (Texts for Students of International Relations, (London: Grotius Society, 2, 1921).
PADOVER, S.K., *Prince Kaunitz and the First Partition of Poland* (London: Eyre and Spottiswoode, 1935).
RAPOPORT, A., *Fights, Games and Debates* (Ann Arbor: University of Michigan, 1960).
RAUMER, K. von, *Ewiger Friede. Friedensrufe und Friedenspläne seit der Renaissance* (Freiburg and Munich: Oldenbourg, 1953).
REISMAN, W.M. (ed.), *Toward World Order and Human Dignity. Essays in honor of M.S. McDougal* (New York: Free Press, 1977).
SAINT PIERRE, C.I. Castel de, *Projet pour rendre la paix perpétuelle en Europe* (Utrecht, 1712).
SCHELLING, T.C., *The Strategy of Conflict* (London: Oxford University Press, 1963).
WALL, G.R., *Bipolarization and the International System, 1946-1970* (Stockholm: The Swedish Institute of International Affairs, 1972).
WEIZSÄCKER, C.F. von, *Wege in der Gefahr* (Munich: Hanser, 1977).
WILLIAMS, P., *Conflict, Confrontation and Diplomacy* (New York: Halsted, 1975).

Articles

ANDERSON, M.S., "Eighteenth century theories of the balance of power," in HATTON, R. and ANDERSON, M.S. (eds.), *Studies in Diplomatic History* (London: Longmans, 1970), pp. 183-199.
DUNN, L.A. and OVERHOLT, W.H., "The next phase in nuclear proliferation research," 20 *Orbis* (1976), pp. 497-524.
HERZ, J.H., "The rise and demise of the territorial state," in 9 *World Politics* (1957), pp. 474-493.
LEWIS, J.V., "Jean Bodin's 'Logic of Sovereignty,'" 16 *Political Studies* (1968), pp. 206-222.
MAURSETH, P., "Balance of power thinking from the Renaissance to the French revolution," 1 *Journal of Peace Research* (1964), pp. 120-136.
MURPHY, O.T., "Charles Gravier de Vergennes: profile of an old régime diplomat," 83 *Political Science Quarterly* (1968), pp. 400-418.
NYS, E., "La theorie de l'équilibre européenne," 25 *Revue de droit international* (1893), pp. 34-57.
PURVES, R., "Prolegomena to Utopian International Projects," in ALEXANDROWICZ, C.H. (ed.), *Grotian Society Papers* (1968), (The Hague: Nijhoff; 1970), pp. 100-110.
VAGTS, A., "The balance of power: growth of an idea," *World Politics* (1948), New Haven, Conn.: Yale University, Institute of International Studies, pp. 82-101.
VINER, J., "English theories of foreign trade before Adam Smith," 38 *Journal of Political Economy* (1930), pp. 249-301 and 404-757.
WOHLSTETTER, A., "Spreading the bomb without quite breaking the rules," *Foreign Policy* (Winter 1976/7), pp. 88-96 and 145-179.
WOHLSTETTER, R., "Terror on a grand scale," 18 *Survival* (1976), pp. 98-104.

CHAPTER 4

BOOKS

BECKER, C., *The Heavenly City of the Eighteenth Century Philosopher* (New Haven, Conn.: Yale University Press, 1959).

COBBAN, A., *Rousseau and the Modern State* (London: Allen and Unwin, 1934).

FRIEDRICH, C.J., *Inevitable Peace* (Cambridge, Mass.: Cambridge University Press, 1948).

GALSTON, W.A., *Kant and the Problem of History* (Chicago: University of Chicago, 1975).

KAMENKA, E. and NEALE, R.S. (eds.), *Feudalism, Capitalism and Beyond* (London: Arnold, 1975).

KANT, I., *Idea of a Universal History of a Cosmological Plan* (Hanover, N.H.: The Sociological Press, 1927).

———, *Kritik der reinen Vernunft* (Riga: Hartknoch, 1781).

———, *Zum ewigen Frieden* (Königsberg: Nicolovius, 1795).

KEETON, G.W. and SCHWARZENBERGER, G., *Jeremy Bentham and the Law* (London: Stevens, 1948).

FOX-GENOVESE, E., *The Origins of Physiocracy* (London: Cornell University Press, 1976).

NUTTALL, E.M. (ed.), *A Project of Perpetual Peace: Rousseau's Essay,* translated from Abbé Castel de St. Pierre (London: Cobden Sanderson, 1927).

REISS, H. (ed.), *Kant's Political Writings* (London: Cambridge University Press, 1970).

WALTZ, K.N., *Man, the State and War* (London: American University Publishers' Group, 1975).

Articles

HOFFMAN, S., "Rousseau on war and peace," 57 *American Political Science Review* (1963), pp. 317-333.

LAUTERPACHT, Sir Hersch, "Spinoza and international law," 8 *British Yearbook of International Law* (1927), pp. 89-107.

———, "The Grotian tradition in international law," 27 *British Yearbook of International Law* (1946), pp. 1-53.

LEVIN, M., "Rousseau on independence," 18 *Political Studies* (1970), pp. 497-513.

PERKINS, M.L., "Rousseau on history, liberty and national survival," 53 *Studies on Voltaire and the Eighteenth Century* (1967), pp. 79-169.

PURVES, R., "Prolegomena to utopian international projects," in ALEXANDROWICZ, C.H. (ed.), *Grotian Society Papers,* 1968 (The Hague: Nijhoff, 1970), pp. 100-110.

SHKLAR, J.N., "Rousseau's two models: Sparta and the age of gold," 81 *Political Science Quarterly* (1966), pp. 25-51.

WALTZ, K.N., "Kant, liberalism and war," 56 *American Political Science Review* (1962), pp. 331-340.

CHAPTER 5

Books

ALMEYDA, C., *Hacia una teoría del estado* (Santiago: Prensa Latinoamericana, 1948).

AVINERI, S., *The Social and Political Thought of Karl Marx* (London: Cambridge University Press, 1971).

ENGELS, F., *The Dialectics of Nature* (tr: Moscow: Foreign Languages Publishing House, 1954).

GADAMER, H.G., *Hegel's Dialektik* (tr. by P.C. Smith; New Haven: Yale University Press, 1976).

HEGEL, G.W.F., *Die Phänomenologie des Geistes* (Frankfurt: Ullstein, 1970).

———, *Naturrecht und Staatswissenschaft im Grundrisse: Grundlinien der Philosophie des Rechts* (Stuttgart: Reclam, 1870).

HOOK, S. *From Hegel to Marx* (London: Gollancz, 1936).

HYPPOLITE, J., *Studies on Marx and Hegel* (London: Heinemann Educational, 1969).

JAY, M., *The Dialectical Imagination: A history of the Frankfurt School and the Institute of Social Research, 1923-1950* (Boston: Little Brown, 1973).

KORSCH, K., *Marxism and Philosophy* (tr. by F. Halliday. London: NLB, 1970).

LOEWENBERG, J. (ed.), *Hegel: Selections* (Cambridge, Mass.: Cambridge University Press, 1929).

LOEWITH, K. *From Hegel to Nietzsche* (London: Constable, 1964).

O'BRIEN, G.D., *Hegel on Reason and History* (Chicago: Chicago University Press, 1976).

PELCZYNSKI, Z.A., *Hegel's Political Philosophy: Problems and Perspectives* (London: Cambridge University Press, 1972).

ROSENZWEIG, F., *Hegel und der Staat* (Munich and Berlin, 1920).

SANDERSON, J.B., *An Introduction to the Political Thought of Marx and Engels* (London: Longmans, 1969).

TAYLOR, C., *Hegel* (London: Cambridge University Press, 1975).

WEISS, F.G. (ed.), *Hegel: Beyond Epistemology* (Leyden: Nijhoff, 1974).

Articles

ADORNO, F., "Dialettica e politica in Platone," 20 *Atti e memorie dell'Accademia Toscana di Scienze e Lettere* ("La Columbaria," 1955; 1956), pp. 97-200.

AVINERI, S., "The problem of war in Hegel's thought," 22 *Journal of the History of Ideas* (1961), pp. 463-474.

HASSNER, P., "Les concepts de guerre et de paix chez Kant," 11 *Revue française de science politique* (1961), pp. 642-670.

CHAPTER 6

Books

ARON, R., *War and Industrial Society* (London: Oxford University Press, 1958).

BAKER, K.M., *Condorcet: from Natural Philosophy to Social Mathematics* (London: University of Chicago Press, 1975).

BLAU, P.M., *Exchange and Power in Social Life* (New York: John Wiley, 1964).

BOSANQUET, H., *Free Trade and Peace in the Nineteenth Century* (New York: Putnam, 1924).

COBDEN, R., *Speeches* (London: Gilbert, 1849).

COMTE, A., *Cours de philosophie positive.* ed. by M. Serres and others. (Paris: Hermann, 1975).

CONDORCET, Marquis de, *Esquisse d'un tableau historique du progrès de l'esprit humain;* Ouvrage posthume; (Paris, 1795).

EVANS, J.D.G., *Aristotle's Concept of Dialectic* (Cambridge: Cambridge University Press, 1977).

GODWIN, W., *Enquiry Concerning Political Justice and its Influence on Morals and Happiness* (London: Robinson, 1798).

GREEN, T.H., *Lectures on the Principles of Political Obligation* (London: Longman, 1958).

GROOM, A.J.R. and TAYLOR, P. (eds.), *Functionalism: Theory and Practice in International Relations* (London: University of London Press, 1975).

HIRST, F.W. (ed.), *Free Trade and other Fundamental Doctrines of the Manchester School* (London: Harper; New York: Kelly, 1968).

HOBSON, J.A., *Richard Cobden, the International Man* (London: Fisher Unwin, 1918).

HOLLIS, M. and NELL, E., *Rational Economic Man* (Cambridge: Cambridge University Press, 1975).

HORKHEIMER, M., *Verwaltete Welt* (Zürich: Arche, 1970).

IONESCU, G. (ed.), *The Political Thought of Saint-Simon* (London: Oxford University Press, 1976).

JOHNSON, E.A.J., *Predecessors of Adam Smith* (New York: Prentice Hall, 1960).

KEETON, G.W. and SCHWARZENBERGER, G., *Jeremy Bentham and the Law* (London: Stevens, 1948).

KEOHANE, R. and NYE, R. (eds.), *Transnational Relations and World Politics* (Cambridge, Mass.: Harvard University Press, 1973).

MARKHAM, F.M.H. (ed.), *Henri, Comte de Saint-Simon. Selected Writings* (London: English Universities Press, 1952).

MEEK, R.L. (ed.), *Turgot on Progress, Sociology and Economics* (London: Cambridge University Press, 1973).

MITRANY, D., *A Working Peace System* (London: Oxford University Press, 1946).

MYRDAL, G., *Beyond the Welfare State* (New Haven, Conn.: Yale University Press, 1960).

PENTLAND, C., *International Theory and European Integration* (London: Faber, 1973).

PLAMENATZ, J.P., *The English Utilitarians* (Oxford: Blackwell, 1958).

PROUDHON, P.J., *La guerre et la paix* (Brussels: Lavroix, 1861).

READ, D., *Cobden and Bright: A Victorian Partnership* (London: Arnold, 1968).

REISMAN, D.A., *Adam Smith's Sociological Economics* (London: Croom Helm, 1976).

SCHWARTZ, P., *The New Political Economy of J.S. Mill* (London: Weidenfeld and Nicolson, 1973).

SEWELL, J.P., *Functionalism in World Politics* (Princeton, N.J.: Princeton University Press, 1960).

SILBERNER, E., *La guerre dans la pensée politique du XVIe au XVIIIe siècle* (Paris: Pedone, 1939).

——— , *The Problem of War in Nineteenth Century Economic Thought* (Princeton, N.J.: Princeton University Press, 1946).

SMITH, A.D., *The Concept of Social Change. A Critique of the Functionalist Theory of Social Change* (London: Routledge and Kegan Paul, 1974).

SPENCER, H., *Man versus the State* (London and Edinburgh: William & Norgate, 1884).

VILLAGRAN, F.K., *Integración Económica Centroamericana* (Guatemala City: Universidad de San Carlos, 1967).

WELLS, H.G., *A Modern Utopia* (London: Chapman and Hall, 1905).

Articles

FLOURNOY, F.R., "British liberal theories of international relations, 1848-1898," 7 *Journal of the History of Ideas* (1946), pp. 195-217.

HALLIDAY, R.J., "John Stuart Mill's idea of Politics," 18 *Political Studies* (1970), pp. 461-477.

MILLER, K.W., "John Stuart Mill's theories of international relations," 22 *Journal of the History of Ideas* (1961), pp. 493-514.

SIMON, W.M., "History of utopia: Saint-Simon and the idea of progress," 17 *Journal of the History of Ideas* (1956), pp. 311-331.

CHAPTER 7

Books

ARENDT, H., *The Origins of Totalitarianism* (in 2nd. enlarged ed. of *The Burdens of our Time*) (London: Allen and Unwin, 1958).

AVINERI, S., *Karl Marx on Colonialism and Modernisation* (Garden City, N.Y., 1968).

BARAN, P. and SWEEZY, P., *Monopoly Capital* (Harmondsworth: Penguin, 1970).

BROOKFIELD, H., *Interdependence and Development* (London: Methuen, 1975).

BUKHARIN, N.I., *Imperialism and the World Economy* (London: Martin Lawrence, 1929).

CARDOSO, F.H., *Ideologías de la burguesía industrial en sociedades dependientes* (Mexico City: Siglo Veintiuno, 1971).

––– and FALETTO, E., *Dependencia y desarrollo en América Latina* (Mexico City: Siglo Veintiuno, 1971).

COHEN, B.J., *The Question of Imperialism. The Political Economy of Dominance and Dependence* (New York: Basic Books, 1973).

DOS SANTOS, T., *El nuevo carácter de la dependencia* (Santiago: Universidad de Chile, 1968).

EMMANUEL, A., *L'échange inégal. Essai sur les antagonismes dans les rapports économiques internationaux.* (Paris: François Maspero, 1969).

ENGELS, F. and MARX, K., *On Colonialism* (London: Lawrence and Wishart, 1960).

FANON, F., *The Wretched of the Earth* (London: McGibbon and Kee, 1965).

FRANK, G.A., *Capitalism and Underdevelopment in Latin America* (Harmondsworth: Penguin, 1971).

FREYMOND, J., *Lénine et l'Impérialisme* (Lausanne: Payot, 1951).

GALBRAITH, K., *The New Industrial State* (Harmondsworth: Penguin, 1969).

GRIFFIN, K.B., *Underdevelopment in Spanish America* (London: Allen and Unwin, 1969).

HILFERDING, R., *Das Finanzkapital* (Vienna: Brand, 1910).

HINKELAMERT, F., *Dialéctica del Desarrollo Desigual* (Valparaiso: Universidad Católica, 1970).

HOBSON, J.A., *Imperialism* (London: Allen and Unwin, 1907).

JAGUARIBE, H., *La Dominación de América Latina* (Lima: Moncloa, 1968).

––– and others, *La dependencia político-económica de América Latina* (Mexico City: Siglo Veintiuno, 1972).

KAUTSKY, J.H., *Political Change in Underdeveloped Countries* (London: Wiley, 1962).

KAY, G., *Development and Underdevelopment. A Marxist Analysis.* (London: Macmillan, 1975).

KEMP, T., *Theories of Imperialism* (London: Dobson, 1967).

KINDLEBERGER, C. (ed.), *The International Corporation* (Cambridge, Mass.: M.I.T. Press, 1970).

LENIN, V.I., *Imperialism: The Highest Stage of Capitalism.* (Moscow: Foreign Languages Publishing House, 1947).

LICHTHEIM, G., *Imperialism* (London: Allen Lane, 1971).

LIST, G.F., *The National System of Political Economy* (London: Longman, 1904).

LUXEMBURG, R. and BUKHARIN, N., *Imperialism and the Accumulation of Capital* (London: Allen Lane, 1972).

MARINI, R.M., *Subdesarrollo y Revolución* (Mexico City: Siglo Veintiuno, 1969).

MERHAV, V.M., *Dependencia Tecnológica, Monopolio y Crecimiento* (Buenos Aires: Ediciones Periferia, 1972).

MODRZHINSKAYA, E.D., *Kosmopolitizm–imperialisticheskaya ideologiya poroboshcheniya natsii* (Moscow: Gosizdat, 1958).

MODRZHINSKAYA, E.D., *Raspad kolonialnoi sistemy i ideologiya imperializma* (Moscow: Gosizdat, 1965).

NKRUMAH, K., *Neo-Colonialism, the Last Stage of Imperialism* (London: Nelson, 1965 ed.).

OWEN, R. and SUTCLIFFE (eds.), *Studies in the Theory of Imperialism* (London: Longman, 1972).

OXAAL, I. and others (eds.), *Beyond the Sociology of Development, Economy and Society in Latin America and Africa* (London: Routledge and Kegan Paul, 1975).

PASHUKANIS, E.B., *Imperializm i kolonialnaya politika. Kurs lektsii* (Moscow: Izdatelstvo Kommunisticheskoi Akademii, 1928).

RADICE, H., *International Forms and Modern Imperialism* (Harmondsworth: Penguin, 1975).

RHODES, R.I. (ed.), *Imperialism and Underdevelopment: a Reader* (New York: Monthly Review Press, 1970).

SCHMIDT, J.L., *Entwicklungsländer* (Berlin: Die Wirtschaft, 1974).

SCHUMPETER, J., *Imperialism and Social Classes,* ed. H. Norden (Oxford: Blackwell, 1952).

SEMMEL, B., *Imperialism and Social Reform* (London: Allen and Unwin, 1960).

SLOAN, P., *Marx and the Orthodox Economists* (Oxford: Blackwell, 1973).

STRACHEY, J., *The End of Empire* (London: Gollancz, 1959).

STRAUSS, W.L., *Joseph Chamberlain and the Theory of Imperialism* (Washington: American Council on Public Affairs, 1942).

WEISS, T.G., *International Bureaucracy* (Lexington: Lexington Books, 1975).

Articles

AMIN, A., "Accumulation and development: A theoretical model," 1 *Review of African Political Economy* (1974), pp. 9-26.

BERNARDIN-HALDEMANN, V., "L'idéologie de la CEPAL," 2 *Études internationales* (1974), pp. 123-142.

CARDOSO, F.H., "Notas sobre el estado actual de los estudios sobre dependencia," in SIERRA, J. (ed.), *Desarrollo latinoamericano. Ensayos críticos* (Mexico City: Fondo de Cultura Económica, 1974).

CHASE-DUNN, C., "The effects of international economic dependence on development and inequality: A cross-national study," 40 *American Sociology Review* (1975), pp. 720-730.

FERRER, A., "La dependencia scientifica y tecnológica en el contexto internacional y sus implicaciones para la transferencia de tecnología," 15 *Desarrollo Económico* (1976), pp. 565-580.

FURTADO, C., "The Brazilian model," 22 *Social and Economic Studies* (1973), pp. 122-131.

GALTUNG, J., "A structural theory of imperialism," 2 *Journal of Peace Research* (1971), pp. 81-117.

GIRVAN, N., "Teorías de dependencia económica en el Caribe y Latinoamérica comparativo," 6 *Estudios Internacionales* (1973), pp. 23-60.

KNORR, K., "Theories of imperialism," 4 *World Politics* (1951), pp. 402-431.

KOCHEVRIN, Y., "Burzhuaznye teorii krupnoi korporatsii i apologiya menzhevizma," 10 *Mirovaya Ekonomika i mezhdunarodnye otnoshenya* (1976), pp. 43-54.

NURSEY-BRAY, P., "Marxism and existentialism in the thought of Frantz Fanon," 20 *Political Studies* (1972), pp. 152-168.

O'BRIEN, P., "A critique of Latin American theories of dependency," *Institute of Latin American Studies (Glasgow), Occasional Papers,* No. 12 (1975).

PATEL, S.J., "The technological dependence of developing countries," 12 *Journal of African Studies* (1974), pp. 1-18.

ROXBOROUGH, I., "Dependency theory in the sociology of development: some theoretical problems," 1 *West African Journal of Sociology and Political Science* (1976), pp. 116-133.

SHISHKOV, Y., "Mezhdunarodnye sverkhmonopoli i neravnomernost razvitiya kapitalizma," *Mirovaya Ekonomika i mezhdunarodnye otnoshenya* (1973), pp. 36-52.

SUNKEL, O., "Big business and dependencia," 50 *Foreign Affairs* (1972), pp. 517-531.
TARG, H., "Global dominance and dependence: post-industrialism and international relations theory," *International Studies Quarterly* (1976), pp. 461-482.

CHAPTER 8

Books

ADLER, E., *Herder und die deutsche Aufklärung* (Zürich: Europa-Verlag, 1970).
BARNARD, F.M., *Herder's Social and Political Thought: from Enlightenment to Nationalism* (Oxford: Clarendon Press, 1965).
BAUER, O., *Die Sozialdemokratie und die Nationalitätenfrage* (Vienna: Volksbuchhandlung, 1907).
BERLIN, Sir Isiah, *Vico and Herder: Two Studies in the History of Ideas* (London: Hogarth Press, 1976).
BOERSNER, D., *The Bolsheviks and the National and Colonial Question* (Geneva; Institut de Hautes Études Internationales, 1957).
BUNZL, J., *Klassenkampf in der Diaspora. Zur Geschichte der jüdischen Arbeiterbewegung* (Vienna: Europa-Verlag, 1975).
CARR, E.H., *Nationalism and After* (London: Macmillan, 1945).
ENGELS, F., *The Russian Menace* (London: Allen and Unwin, 1953) (original edition, 1849).
ENLOE, C.H., *Ethnic Conflict and Political Development* (Boston: Little Brown, 1973).
FOX, R.W., *Marx, Engels and Lenin on the Irish Revolution* (London: Modern Books, 1933).
HERMAN, S.N., *Israelis and Jews. The Continuity of an Identity.* (New York: Random House, 1970).
HINSLEY, F.H., *Nationalism and the International System* (London: Hodder and Stoughton, 1973).
JOLL, J., *The Second International, 1889-1914* (London: Weidenfeld and Nicolson, 1955).
KAUTSKY, K., *Nationalstaat, imperialistischer Staat und Staatenbund* (Nuremberg: 1910).
KAMENKA, E. (ed.), *Nationalism: The Nature and Evolution of an Idea* (London: Arnold, 1976).
KOHN, H., *Pan-Slavism: Its History and Ideology* (New York: University of Notre Dame, Indiana, 1953).
———, *Prophets and Peoples. Studies in Nineteenth-Century Nationalism* (New York: Macmillan, 1946).
KUPER, L., *Race, Class and Power* (London: Duckworth, 1974).
LESER, N., *Die Odyssee des Marxismus* (Vienna: Molden, 1971).
MEINECKE, F., *Weltbürgertum und Nationalstaat* (Munich and Berlin, 1908).
MOMMSEN, H., *Die Sozialdemokratie und die Nationalitätenfrage im habsburgischen Vielvölkerstaat* (Vienna: Europa-Verlag. 1972).
RENAN, E., *Qu'est-ce qu'une Nation? Conférence faite en Sorbonne* (Paris: Calmann Lévy, 1882).
RENNER, K., *Der Kampf der österreichischen Nationen um den Staat* (Vienna: Volksbuchhandlung, 1902).
SHAHEEN, S., *The Communist Theory of Self-Determination* (The Hague: W. van Hoeve, 1956).
SMITH, A.D., *Theories of Nationalism* (London: Duckworth, 1971).
STALIN, J.V., *Marxism and the National and Colonial Question* (ed. A. Fineberg.) (London: Martin Lawrence, 1915).

VERGNAND, P., *L'idée de la nationalité et de la libre disposition des peuples dans ses rapports avec l'idée de l'État* (Geneva: Etudes d'histoire économique, politique et sociale, No. 10, 1955).

WELL, G., *L'Europe du XIXe siècle et l'idée de nationalité* (Paris: Michel, 1938).

WHITAKER, A.P. and JORDAN, D.C., *Nationalism in Contemporary Latin America* (New York: Free Press, and London: Collier, Macmillan, 1966).

Articles

COBBAN, A., "Edmund Burke and the origins of the theory of nationality," 2 *The Cambridge History Journal* (1926), pp. 36-47.

DAVIS, H.B., "Nations, colonies and classes: the position of Marx and Engels," 29 *Science and Society* (1965), pp. 26-43.

LYNN, R., "The sociobiology of nationalism," *New Society,* July 1, 1976, pp. ll-14.

PERES, Y., "Modernisation and nationalism: The identity of the Israeli Arab," 24 *Middle East Journal* (1970), pp. 479-492.

PETRUS, J.A., "Marx and Engels on the national question," 33 *Journal of Politics* (1971), pp. 797-825.

CHAPTER 9

Books

AMOUDRUZ, M., *Proudhon et l'Europe* (Paris: Montchrétien, 1945).

BAKUNIN, M.A., *Gosudarstvennost i anarkhiya* (Leyden: International Institute of Social History, 1967).

BODIN, J., *Six livres de la République* (Paris: Puys, 1576).

BOURGEOIS, N., *Les théories du droit international chez Proudhon. Le fédéralisme et la paix.* (Paris: Marcel Rivière, 1927).

DAVIES, Lord, *A Federated Europe* (London: Gollancz, 1940).

——— , *Nearing the Abyss* (London: Constable, 1936).

——— , *The Problem of the Twentieth Century* (London: Benn, 1930).

FRANTZ, C., *Der Föderalismus, als das leitende Prinzip für die sociale, staatliche und internationale Organisation* (Mainz: Kirchheim, 1879).

HAMILTON, A. and others, *The Federalist*, 1789 (New York: New America Library, 1961).

HEPNER, B.P., *Bakounine et le panslavisme révolutionnaire* (Paris: Rivière, 1950).

HODÉ, J., *L'Idee de fédéralisme internationale dans l'histoire* (Paris: Pedone, 1921).

KROPOTKIN, P.A., *The State: its Historical Role* (London: Freedom Office, 1897).

——— , *Mutual Aid* (Harmondsworth: Penguin, 1939).

LEHNING, A. (ed.), *Archives Bakounine*, Vol. 5 (Leyden: Brill, 1976).

MILL, J.S., *Considerations on Representative Government* (London: Parker, 1845).

PROUDHON, J.P., *Du principe fédératif* (Paris: Dentu, 1863).

———, *L'Idée générale de la Révolution du XIXe siècle* (Paris: Garnier Frères, 1851).

PUFENDORF, S., *Gründlicher Bericht von dem Zustande des Heiligen Reichs Teutscher Nation,* (1667) (Leipzig: 1715 ed.)

RENOUVIN, P., *L'Idée de fédération européenne dans la pensée politique du XIXe siècle* (Oxford: Clarendon Press, 1949).

RITTER, A., *The Political Thought of Pierre-Joseph Proudhon* (Princeton, N.J.: Princeton University Press, 1969).

STREIT, C.K., *Union Now: Proposal for a Federal Union of the Democracies of the North Atlantic* (London: Right Book Club, 1939).

VERGNAND, P., *L'Idée de la nationalité et de la libre disposition des peuples dans ses rapports avec l'idée de l'État* (Geneva: Études d'histoire économique, politique et sociale, No. 10; 1955).

WOODCOCK, G. (ed.), *The Anarchist Reader* (London: Harvester Press, 1977).

ARTICLES

BELOFF, M., "Federalism as a model for international integration," 13 *Yearbook of World Affairs* (1969), pp. 188-204.

HAYEK, F.A. von, "Economic conditions of inter-state federalism," 5 *New Commonwealth Quarterly* (1939-1940), pp. 131-149.

PAINCHAUD, P., "Fédéralisme et théories de politique étrangère," 4 *Études Internationales* (1974), pp. 25-44.

RIKER, W.H., "Dutch and American federalism," 18 *Journal of the History of Ideas* (1957), pp. 495-501.

WEISS, T., "The tradition of philosophical anarchism and future directions in World Policy," 12 *Journal of Peace Research* (1975), pp. 1-17.

WOOTTON, Dame Barbara, "Economic Problems of Federal Union," 5 *New Commonwealth Quarterly* (1939-1940), pp. 150-156.

CHAPTER 10

Books

ANGELL, Sir Norman, *The Great Illusion* (London: Heinemann, 1910).

BEARD, C.A., *The Idea of National Interest* (New York: Macmillan, 1934).

CARR, E.H., *The Twenty Years Crisis: An Introduction to the Study of International Relations* (London: Macmillan, 1939).

CURTIS, L., *Civitas Dei*, 3. vols. (London: Macmillan, 1934-1937).

HEEREN, A.H.L., *Historische Werke* (Göttingen: Röwer, 1821-1826).

HOLBRAAD, C., *The Concert of Europe* (London: Longman, 1970).

KEGLEY, C.W. and BRETALL, R.W. (eds.), *Reinhold Niebuhr* (New York: Macmillan, 1956).

KISSINGER, A.H., *A World Restored* (New York: Grosset, 1964).

LADD, W., *An Essay on a Congress of Nations for the Adjustment of International Disputes without Resort to Arms* (original edition, 1840) (Columbia: Carnegie Endowment for International Peace, 1916).

MARGERIE, B. de, *Reinhold Niebuhr, théologicien de la communauté mondiale* (Paris: Brouwer, 1969).

MARTIN, L.W., *Peace Without Victory: Woodrow Wilson and the British Liberals* (New Haven: Yale University Press, 1918).

MURRAY, G., *The League of Nations and the Democratic Idea* (London: Oxford University Press, 1918).

PADOVER, S.K. (ed.), *Wilson's Ideals* (Washington: American Council of Public Affairs, 1943).

PORTER, B. (ed.), *The Aberystwyth Papers. International Politics, 1919-1969* (London: Oxford University Press, 1972).

SCHWARZENBERGER, G., *Power Politics* (London: Cape, 1941).

———, *Power Politics* (London: Stevens, 1964).

———, *The League of Nations and World Order* (London: Constable, 1936).

———, *William Ladd* (London: Constable, 1935).

STERLING, R.W., *Ethics in a World of Power. The Political Ideas of Meinecke.* (Princeton, N.J.: Princeton University Press, 1958).

TOYNBEE, A., *The World after the Peace Conference; being an epilogue to the "History of the Peace Conference of Paris" (ed. by Temperley), and a prologue to the "Survey of International Affairs," 1920-1923* (London: Royal Institute of International Affairs, 1925).

TRIEPEL, H., *Die Hegemonie. Ein Buch von führenden Staaten* (Stuttgart: Kohlhammer, 1938).

WOLFERS, A. and MARTIN, L.W. (eds.), *The Anglo-American Tradition in Foreign Affairs* (New Haven: Yale University Press, 1956).

ZIMMERN, Sir Alfred, *The Prospects of Civilisation* (London: Oxford University Press, 1939).

Articles

BIRN, D.S., "The League of Nations Union and collective security," 9 *Journal of Contemporary History* 1974), pp. 131-159.

BUTTERFIELD, H., "The scientific v. the moralistic approach in international affairs," 27 *International Affairs* (1951), pp. 411-422.

JOHNSTON, W., "E.H. Carr's theory of international relations: a critique," 29 *Journal of Politics* (1967), pp. 861-885.

MORGAN, R., "E.H. Carr and the study of international relations" in ABRAMSKY, C. and WILLIAMS, B.J. (eds.), *Essays in Honour of E.H. Carr* (London: Macmillan, 1974), pp. 171-182.

THOMPSON, K.W., "Beyond national interest: a critical evaluation of Reinhold Niebuhr's theory of international politics," 17 *Review of Politics*, pp. 167-180.

——— , "Mr. Toynbee and world politics," 13 *World Politics* (1956), pp. 379-391.

ZIMMERN, Sir Alfred, "The influence of public opinion on foreign policy," Geneva Institute of International Relations, *Problems of Peace* (1928), pp. 299-320.

CHAPTER 11

Books

BERLIN, Sir Isiah, *Karl Marx* (London: Oxford University Press, 1939).

BRETTON, P. and CHAUDET, M., *La Coexistence Pacifique* (Paris: Armand Colin, 1971).

BUKHARIN, N.I., *Ekonomika perekhodnovo perioda* (Moscow: Gosizdat, 1920).

——— , and PREOBRAZHENSKY, E.A., *The ABC of Communism* (Harmondsworth: Penguin, 1967 ed.).

CARR, E.H., *A History of Soviet Russia. Socialism in One Country, 1924-1926*, Vol. 3 (London: Macmillan, 1964).

DAY, R.B., *Leon Trotsky and the Politics of Isolation* (London: Cambridge University Press, 1973).

ENGELS, F., *Principles of Communism* (New York: Monthly Review, 1847).

FOURIER, C., *L'Unité universelle* (original edition, 1842; under title of *L'Harmonie universelle*) (Paris, 1949).

HORKHEIMER, M., *Kritische Theorie. Eine Dokumentation* (ed. A. Schmidt) (Frankfurt: Fischer, 1968).

KOROVIN, E.A., *Mezhdunarodnoye pravo perehodnovo vremeni* (Moscow: Gosizdat, 1923).

LENIN, V.I., *State and Revolution* (London: Allen and Unwin, 1919).

MARCUSE, H., *Reason and Revolution: Hegel and the Rise of Social Theory* (London: Routledge and Kegan Paul, 1967 ed.).

——— , *Soviet Marxism: A critical analysis.* (Ithaca: Columbia University Press, 1958).

PREOBRAZHENSKY, E.A., *Novaya Ekonomika* (Moscow: Gosizdat, 1926).

SAMPSON, R.V., *Tolstoy: The discovery of peace.* (London: H.E.B., 1973).

SLATER, P., *Origin and Significance of the Frankfurt School* (London: Routledge and Kegan Paul, 1977).

TROTSKY, L.D., *Permanentnaya Revolutsiya* (Berlin: Izdatelstvo "Granit," 1930).

Articles

BERKI, R.N., "On Marxian thought and the problem of international relations," 24 *World Politics* (1971), pp. 80-105.

BURIN, F.S., "The communist doctrine of the inevitability of war," 57 *American Journal of International Law* (1966), pp. 334-354.

GOORMAGHTIGH, J., "International relations as a field of study in the Soviet Union," 28 *Yearbook of World Affairs* (1974), pp. 250-261.

JANOS, A.C., "The communist theory of the state and revolution" in BLACK, C.E. and THORNTON, T.P. (eds.), *Communism and Revolution* (Princeton, N.J.: Princeton University Press, 1964).

JONES, C.D., "Just wars and limited wars: restraints on the use of the Soviet armed forces," 17 *World Politics* (1975), pp. 44-68.

KOROVIN, E.A., "Proletarian internationalism and international law," *Soviet Yearbook of International Law* (1958), pp. 50-73.

KRYLOV, S., "Les notions principales du droit international," 70 *Receuil de Cours* (1947), pp. 411-475.

LASSWELL, H.D., "Inevitable war," 2 *World Politics* (1949-1950), pp. 1-39.

THOMPSON, W.S., "Toward a Communist international system," 20 *Orbis* (1977), pp. 841-856.

TUNKIN, G.I., "Forty years of co-existence and international law," *Soviet Yearbook of International Law* (1958), pp. 15-49.

——— , "Printsip mirnovo sososuvshchvovaniya," 7 *Gosudarstvo i Pravo* (1963), pp. 26-37.

CHAPTER 12

(a) General

Books

COPLIN, W.D., *Introduction to International Politics: A Theoretical Overview* (New York: Rand McNally, 1974).

DOUGHERTY, J.E. and PFALTZGRAFF (eds.), *Contending Theories of International Relations* (Philadelphia: Lippincott, 1971).

KAPLAN, M.A. (ed.), *New Approaches to International Relations* (New York: St. Martin's, 1968).

KNORR, K. and ROSENAU, J. (eds.), *Contending Approaches to International Politics* (Princeton, N.J.: Princeton University Press, 1969).

LIEBER, R.J., *Theory and World Politics* (London: Allen and Unwin, 1972).

ZINNES, D.A., *Contemporary Research in International Relations* (London: Cassell and Collier Macmillan, 1976).

Articles

HOLSTI, K.J., "Retreat from utopia: international relations theory, 1945-1970," 4 *Canadian Journal of Political Science* (1971), pp. 165-177.

(b) Ecological Approaches

Books

FREEMAN, C. and others, *Thinking about the Future: A Critique of the Limits to Growth* (London: Chatto and Windus, 1973).

SPROUT, H. and M., *The Ecological Perspective of Human Affairs* (Princeton, N.J.: Princeton University Press, 1965).

——— , *Towards a Politics of the Planet Earth* (New York: van Nostrand, 1971).

TOYNBEE, A., *Mankind and Mother Earth* (London: Oxford University Press, 1976).

Articles

SHIELDS, L.P. and OTT, M.C., "The environmental crisis: international and supranational approaches," 4 *International Relations* (1974), pp. 629-648.

(c) Historical Approaches

Books

BARZUN, J., *Clio and the Doctors: Psycho-History, Quanto-History and History* (Chicago: University of Chicago Press, 1975).

BORCHARDT, K., *Dreht sich die Geschichte um?* (Ebenhausen: Langewiesche Brandt, 1975).

BUTTERFIELD, H., *History as the Emancipation of the Past* (London: London School of Economics, 1956).

FEBVRE, L., *A New Kind of History and Other Essays,* ed. by P. Burke (New York: Harper and Row, 1973).

FINLEY, M.I. (ed.), *The Use and Abuse of History* (London: Chatto and Windus, 1975).

FLECHTHEIM, O.P., *History and Futurology* (Meisenheim: Haim, 1966).

GARDINER, P. (ed.), *The Philosophy of History* (London: Oxford University Press, 1975).

HERTZLER, J.O., *The History of Utopian Thought* (London: Allen and Unwin, 1923).

HEXTER, J.H., *Doing History* (London: Allen and Unwin, 1972).

LAUE, T.H. von, *Ranke. The Formative Years.* (Princeton, N.J.: Princeton University Press, 1950).

MANUEL, F.E., *Freedom from History* (London: University of London Press, 1972).

POPPER, Sir Karl, *The Poverty of Historicism* (New York: Harper and Row, 1964).

TOYNBEE, A., *A Study of History, Vol. 12: Reconsideration* (London: Oxford University Press, 1961).

WALLERSTEIN, I., *The Modern World System: Capitalist Agriculture and the Origins of the European World Economy in the Sixteenth Century* (London: Academic Press, 1974).

HALL, A.R. and SMITH, N. (eds.), *1 History of Technology* (London: Mansell Information Publishing, 1976).

(d) Philosophical Approaches

Books

BENTWICH, N., *The Religious Foundations of Internationalism* (London: Allen and Unwin, 1933).

BLOCH, E., *Das Prinzip Hoffnung* (Berlin: Aufbau, 1954).

——— , *Geist der Utopie* (Munich: Duncker und Humblot, 1972).

———, *Das Materialismus-Problem. Seine Geschichte und Substanz* (Frankfurt: Suhrkamp, 1972).

——— , *Naturrecht und menschliche Würde* (Frankfurt: Suhrkamp, 1961). *

BRAILLARD, P., *Philosophie et relations internationales* (Geneva: Institut des Hautes Études Internationales, 1974).

CRESPIGNY, A. de and MINOGUE, K., *Contemporary Political Philosophers* (London: Methuen, 1976).

GRENE, M., *Introduction to Existentialism* (Chicago: Phoenix Books, 1959).

HEIDEGGER, M., *The End of Philosophy* (London: Souvenir Press, 1975).

JASPERS, K., *The Future of Mankind* (London: University of Chicago Press, 1961).

KOLAKOWSKI, L., *Positivist Philosophy* (Harmondsworth: Penguin, 1972).

LEM, S., *Summae technologicae* (Frankfurt: Insel Verlag, 1977).

MACQUARIE, J., *An Existentialist Theology. A comparison of Heidegger and Bultmann* (New York and London: Pelican, 1973).

ODAJNYK, W., *Marxism and Existentialism* (New York: Doubleday, 1965).

OSGOOD, R.E. and TUCKER, R.W., *Force, Order and Justice* (Baltimore, Johns Hopkins, 1967).

RUSSELL, B., *Has Man a Future?* (London: Allen and Unwin, 1961).

SAMPSON, R.V., *Tolstoy: The Discovery of Peace.* (London: Heinemann, 1973).

TILLICH, P., *Christianity and the Encounter of World Religions* (London: Columbia University Press, 1963).

WILLIAMS, R., *Culture and Society, 1750-1950* (London: Chatto and Windus, 1958).

Articles

COX, R., "The role of philosophy in the theory of international relations," 29 *Social Research* (1962), pp. 261-292.

HEIDEGGER, M., "Die Frage nach der Technik," 3 *Jahrbuch Gestalt und Gedanke* (1954), pp. 70-108.

McCOT, C.N.R., "On the revival of classical philosophy," 35 *Review of Politics* (1973), pp. 161-179.

VITAL, D., "On approaches to a study of international relations, or back to Machiavelli," 19 *World Politics* (1967), pp. 551-562.

(e) Psychological Approaches

Books

ALEXANDER, F.G., *The Scope of Psychoanalysis* (New York: Basic Books, 1961).

COSER, L., *The Functions of Social Conflict* (London: Routledge and Kegan Paul, 1956).

DEDRING, J., *Recent Advances in Peace and Conflict Research: A Critical Survey.* (London and Beverly Hills: Sage Publications, 1976).

DEUTSCH, M., *The Resolution of Conflict* (New Haven, Conn.: Yale University Press, 1973).

___ and KRAUS, R.M., *Theories in Social Psychology* (New York: Basic Books, 1965).

DOOB, L.W. (ed.), *Resolving Conflict in Africa. The Fermeda Workshop* (New Haven: Yale University Press, 1970).

FENICHEL, O., *Problems of Psychoanalytical Technique* (Albany: The Psychoanalytic Quarterly, 1941).

FERENCZI, S. and RANK, O., *The Development of Psychoanalysis* (New York: Nervous and Mental Disturbance Publications, 1925).

FREUD, S., *Group Psychology and the Analysis of the Ego* (original publication, 1921) (New York: Liverwright, 1949).

FOULKES, S.H., *Group Analytic Psychotherapy: Methods and Principles* (London: Gordon and Breach, 1975).

___ , *Therapeutic Group Analysis* (London: Allen and Unwin, 1964).

FROMM, E., *The Crisis in Psychoanalysis: Essays on Freud, Marx and Social Psychology* (Harmondsworth: Penguin, 1973).

GUETZKOW, H.A. and others (eds.), *Simulation in International Relations* (Englewood Cliffs: Prentice Hall, 1973).

HAAS, M., *International Conflict* (New York: Bobbs-Merrill, 1974).

HARE, A.P., *Handbook of Small Group Experience* (New York: Free Press, 1977).

HERMANN, C.F. (ed.), *International Crises* (New York: Collier-Macmillan, 1971).

LEVINE, R.A. and CAMPBELL, D.T., *Ethnocentrism, Theories of Conflict, Ethnic Attitudes and Group Behavior* (New York: John Wiley, 1972).

LEWIN, K., *Field Theory in Social Science: Selected Theoretical Papers* (London: Tavistock, 1952).

McIVER, R.M. (ed.), *Civilization and Group Relationships* (New York: Institute for Religious and Social Studies, 1945).

MEGARGEE, E.I. and HOKANSON, J.E. (eds.), *The Dynamics of Aggression. Individual, Group, and International Analysis.* (New York: Harper and Row, 1970).

MILLS, T.M., *The Sociology of Small Groups* (Englewood Cliffs: Prentice Hall, 1967).

MODRZHINSKAYA, E.D., *Problemy voina i mira: Kritika sovremennykh burzhuaznykh sotsialno - filosofskikh kontseptsii* (Moscow: Gosizdat, 1967).

MOROZOV, G.I. and others, *Obshchestvennost i problemy voiny i mira* (Moscow: Izdatelstvo "Mezhdunarodniye otnosheniya," 1976).

NICHOLSON, M.L., *Conflict Analysis* (London: English Universities Press, 1970).

POHLEN, M., *Gruppenanalyse* (Göttingen: Vandenhoeck, 1972).

ROSENBAUM, M. and SNADOWSKY, A. (eds.), *The Intensive Group Experience* (New York: Free Press, 1977).

SHERIF, M., *Group Conflict and Co-operation* (London: Routledge and Kegan Paul, 1966).

——— , and others, *Intergroup Conflict and Co-Operation: the Robber's Cave Experiment* (Oklahoma: The University Book Exchange, 1961).

——— (ed.), *Intergroup Relations and Leadership* (New York and London: Wiley, 1962).

WHITAKER, D.S. and LIEBERMAN, M., *Psychotherapy Through Group Process* (London: Tavistock Publications, 1965).

WILLIAMS, P., *Crisis Management: Confrontation and Diplomacy in the Nuclear Age* (London: Robertson, 1976).

WOLBERG, L.R. and SCHWARTZ, E.K. (eds.), *Group Therapy 1973: An Overview* (New York: Intercontinental Medical Book Corporation, 1973).

YOUNG, O.R., *The Intermediaries: Third Parties in International Crises* (Princeton, N.J.: Princeton University Press, 1967).

Articles

BANKS, M.H. and MITCHELL, C., "Conflict theory, peace research and the analysis of communal conflicts," 3 *Millennium* (1974-1975), pp. 252-267.

BANKS, M.H., GROOM, A., and OPPENHEIM, A.N., "Gaming and simulation in international relations," 16 *Political Studies* (1968), pp. 1-17.

GURR, T.R., "Psychological factors in civil violence," 20 *World Politics* (1968), pp. 245-278.

SCHINDLER, W., "Suggestive momente in der psychoanalyse," 9 *Praxis der Psychotherapie* (1966), pp. 267-279.

——— , "Entwicklung der Gruppen-Psychotherapie," 21 *Praxis der Psychotherapie* (1976), pp. 59-67.

(f) Scientist and Behavioural Approaches

Books

AKADEMIYA NAUK SSSR. INSTITUT MIROVOY EKONOMIKI i MEZHDURNA-RODNYKH OTNOSHENIYA, i INSTITUT S.SH.A., *Mezhdunarodniye Konflikty* (Moscow: Isdatelstvo "Mezhdunarodniye Konflikty," 1972).

ANDRESKI, S., *Social Sciences as Sorcery* (London: Deutsch, 1972).

BERLINSKI, D., *On Systems Analysis* (Cambridge, Mass.: MIT Press, 1976).

BERTALANFEY, L., *General Systems Theory: Foundations, Development, Applications* (New York: Braziller, 1973).

BUCKLEY, W. (ed.), *Modern Systems Research for the Behavioral Scientist* (Chicago. Aldine, 1968).

BURTON, J.W., *Conflict and Communication: The Uses of Controlled Communication in International Relations* (London: Macmillan, 1969).

——— , *Systems, States, Diplomacy and Rules* (London: Cambridge University Press, 1968).

CASSIRER, E., *The Problem of Knowledge: Philosophy, Science and History Since Hegel* (New Haven: Yale University Press, 1950).

CENTER FOR THE ANALYSIS OF CONFLICT, *The Study of World Society: A London Perspective* (Pittsburgh: University Center for International Studies, 1974).

COSER, L.S., *The Functions of Social Conflict* (London: Routledge and Kegan Paul, 1964).

DEUTSCH, K.W., *The Nerves of Government* (New York: Free Press, 1963).

EASTON, D., *A Systems Analysis of Political Life* (New York: Wiley, 1965).

EDMEAD, F., *Analysis and Prediction in International Mediation* (New York: UNITAR, 1971).

ELCOCK, H., *Political Behaviour* (London: Methuen, 1976).

ENGELS, F., *Die Entwicklung des Sozialismus von der Utopie zur Wissenschaft* (original edition, 1883) (Berlin: 1891).

ARRELL, J.C. and SMITH, A.C. (eds.), *Image and Reality in World Politics* (New York: Columbia University Press, 1971).

FEDDER, E.H. (ed.), *Methodological Concerns and International Studies* (St. Louis, Mo: University of Missouri, 1970).

FEYERABEND, P., *Against Method: Outline of an Anarchistic Method of Knowledge* (New York: Humanities Press, 1975).

FORRESTER, J.W., *World Dynamics* (Cambridge, Mass.: Wright-Allen Press, 1972).

HABERMAS, J., *Legitimation Crisis* (London: Heinemann, 1976).

HARAWYA, D.J., *Crystals, Fabrics and Fields: Metaphors of Organicism in Twentieth Century Developmental Biology* (New Haven: Yale University, 1976).

KELMAN, H.C., *International Behavior* (New York: Rinehart and Winston, 1965).

LASZLO, E., *The Systems View of the World* (New York: Braziller, 1972).

McCOY and PLAYFORD, J. (eds.), *Apolitical Politics: A Critique of Behavioralism* (New York: Crowell, 1967).

MORGAN, R. (ed.), *The Study of International Affairs: Essays in Honour of Kenneth Younger* (London: Oxford University Press, 1972).

MUELLER, J.E. (ed.), *Approaches to Measurement in International Relations* (New York: Appleton-Century-Crofts, 1969).

NORTH, R.C., *Content Analysis: a Handbook with Application for the Study of International Crisis* (Evanston, Ill.: Northwestern University Press, 1963).

PETTMAN, R., *Human Behaviour and World Politics* (London: Macmillan, 1977).

ROSENAU, J.N., *International Studies and the Social Sciences: Problems, Priorities and Prospects in the U.S.* (London and Beverly Hills: Sage Publications, 1973).

SAID, A.A. (ed.), *Theory of International Relations: The Crisis of Relevance* (Engle-wood Cliffs: Prentice Hall, 1968).

SINGER, J.D. (ed.), *Human Behavior and International Politics* (Chicago: Rand Mc-Nally, 1965).

—— , *Quantitative International Politics* (New York: Free Press, 1968).

—— , *Theorizing about International Politics* (Chicago: Rand McNally, 1965).

STAGNER, R., *Psychological Aspects of International Conflict* (Belmont: Brooks-Cole 1967).

STEINBRUNER, J., *Cybernetic Theory of Decision* (Princeton, N.J.: Princton University Press, 1974).

VUCINICH, A., *Social Thought in Tsarist Russia: The Quest for a General Science of Society, 1861-1917* (Chicago: University of Chicago Press, 1976).

WELTMANN, J.J., *Systems Theory in International Relations: A Study in Metaphoric Hypertrophy* (Lexington: Lexington Books, 1973).

WILSON, E.O., *Sociobiology: The New Synthesis* (Cambridge, Mass.: Belknap Press, 1976).

YOUNG, O.R., *A Systemic Approach to International Politics* (Princeton, N.J.: Princeton University Press, 1968).

Articles

BALES, R.F., "A set of Categories for the analysis of small group interaction," 15 *American Sociological Review* (1950), pp. 257-263.

EASTON, D., "The new revolution in political science," 63 *American Political Science Review* (1969), pp. 1051-1061.

FINNEGAN, R.B., "International relations: the disputed search for a method," 36 *Review of Politics* (1972), pp. 40-66.

GORMAN, R., "On the inadequacies of non-philosophical political science: a critical analysis of decision-making," 14 *International Studies Quarterly* (1970), pp. 395-411.

LIJPHART, A., "The structure of theoretical revolutions in international relations," 18 *International Studies Quarterly* (1974), pp. 41-74.

NICHOLSON, M.B., "Mathematical models in the study of international relations," 22 *Yearbook of World Affairs* (1968), pp. 47-63.

RUMMEL, R., "Indicators of cross-national and international patterns," 63 *American Political Science Review* (1969), pp. 127-147.

SINGER, J.D., "The relevance of the behavioral sciences to the study of international relations," 6 *Behavioral Science* (1961), pp. 324-335.

YALEM, R.J., "Prolegomena on the post-behavioral revolution in international studies," 16 *Orbis* (1973), pp. 1032-1042.

(g) Sociological Approaches
Books
BELL, D., *The Coming of Post-Industrial Society* (London: Heinemann, 1974).

BERRY, A., *The Next Ten Thousand Years* (New York: Saturday Review Press, 1975).

BIDEZ, J., *La Cité du Monde et la cité du soleil chez les Stoïciens* (Paris and Brussels: "Bulletins de l'Academie royale de Belgique," 1932).

BLAU, P.M., *Exchange and Power in Social Life* (New York: Wiley, 1964).

BLOOMFIELD, P., *Imaginary Worlds; or, the Evolution of Utopia* (London: Hamish Hamilton, 1932).

HILLEGAS, M.R., *The Future as Nightmare: H.G. Wells and the Anti-Utopians* (New York: Oxford University Press, 1968).

HORKHEIMER, M., *Verwaltete Welt* (Zürich: Arche, 1970).

KEOHANE, R.O. and NYE, J.S., *Power and Independence: World Politics in Transition* (Boston: Little Brown, 1977).

KOTHARI, R., *Footsteps into the Future: Diagnosis of the Present World and a Design for an Alternative* (Amsterdam: North Holland Publishing, 1975).

LANDHEER, B., LOENEN, J.H.M.M., and POLAK, F.L. (eds.), *Worldsociety* (The Hague: Nijhoff, 1971).

MANNHEIM, K., *Ideology and Utopia* (original edition, 1935) (London: Routledge and Kegan Paul, 1960).

MORGAN, A.E., *Nowhere Was Somewhere: How History Makes Utopias and How Utopias Make History* (North Carolina University Press, and Oxford University Press, 1947).

NORTHEDGE, F.S., *The International Political System* (London: Faber, 1976).

RUMMEL, R.J., *Understanding Conflict and War, Vol. I* (New York and London: Sage Publications, dist. by John Wiley, 1975).

RUSSELL, B.M., *Economic Theories of International Politics* (Chicago: Markham, 1968).

INDEX

(Note: the index contains authors' names only if they appear in the text.)

ABOUT THE AUTHOR

DR. F. PARKINSON is Senior Lecturer at University College London, where he has been teaching since 1952. He is a graduate of the University of London, and a World War II veteran of the British army. He was Assistant Director of the London Institute of World Affairs from 1967 to 1970, and from 1957-1970 Assistant and Managing Editor of the Institute's *Year Book of World Affairs* of which he currently is serving as chairman of the panel of advisors to the editorial board. Dr. Parkinson has traveled throughout the world and has contributed numerous articles to scholarly journals. He is the author of *Latin America, the Cold War, and the World Powers, 1945-1973* (Beverly Hills: Sage Publications, 1974).

JX 1305 .P37 1977

Parkinson, F.   nternational rela-
                                      e history of
The philosophy of   n. -- Beverly
  international relations   Publications,

                        ... (Sage library of so-
cial research ; v. 52)

      ISBN 0-8039-0689-7. ISBN 0-8039-0690-
0 pbk.

      1.International relations--History.
      I.Title.
JX1305.P37   327'.01

                                    77-11197
                                    MARC

DELTA COLLEGE

LEARNING RESOURCES

OVERDUE FINE

OVERDUES 5¢
PER DAY.

RESERVE MATERIALS
10¢ EACH HOUR THEREAFTER